THE
BROTHERHOOD

THE BROTHERHOOD

AMERICA'S NEXT GREAT ENEMY

ERICK STAKELBECK

REGNERY
Publishing, Inc.

An Eagle Publishing Company • Washington, DC

Cataloging-in-Publication data on file with the Library of Congress

ISBN 978-1-62157-033-2

Published in the United States by
Regnery Publishing, Inc.
One Massachusetts Avenue NW
Washington, DC 20001
www.Regnery.com

Manufactured in the United States of America
10 9 8 7 6 5 4 3 2 1

Books are available in quantity for promotional or premium use. Write to Director of Special Sales, Regnery Publishing, Inc., One Massachusetts Avenue NW, Washington, DC 20001, for information on discounts and terms, or call (202) 216-0600.

Distributed to the trade by
Perseus Distribution
250 West 57th Street
New York, NY 10107

Dedicated to my beautiful girls, Lori, Juliana, and Leah.

"An excellent wife is the crown of her husband."
—Proverbs 12:4

"Children are a heritage from the LORD."
—Psalm 127:3

CONTENTS

"*I have set watchmen upon your walls,*
O Jerusalem, who shall never hold their peace day nor night:
you that make mention of the LORD, keep not silence."

—*Isaiah* 62:6

MEET THE BROTHERHOOD

The alleged leader of Germany's Muslim Brotherhood punched me.

It was actually more of a playful nudge of my right shoulder, something an old friend might do while busting your chops. Yet I had met Ibrahim el-Zayat only minutes before.

"You should have asked me for some names," el-Zayat said as we stood in the lobby of a Cologne hotel. "I could have put you in touch with all the right people."

I had just informed him that I had contacted a few leading Islamist figures in his home base of Cologne and gotten no response. Hence, the nudge and a look of feigned exasperation. *How long must I suffer this infidel?*

In reality, I wasn't too upset at the lack of response from Cologne's Islamists. El-Zayat was the one I really wanted. He's been called "one of the most influential Islamists in Europe"[1] and "a quintessential New Western [Muslim] Brother."[2] Likewise, the *Global Muslim Brotherhood Daily Report*, a comprehensive intelligence digest, regularly refers to el-Zayat as "the leader of the Muslim Brotherhood in Germany."[3]

Since I was writing a book about the Brotherhood, el-Zayat seemed a good place to start. But in the run-up to our meeting in late June 2012, I had all but given up on interviewing him. For weeks, I had sent el-Zayat emails saying I was coming to Germany and would love to get together. His responses were infrequent and noncommittal. Finally, on my last night in Germany and after a long day of interview shoots, my cell phone rang as I was heading back to my hotel. To my great surprise, it was Ibrahim el-Zayat.

"I can meet you at your hotel in thirty minutes," he said. "But I can't stay long."

My cameraman and I grabbed a quick bite, set up for the interview shoot and waited. And waited. Just when we thought el-Zayat might not show, he came bounding through the hotel's front entrance. Clad in a smart suit and designer eyeglasses and sporting a wavy, salt-and-pepper mane and neatly trimmed beard, el-Zayat looked more like a European diplomat than "a spider in the web of Islamist organizations," as one German security official described him.[4]

That alleged web has many strands. El-Zayat, according to *Wall Street Journal* reporter Ian Johnson, "seemed to have either founded or been closely involved with every recently established Muslim Brotherhood–related group in Europe."[5] The list includes The Federation of Islamic Organisations in Europe (FIOE)—widely considered the Brotherhood's lobbying arm on the Old Continent—as well as the World Assembly of Muslim Youth (WAMY), a Saudi-created group for which el-Zayat acted as European representative. El-Zayat also served for nearly a decade as head of the Islamic Society of Germany (IGD), an organization with long-time ties to top Brotherhood leaders in Germany and abroad.

In short, Ibrahim el-Zayat is an extremely well connected mover and shaker who, despite his youth, has been a major player on Europe's Islamist scene for years. Born in Germany in 1968 to an Egyptian Muslim father and a German mother who converted to Islam, el-Zayat has spent most of his life in Deutschland but is well traveled and speaks fluent English. After studying law and economics at German universities, he went on to become a successful businessman and marry a doctor (his wife is the niece of famed Turkish Islamist Necmettin Erbakan).

Needless to say, Germany has been very good to el-Zayat. Yet he seemed to have little affinity for his homeland as he spoke to me of Germany's supposed intolerance for its 4.3 million-strong Muslim community.

"From the Muslim community's side, it is that you feel not part of the country," he told me as we sat in a small conference room. "Because many people have the deep understanding that they have done the utmost to be part of Germany, but the society is refusing them.... Germany has a lot of parts now which are no longer multicultural but now monocultural, and this is a challenge for everybody."

A challenge indeed: particularly for non-Muslims in places like London, Madrid, and Boston who've seen Muslim immigrants unleash deadly terror on their cities in recent years.

I've visited many of the type of unassimilated, "monocultural" Islamic communities el-Zayat describes and have reported on them extensively. From Berlin to Brussels to suburban Paris to Dearborn, Michigan, Muslim immigrants are segregating themselves from their host societies and setting up Islamic enclaves that are often no-go zones for non-Muslims, including police.

It's hard to see why a committed Islamist like el-Zayat would frown on this development. The Muslim Brotherhood's leading global ideologue and Spiritual Guide, Sheikh Yusuf al-Qaradawi (whom el-Zayat praises effusively), is the driving force behind the Brotherhood's

state-within-a-state strategy for the West. And el-Zayat himself is helping to spearhead the rapid construction of mosques throughout
Europe.

A Cologne newspaper featured a profile of el-Zayat describing him
as the chief representative of an organization called European Mosque
Construction and Support. In that capacity, el-Zayat reportedly maintains more than six hundred mosques across Europe and helps with
the construction and renovation of countless others.[6] According to
the Muslim Brotherhood's own documents, mosques, or "Islamic
centers," are meant to serve as the "beehives" of the parallel Muslim
societies the Brotherhood envisions in Europe and the United States.[7]
Coincidence?

When el-Zayat's involvement in a mosque project becomes known,
locals often protest—his reputation as a Muslim Brotherhood–connected
figure precedes him. He is well aware of the baggage he carries in the eyes
of non-Muslims and shared a simple, very Brotherhood-esque solution
in an interview with the *Wall Street Journal*'s Ian Johnson:

> If a plan to build a mosque is made public, everyone is against
> it. Mosques must always be built secretly … if it's not public,
> you can build any mosque, regardless of who's behind it. You
> just have to keep it secret.[8]

This strategy of deception—or *taqiyya*—has paid big dividends for
el-Zayat. It has also attracted the attention of German authorities, who
have investigated his business dealings over the years but have yet to
indict him on any charges.

Although the government scrutiny and ensuing bad press have forced
el-Zayat to keep a lower public profile, once we began our interview, he
settled almost immediately into his familiar role of crafty spokesman for
the Islamist cause.

The Muslim Brotherhood's Mohammed Morsi had been declared the victor in Egypt's presidential election just hours earlier, and el-Zayat was clearly pleased.

"I think it is a big success for Egypt and for the democratic change process that you have Mohammed Morsi now as president," he crowed.

To hear "Mohammed Morsi" and "democratic change" uttered in the same sentence now sounds absurd, given Egypt's wholesale descent into Islamist chaos under Morsi's rule. Of course, to those of us who've long warned that the Muslim Brotherhood is a radical, anti-American organization that spawned al-Qaeda and Hamas and actively calls for the destruction of Israel, the idea of Morsi as Cairo's version of Thomas Jefferson has always been not only ludicrous, but downright dangerous.

Yet at the time of Morsi's election in 2012, Western media and governments were still enraptured by the so-called Arab Spring (some still are, despite its disastrous results) and had much invested in the notion of a supposedly moderate, pragmatic Muslim Brotherhood taking the reins in Egypt.

Whether el-Zayat assumed I was among this sizable, pro-Brotherhood camp is unclear. Regardless, he plowed ahead with talking points that would leave the average *New York Times* or BBC journo positively smitten (as if the playful love tap on the shoulder wouldn't have already done the trick).

"I believe that for many years we had only a lot of misinformation and misconceptions about...the Muslim Brotherhood," el-Zayat said. "You had information mainly filtered by governments who have been oppressive...and I think that this should be overcome and I hope that it's overcome."

He needn't have worried. Ever since the outbreak of the Egyptian revolution in January 2011, the Obama administration and its mainstream media minions have been hard at work recasting the Brotherhood as (in el-Zayat's words) a "reform movement" that is "evolving" and worthy of more than a billion dollars in American taxpayer aid, even given our massive debt.

"I think what is special about the Muslim Brotherhood in the end...," el-Zayat continued, now clearly hitting his stride, "is what you could describe as a thought which is combining Islam with modern life. And this starts with [Jamal al-Din] al-Afghani and Rashid Rida and it comes to Hassan al-Banna—who had been the founder of the Muslim Brotherhood but who had a completely different stance on things."

Al-Afghani and Rida were two seminal Islamists who helped inspire al-Banna's "stance on things" prior to his formation of the Muslim Brotherhood in 1928—a stance that included, as we'll see shortly, a hatred for the West and Jews and a desire to reestablish the global Islamic caliphate, with an Egypt ruled by sharia law as its centerpiece.

When I pressed el-Zayat on al-Banna's clear directives for Muslim Brothers to wage armed jihad against non-believers, he didn't skip a beat.

"The concept of jihad as it has been presented by al-Banna—as the 'Big Jihad'—is the jihad *in* us," el-Zayat calmly explained. "As to fight...against all the bad evil that is within you. This is the real jihad that you have to overcome."

The hundreds of millions of men, women, and children who have lost their lives to jihad—as in, holy war for Allah, it's traditional and primary meaning—over the past 1,400 years would likely beg to differ with el-Zayat's assessment. But the Brotherhood's good friends on the political Left, most of whom know not a shred of Islamic history and have never picked up a Koran in their lives, simply nod in mindless agreement. After all, this jihad stuff sounds like it would fit in perfectly at their next yoga class.

Polished, eloquent, and charming, el-Zayat would seem the ideal spokesman for the Muslim Brotherhood (MB) and its agenda in the unsuspecting West. The only hitch is that he steadfastly denies being a member of the group. In 2007, the MB's official English-language website, Ikhwanweb, identified him as a Brotherhood member but later retracted the claim and published a denial from el-Zayat.[9] Additionally, when a German parliamentarian said that el-Zayat was "clearly a functionary" of the Brotherhood, he sued her (unsuccessfully).[10]

The Egyptian government under Hosni Mubarak also maintained that el-Zayat belonged to the Brotherhood. In 2008, it convicted him in absentia and sentenced him to ten years in prison on charges of funding the MB in Egypt (the Brotherhood was banned under Mubarak). As you might have suspected, el-Zayat's conviction was thrown out after the Mubarak regime was toppled, and he received an official pardon from Morsi in July 2012.[11]

Member or not, el-Zayat plays a unique role in the Muslim Brotherhood's ideological universe. He's forged close connections with top global Brotherhood leaders and clearly shares and promotes the movement's worldview. Still, he, like other MB-connected individuals in the West whom I've interviewed—some of whom you'll meet in this book—disavows any sort of formal relationship with the Brotherhood.

Doing so has helped these "New Western Brothers"—as Italian terrorism expert Lorenzo Vidino calls them[12]—largely avoid the stigma that the Muslim Brotherhood carries. Or used to carry. Indeed, the MB's much-deserved reputation for violence, radicalism, anti-Americanism, and anti-Semitism is rapidly disappearing in the Age of Obama. The concept of engagement with the Muslim Brotherhood is no longer only whispered about at D.C. cocktail parties—it has become the official policy of the United States government.

We're nearing a point where el-Zayat and his Western cohorts may not even have to bother playing a double game anymore. The Muslim Brotherhood and its affiliates are coming to power throughout the Middle East and North Africa, with the full support of Western governments—the Obama administration chief among them. In essence, the Brotherhood, which had moved in the shadows for most of its existence, has suddenly gone mainstream.

When an organization's members (and "non-members") become frequent guests at the White House and European Parliament and lead governments that receive billions in Western funding and weaponry, it's safe to say that any stigma that once existed is out the window. As a result, the day is fast approaching in Europe and the United States when allegations of membership in the Muslim Brotherhood will be greeted with a collective shrug of the shoulders by Islamists and Western officials alike.

The Muslim Brotherhood, the granddaddy of them all when it comes to modern-day Islamic terrorist groups, is now considered polite company in Western capitals. In the process, it hasn't had to change its core beliefs one iota: America as we know it must still be destroyed, Israel must still be wiped from the face of the earth, the global Islamic super-state, or caliphate, must still be reborn, and Islamic sharia law must still be imposed upon one and all—whether we want it or not. In other words, the Brothers espouse the same platform today that they did upon their founding nearly a century ago—a fact that seems not to bother President Obama and his foreign policy team in the least.

"Let me know when your report airs," Ibrahim el-Zayat said as he prepared to depart our interview and move on to yet another appointment. "I look forward to seeing it."

The wind was at el-Zayat's back as he bade me farewell and strode off into the warm Cologne night. His side was winning. And he knew it.

CHAPTER ONE

ISLAMIST WINTER IS COMING

"The Arab Spring will weaken al-Qaeda. Of that, I am sure."

Strike one.

It was June 2012, and I was at the Council of the European Union in Brussels, chatting with one of the EU's top counterterrorism officials as we prepared to do an interview. He holds a position that is central to securing Europe from a rising tide of jihadist mayhem, much of which stems from its own growing Muslim communities. An important man, for certain: with zero understanding of the Islamist ideology that drives terrorism and animates a large slice of the Muslim world.

"The Muslim Brotherhood will work against the terrorists," he continued, offering the standard view of Western bureaucrats, led by the Obama White House, that have doubled as cheerleaders for the MB and its supposed "moderate" brand of Islamism.

1

Strike two.

As we sat down to begin the interview, our distinguished Eurocrat asked what we would be discussing. "Iran, Hezbollah, al-Qaeda, and the Muslim Brotherhood," I replied. "Let's just focus on al-Qaeda," he answered. "I'm not as strong on the others."

My cameraman had to stop me from falling out of my chair. This was one of the European Union's top counterterrorism officials, and he wasn't up to speed on the world's number one state sponsor of terrorism (Iran), its most lethal terrorist paramilitary organization (Hezbollah), and its number one purveyor of jihadist ideology (the Brotherhood)?

Automatic strike three. And the interview hadn't even started yet.

Our European friend's tunnel vision regarding al-Qaeda is a sickness that is endemic to Western capitals. In focusing the overwhelming bulk of their counterterrorism energies on stopping al-Qaeda, U.S. and European officials have watched impotently as Iran, Hezbollah, and the Muslim Brotherhood—all three even greater threats than AQ, for different reasons—have grown in strength and influence.

Incidentally, so has al-Qaeda—President Obama's disingenuous message to audiences during the 2012 presidential campaign, that "al Qaeda is on its heels," "decimated," and "on the path to defeat" notwithstanding.[1] He continued to trumpet this false narrative and shamelessly mislead the American people even after al-Qaeda–linked jihadists rampaged the U.S. consulate in Benghazi, on September 11, 2012—killing four Americans— and stormed U.S. Embassies in Egypt, Tunisia, and Yemen that same week.

What President Obama conveniently left out of his campaign stump speech was the fact that al-Qaeda and its affiliates and allies now cover more geographical ground than they did on 9/11. From its main base in Pakistan's tribal regions, AQ has spread its tentacles into Yemen, Somalia, Sinai, Syria, Nigeria, Libya, Iraq, Europe, and the Sahara desert region encompassing northern Mali and southern Algeria. At the same time, the terror group's murderous ideology has inspired a wave of homegrown and immigrant jihadists to attack their host countries in the West.

Don't worry though, folks: Osama bin Laden is dead. Which means Bush's bogus War on Terror is over. We can pack our bags and go home now. That little flare-up in Boston? An isolated incident carried out by two lone wolves who misinterpreted the inherently peaceful teachings of a great religion. Anyway, this "violent extremism" stuff is distracting our president from much more pressing matters at home, like instituting Obamacare and keeping his promise to "fundamentally transform America."

While he's busy doing that, Islamists are fundamentally transforming large swaths of the Middle East and North Africa. And we've decided to cast our lot with the most dangerous of them all: the Muslim Brotherhood.

———

"The shari'a, then the shari'a, and finally, the shari'a."

Mohammed Morsi was on a roll. It was May 2012, just prior to his victory in Egypt's historic presidential election, and Morsi was providing an adoring audience of Egyptian Islamists a vision of things to come under his leadership.

"This nation will enjoy blessing and revival only through the Islamic shari'a," he bellowed. "I take an oath before Allah and before you all that regardless of the actual text [of the Egyptian constitution]...Allah willing, the text will truly reflect [the sharia], as will be agreed upon by the Egyptian people, by the Islamic scholars, and by legal and constitutional experts."[2]

Thick-necked, humorless, and podium-pounding, Morsi represents the polar opposite of the dashing and verbose Ibrahim el-Zayat. The differences extend into the tactical realm as well. Whereas el-Zayat has always followed the trusted Muslim Brotherhood blueprint of slow, stealthy Islamization, Morsi and his ironically named Freedom and Justice Party have thrown gradualism out the window since taking power in Egypt. The result has been a headlong dive into sharia madness for the Arab world's most populous and influential country.

The Islamic sharia system that Morsi and the Brothers so lustily desire for Egypt—and are well on their way to achieving—means a few things: women will be oppressed, Christians and other religious minorities will be persecuted, homosexuals will be executed, political dissidents will be imprisoned and tortured, the extinction of Israel will become a chief foreign policy goal, and the West—the United States in particular—will be demonized as the eternal enemy of Islam and a tool of the hated Jews.

At least four of these sharia harbingers are already occurring with alarming frequency in the new, Muslim Brotherhood–dominated Egypt—and things promise to get worse, quickly. The implementation of Islamic sharia law means that freedoms of speech, conscience, religion, and thought, if they existed before, are brutally repressed. For examples, look at Iran, northern Sudan, and the mini-Islamic emirate of Gaza, run by the Muslim Brotherhood's Palestinian branch, Hamas. Such was life under the Taliban in Afghanistan as well, and such will be life in Egypt one day, probably soon, unless civil war, economic collapse, and famine tear the country apart first. You can take it to the bank (no interest allowed, since we're staying sharia compliant).

"Listen, the Muslim Brothers fought for 84 years to reach power and impose sharia," Israel's former ambassador to Egypt, Zvi Mazel, told me during an interview in his Jerusalem home in late 2012. "Now that they are in power, will they say, 'Okay, now we are going to become modern people. We are going for high tech and Allah is not important'? No, it's impossible."

Indeed. During his aforementioned "Sharia Speech" in May 2012, Morsi shared a bit more of his worldview and the kind of modernizing, forward-thinking policy prescriptions he would bring to the office of Egypt's presidency:

Mohammed Morsi: [In the 1920s, the Egyptians] said: "The constitution is our Koran." They wanted to show that the constitution is a great thing. But Imam [Hassan] al-Banna, Allah's mercy upon him, said to them: "No, the Koran is our constitution."

The Koran was and will continue to be our constitution. The Koran will continue to be our constitution! The Koran is our constitution!

Crowd: The Koran is our constitution!

Morsi: The Prophet Mohammed is our leader!

Crowd: The Prophet Mohammed is our leader!

Morsi: Jihad is our path!

Crowd: Jihad is our path!

Morsi: And death for the sake of Allah is our most lofty aspiration!

Crowd: And death for the sake of Allah is our most lofty aspiration!

Morsi: Above all—Allah is our goal.[3]

Is it any wonder that Egypt's beleaguered Coptic Christians—who not long ago comprised 10 percent of the country's population—are leaving in ever-growing numbers now that Morsi is in power?

Incidentally, Morsi's harangue was neither spontaneous nor original. He simply—and intentionally—paraphrased the longtime motto of the Muslim Brotherhood:

> Allah is our objective. The Prophet is our leader. Qur'an is our law. Jihad is our way. Dying in the way of Allah is our highest hope.

In other words: total, unwavering devotion to imposing fundamentalist Islam—by the sword if necessary—upon the world, with a ghoulish veneration of violent death to boot. The slogan is the same today as it was eighty-five years ago. And it will be the same eighty-five years from now. The Brotherhood, unlike the flatlining Western societies it is slowly helping transform from within, does not compromise on its core beliefs. It does not do tweaks or reboots. It's all Allah, Mohammed, the Koran, jihad, and violent martyrdom, all the time—take it or leave it, infidels. Americans, meet your new "ally" in the Middle East.

What Mohammed Morsi did in his May 2012 speech—one which was utterly ignored by Western media—was the same thing that a long succession of Brotherhood leaders have done before him. He simply laid down the gauntlet and reiterated the Brotherhood's longstanding, bedrock principles to Egyptians and to the world. All who are shocked by Morsi's subsequent moves as president have no one to blame but themselves. They weren't listening.

If they were, they would have known that the Brotherhood's official rallying cry has remained the same ever since its founding by a fervently Islamist schoolteacher named Hassan al-Banna in the Egyptian port city of Ismailia in 1928. Al-Banna, who was heavily influenced by the extremist Wahhabi Islam of Saudi Arabia, was disgusted by British colonial rule and the non-Muslim influence it brought to Egypt. He blamed the country's downtrodden state of affairs on what he perceived as its drift away from Islam.

Al-Banna's slogan, "Islam is the answer," spread like wildfire and the Brotherhood—also known as the *Ikhwan* or the Society of the Muslim Brothers—went from seven members at its founding to as many as two million by the late 1940s.[4] Indeed, al-Banna's anti-Western message of Muslim superiority (which also included generous doses of jihad incitement and anti-Semitism) resonated to such a degree that by 1948—just twenty years after its founding—the Ikhwan had become arguably the most powerful political and cultural force in all of Egypt.

Today, although Egypt remains its main power base, al-Banna's movement knows no national boundaries. The Brotherhood's relentless focus on *dawa*, or proselytization, has helped it make major inroads on six continents. One of its main "settlement" techniques has been its control of mosques, including across the United States and Europe. These frequently mammoth, multi-million-dollar Islamic centers, run by Brotherhood acolytes, are built largely with funds supplied by wealthy donors in the Persian Gulf region, particularly from Saudi Arabia and Qatar.

Thanks to this disciplined, dawa-and-settlement strategy, the Muslim Brotherhood is now present in at least eighty countries, and according to one longtime Brotherhood leader, boasts some 100 million adherents worldwide. The vast majority are not official "members" but all have one thing in common: tireless, fanatical devotion to the Brotherhood's radical ideology.[5] That's bad news for the United States, not to mention Europe, Israel, and any secular-minded Muslim or religious minority who has the misfortune of living under Ikhwan rule.

The seeds for the Ikhwan's meteoric global rise were planted by al-Banna. Above all, he was devastated by the collapse of the Islamic caliphate, which ended with the disbandment of the Turkish-led Ottoman Empire in 1924. The caliphate joined the Muslim world—*or ummah—*

into one unified, Islamic state governed by sharia law and pitted against the West. Al-Banna's ultimate goal was to transform Egypt into an Islamic state en route to reviving this global caliphate and the glories of Islam's heyday. As described in the Brotherhood's seven-point pledge of allegiance, which he devised:

> ...the Muslim Brotherhood should collectively work to restore the international position of the *Umma*. To this end, it will be necessary to liberate occupied Muslim regions. The Brotherhood should restore Muslim honor and superiority; it should promote its civilization and re-establish its culture. A new spirit of oneness should be instilled until the entire *Umma* becomes a heartwarming unity. *In this way the crown and throne of the caliphate of the world can be regained.*[6] [emphasis added]

Translation: world domination. By the way, those "occupied Muslim regions" that must be liberated include any nation that was once part of the Islamic caliphate, including Spain, Sicily, Greece, Bulgaria, the former Yugoslavia, and Israel, among others. In the Islamist worldview, if a nation was conquered and existed under the banner of Islam for even a short amount of time, it must eventually return to the fold: by force, if necessary.

No such force will be needed, however, to cajole the nations of the Middle East and North Africa into caliphate-hood. An April 2013 Pew Forum poll showed that a majority of Muslims throughout those two regions, as well as in South Asia, want sharia law to govern their countries.[7] The numbers are even more stunning when you consider that, as National Review Online's Andrew McCarthy noted, the poll did *not* include Iran, Saudi Arabia, and Sudan, arguably the top three sharia hotbeds in the world.[8]

The bottom line, if the results of the Pew poll are any indication, is that the Brotherhood's aspirations seem to be supported, at least in a general way, by a majority of Muslims around the world. The Arab Spring has brought these forces newfound power, and they have never been closer to achieving al-Banna's caliphate dream than they are today. And make no mistake: today's Muslim Brothers are fully committed to al-Banna's vision of a modern-day caliphate. During a May 2012 rally to launch the presidential campaign of Mohammed Morsi, leading Brotherhood cleric Safwat Hegazy delivered a thunderous sermon declaring that the dawn of a revived Islamic super-state was at hand:

> We can see how the dream of the Islamic Caliphate is being realized, Allah willing, by Dr. Mohamed Morsi and his brothers, his supporters, and his political party. We can see how the great dream, shared by us all—that of the United States of the Arabs...will be restored, Allah willing. The United States of the Arabs will be restored by [Morsi] and his supporters. The capital of the Caliphate—the capital of the United States of the Arabs—will be Jerusalem, Allah willing.[9]

In case you were wondering how Jerusalem—currently the capital of Israel—could possibly become the centerpiece of a new caliphate, Hegazy (who has also promised that the Muslim Brothers will one day be "Masters of the World")[10] filled in the blanks:

> Our capital shall not be Cairo, Mecca, or Medina. It shall be Jerusalem, Allah willing. Our cry shall be: "Millions of martyrs march toward Jerusalem." Millions of martyrs march toward Jerusalem.[11]

Throughout this tirade, Mohammed Morsi sat directly behind Hegazy on stage, smiling and nodding his head in affirmation. Egypt's soon-to-be-president was absolutely enthralled with both Hegazy and the event's master of ceremonies, who led the frenzied audience in chants of "Banish the sleep from the eyes of all Jews" and "Come on, you lovers of martyrdom, you are all Hamas," all under Morsi's watchful eye. It was a fitting coming out party for a man who would soon become the equivalent of a modern day jihadist pharaoh.

Yes, our new "asset" in Cairo is a real piece of work. Video unearthed by the invaluable Middle East Media Research Institute (MEMRI) in January 2013 captured some of Morsi's greatest hits from his appearances on Arabic television. In one lighthearted clip, he called Jews, "bloodsuckers, who attack the Palestinians…warmongers, the descendants of apes and pigs."[12]

The "Jews-as-apes-and-pigs" reference is an old Islamist favorite. Another is armed jihad, which Morsi also encouraged in the video, saying of Israel, "We should employ all forms of resistance against them. There should be military resistance within the land of Palestine against those criminal Zionists."

Interestingly enough, our new partner for peace in the Middle East also referred to America as being among Egypt's "enemies," and called for a worldwide Muslim boycott of U.S. goods. Morsi made these comments in 2010, just two years before his newly elected government would become the recipient of massive U.S. aid.

Morsi, like many top Brotherhood leaders in Egypt, is also an unabashed 9/11 "Truther" who denies that al-Qaeda was behind the deadliest terrorist attack in American history. As Robert Satloff and Eric Trager recounted in the *Washington Post*:

In a May 2010 interview with Brookings Institution scholar Shadi Hamid, Morsi dismissed al-Qaeda's responsibility for the attacks. "When you come and tell me that the plane hit the tower like a knife in butter, then you are insulting us," Hamid reported Morsi as saying. "How did the plane cut through the steel like this? Something must have happened from the inside. It's impossible." Similarly, in 2007, Morsi reportedly declared that the United States "has never presented any evidences [sic] on the identity of those who committed that incident." In 2008, he called for a "huge scientific conference" to analyze "what caused the attack against a massive structure like the two towers."[13]

Of course, Morsi has kept mum about his views on 9/11 since assuming the Egyptian presidency. Why jeopardize all that high-tech American weaponry and cash? Besides, he knows from firsthand experience how easy it is to deceive naïve American *kuffar*. According to Morsi's wife, he joined the Muslim Brotherhood not in his Egyptian homeland, but in America, while he was a student at the University of Southern California in the late 1970s and early 1980s.[14] It's a good bet that Morsi hooked up with some of Cali's finest "Amerikhwan," or U.S.-based Muslim Brothers.

After earning a doctorate in rocket engineering (an area of expertise which could come in handy for his rocket-happy Hamas friends in Gaza), Morsi worked for three years as an assistant professor at Cal State University, Northridge. Two of his children were born in the United States and are U.S. citizens. But by 1985, Morsi had returned to Egypt, where he went on to steadily climb the Brotherhood's ranks and spend time in prison under the Mubarak regime.

Morsi's trajectory—a few years in America, followed by time in Egyptian prisons for his Brotherhood activities—mirrors in some ways that of one of the Brotherhood's greatest icons. Sayyid Qutb lived in the United States from 1948 to 1950, bouncing from New York City to Washington, D.C., to Greeley, Colorado, where he studied at a teachers' college. His hatred for America and for what was, in his eyes, its endless moral vice, grew with each new stop. In Greeley, an idyllic small town where alcohol was banned, Qutb saw a den of iniquity. After attending a dance at a local church, he wrote in disgust:

> The room convulsed with the feverish music from the gramo-phone. Dancing naked legs filled the hall, arms draped around the waists, chests met chests, lips met lips, and the atmosphere was full of love.[15]

Remember, this was the late 1940s, not exactly known as one of the more hedonistic periods in American history. If Qutb visited the United States today, he might spontaneously combust from shock. Instead, he was hanged in Egypt in 1966 after various stints in prison for participating in Brotherhood plots to overthrow the Egyptian government. His ideas, however—cultivated over his years as the Muslim Brotherhood's chief propagandist—still inspire legions of Islamic suicide bombers to combust themselves and others.

Qutb was a frail, bookish introvert who never married. Yet if there were a Jihadist Mount Rushmore carved somewhere deep in the wilds of the Saudi desert, his profile, along with al-Banna's, would surely be among those included. Qutb's writings have played a critical part in the genesis of the entire modern jihadist movement—particularly al-Qaeda (AQ). AQ heavyweights like Osama bin Laden, Ayman al-Zawahiri, and Anwar al-Awlaki (the American-born jihadi cleric killed in a U.S. drone strike in Yemen in 2011) have all cited Qutb as a major inspiration, and Iranian Supreme Leader Ali Khamenei has translated Qutb's books from Arabic to Farsi.[16]

Qutb's seminal work was called *Milestones*. In it, he called for Muslims to return to Islam as practiced in the seventh century. He considered the Muslim societies of his day and their rulers to be living in *jahiliyya*, the state of ignorance that supposedly existed before Islam's prophet Mohammed. Qutb's solution to jahiliyya was endless jihad: first to overthrow insufficiently Islamic rulers and institute sharia states, and then to conquer the entire world for Islam.

Qutb's goal was a global caliphate where non-Muslims (that is, those who survived) lived as oppressed, second-class citizens, or *dhimmis*. This philosophy of worldwide Islamic revolution was laid out in a chapter from *Milestones*, titled, simply, "Jihad":

> It would be naïve to assume that a call is raised to free the whole of humankind throughout the earth, and it is confined to preaching and exposition.... Since the objective of the message of Islam is a decisive declaration of man's freedom...it must employ jihad. It is immaterial whether the homeland of Islam...is in a condition of peace or whether it is threatened by its neighbors.[17]

"Freedom," to Qutb, meant submission to Allah and to sharia law, and throughout the chapter, he criticized the concept that holy war should be a last resort used only for defensive purposes. Islam, he believed, must always be on the offensive, always attacking, always seeking to subjugate, until no opposition remained, because "this struggle is not a temporary phase but an eternal state—an eternal state, as truth and falsehood cannot co-exist on this earth...the eternal struggle for the freedom of man will continue until [Islam] is purified for God."[18] Qutb's violent playbook, which became known as "Qutbism," has been followed by countless Islamic terrorist organizations, most notably, al-Qaeda. As a result, the Brotherhood today often distances itself from him, while at the same time trying to rationalize his incendiary rants. The MBers I've interviewed usually offer something along the lines of, "Many of Qutb's writings have been taken out of context. While some of his ideas are extreme, you have to consider the conditions in which he wrote them, under torture in an Egyptian prison. This experience changed Brother Sayyid and hardened him."

Milestones has caused more death and misery than any prison-produced "literature" in history since Hitler's *Mein Kampf*. Nevertheless, it's not hard to read between the lines that the Brothers believe Qutb is a genius and martyr who is unfairly demonized. They condemn his wanton calls to jihad and global insurrection only because they seek to maintain a moderate veneer before Western audiences. For instance, official Brotherhood websites still feature glowing tributes to Qutb, and the Ikhwan's current Supreme Guide and global leader, Mohammed Badie (who was imprisoned with Qutb in Egypt), has been described as a "devoted disciple" of the jihadi mastermind.[19]

During a February 2013 interview, the Washington Institute for Near East Policy's Eric Trager, who has interviewed Mohammed Morsi face to face, told me that the current Egyptian president is also an adherent of Qutb:

> [Morsi] was considered within the Brotherhood a hardliner—somebody who was there to enforce the Brotherhood's most hardline ideas, whether it came to saying that women and Christians can't even run for the presidency of Egypt, whether it was their foreign policy ideas or their hostility towards Israel.... Morsi is considered the icon of the Qutbists, as one former young Muslim Brother told me...[today's Ikhwan] have re-interpreted Sayyid Qutb as being less focused on violence, less focused on violent revolution, but still focused on revolution and the idea that the only way to achieve a

renaissance is through establishing an Islamic state that can then pursue more global aims.

Those global aims begin with "Cali" and end with "phate."

———————

How did we come to the point where a brazen 9/11 Truther who reveres Sayyid Qutb, considers Jews "apes and pigs," and calls America an enemy is now Egypt's most powerful man—with U.S. backing to boot? There have been a few important, ahem, *milestones* along the way. The most significant may have occurred on February 18, 2011, when Yusuf al-Qaradawi, the Brotherhood's celebrated Spiritual Guide, appeared in Cairo's Tahrir Square. It was the first time al-Qaradawi, who was banned under the Mubarak regime, had set foot on Egyptian soil in thirty years. In a triumphant return, he led Friday prayers for a crowd of hundreds of thousands and gave a sermon calling for the Muslim conquest of Jerusalem.[20]

The young, secular Egyptians so adoringly promoted by the Western media as the Facebook-and-Twitter-savvy face of the revolution—and the future leaders of a new, democratic Egypt—were nowhere to be found. Just a week before, when Mubarak was still desperately clinging to power, al-Qaradawi's presence in Cairo would have been unthinkable. But al-Qaradawi's speech was proof that the Muslim Brotherhood, long the most organized, influential, and ruthless political movement in Egypt, was now firmly in the driver's seat, and would take Egypt in a harshly Islamist direction.

■ In January 2012, Egypt held its first post-Mubarak parliamentary elections. Despite assurances from liberals in the press and academia as well as the State Department that Islamist parties would be marginalized and a secular consensus would emerge, the exact opposite happened—and in stunning, decisive fashion. The Muslim Brotherhood's Freedom and

Justice Party won 48 percent of the seats, while the al-Nour Party, an even more hardline Salafist faction, won 25 percent. Which meant Egypt's parliament would now lie firmly in the hands of sharia-breathing, anti-Western, anti-Semitic Islamists, as voted on by the Egyptian people, as some of us had warned was inevitable. Ain't Middle East "democracy" grand?

■ In April 2012, a delegation from the Muslim Brotherhood's Freedom and Justice Party visited the White House to meet with Obama administration officials—during Easter week, no less. Then-Obama spokesman Tommy Vietor explained the White House visit by stating: "We believe that it is in the interest of the United States to engage with all parties that are committed to democratic principles, especially nonviolence."[21] Yes, he was talking about the Muslim Brotherhood.

The Obama team's view of the Brotherhood as a force for good—a view which flies in the face of reality, facts, and history—has been reflected in the administration's policy of promoting the Islamist organization's interests, not only in Egypt, but everywhere from Libya to Tunisia to Syria to right here in the United States. Indeed, the Obama administration's support for the Muslim Brotherhood has gone a long way toward making the world's first modern Islamic terrorist group mainstream, even as the MB pushes for a new, global Islamist superpower.

■ After months of Muslim Brotherhood officials repeatedly promising that they would not present a candidate for the Egyptian presidency, the MB's Freedom and Justice Party (FJP) did exactly that. At first, the FJP offered Khairat el-Shater, a wily and charismatic Brotherhood veteran who has helped formulate much of the movement's current game plan. When Egypt's interim military government, flexing what was left of its waning influence (it also tried to dissolve the newly elected Islamist parliament), disqualified el-Shater as a candidate, the Brotherhood put Mohammed Morsi in his place. Morsi went on to win a narrow, controversial victory in the June 24, 2012, Egyptian presidential election. The rest, as we've seen, is Islamist history.

■ The idea that Egypt's military could neutralize Morsi and the fledgling Islamist parliament suffered a severe setback on August 12, 2012,
when Morsi forced the retirement of Field Marshal Mohammed Hussein
Tantawi—Egypt's defense minister and a Mubarak-era power broker—as
well as the army chief of staff and other senior generals.[22] It was a bold,
unexpected move that stunned observers—but it shouldn't have. Morsi
and the Brothers were clearly playing for keeps and consolidating power
quickly (on the same day as the sackings, Morsi also issued a declaration
expanding his powers as president). The Egyptian military's response to
these developments was submissive silence—even after Morsi replaced
Tantawi with General Abdel Fatah al-Sissi, a known Brotherhood
sympathizer.

The military's lack of response did not surprise National Review
Online's Andrew McCarthy, who wrote:

> The Egyptian military is a reflection of Egyptian society which,
> as we have now seen in election after election, is dominated
> by Islamists. Indeed, despite the good relations some top
> Egyptian military brass have had with the Pentagon, the fact
> is that some of the most important members of al Qaeda and
> other jihadist organizations have served in the Egyptian armed
> forces.[23]

In March 2013, the *Washington Times* reported that the Brotherhood
was attempting to stack the military and police forces with Islamists and
that overt Islamists were for the first time being admitted to Egypt's
military academy.[24]

■ On September 11, 2012, a mob of Egyptian Islamists—led by the
brother of al-Qaeda leader Ayman al-Zawahiri—rioted outside the U.S.
Embassy in Cairo. Several of them scaled the walls and tore down the
American flag, replacing it with the black flag of al-Qaeda.[25] Morsi made

no public statement of condemnation or regret until three days after the incident, and only after pressure from the Obama White House.[26]

On the same day that the American Embassy in Cairo was stormed, a mob of al-Qaeda–linked terrorists carried out a well-planned, coordinated assault on the U.S. consulate in Benghazi, Libya, that left four Americans dead, including Ambassador J. Christopher Stevens. Then, on September 13 and 14, Islamist mobs stormed the American embassies in Yemen and Tunis, with the Tunisians, like their Egyptian counterparts, raising the black flag of al-Qaeda over the building.[27]

Egypt. Libya. Yemen. Tunisia. All four are so-called "Arab Spring" countries in which the Obama administration supported "regime change"—to disastrous ends.

■ On November 22, 2012, just one day after the *New York Times* published an article in which Obama administration officials praised Morsi effusively for his role in helping to broker a ceasefire between Israel and Hamas, the budding pharaoh made a move for absolute power. Morsi issued a decree banning any opposition to his laws and decisions as president.

The announcement sparked riots and violence in Egypt that, as I write this in May 2013, are still flaring up from time to time around the country. Reports have also surfaced of Brotherhood and Salafi thugs raping women in Cairo,[28] setting up torture chambers to brutalize Morsi's opponents,[29] and enforcing sharia law. In December 2012, Morsi signed into law a new constitution enshrining sharia principles. It was written by the Islamist parliament and approved by 64 percent of Egyptian voters. Tellingly, the sessions during which the constitution was drafted were boycotted by Christians and secularists, who claimed—rightly—that the process had been hijacked by the Brotherhood and its Salafist allies.[30]

For Christians and secularists, things promise only to get worse. But no worries. According to the *New York Times*, "Mr. Obama told aides he was impressed with the Egyptian leader's pragmatic confidence.

He sensed an engineer's precision with surprisingly little ideology." Obama, the *Times* reported, considered Morsi "a straight shooter."[31]

No American president has so sorely misjudged an Islamic leader since Jimmy Carter praised Iran's Ayatollah Khomeini as a "fellow man of faith."[32]

―――――――

For the Muslim Brothers, the glorification of holy war and martyrdom found in their official creed is more than just words. For close to a century, the Brotherhood and its affiliates—which include Hamas—have engaged in terrorism and assassinations. Al-Banna's followers even collaborated with the Nazis in an effort to exterminate the Jews of the Middle East during World War II. A few years later, in 1948, the Brotherhood sent battalions to fight alongside Arab armies in their invasion of Israel.

Today, the Brotherhood refuses to recognize Israel's right to exist and propagates the kind of outlandish, anti-Jewish conspiracy theories that were commonplace in the infamous Nazi propaganda rag, *Der Sturmer*. It's no surprise, then, that the Brotherhood spawned one of Israel's fiercest enemies, the terrorist group Hamas. It is also no surprise that in October 2012, during a visit to an Egyptian mosque, Mohammed Morsi himself took part in prayers that called for Israel's destruction, mouthing "amen" as a cleric railed: "Oh Allah, absolve us of our sins, strengthen us, and grant us victory over the infidels. Oh Allah, destroy the Jews and their supporters. Oh Allah, disperse them, rend them asunder."[33]

Also in October 2012, Mohammed Badie, the Brotherhood's Cairo-based Supreme Guide and overall global leader, declared:

> The time has come for the Islamic nation to unite around one man for the sake of Jerusalem and Palestine. The Jews have

dominated the land, spread corruption on earth, spilled the blood of believers and in their actions profaned holy places, including their own.

Zionists only understand the language of force and will not relent without duress. This will only happen through holy Jihad, high sacrifices and all forms of resistance. The day they realize we will march this path and raise the banner of Jihad for the sake of God, is the day they will relent and stop their tyranny.[34]

Badie's jihadist bile isn't reserved solely for the Jews, mind you. After all, a proper Islamist can't take a swipe at the Little Satan, Israel, without also hitting the Great Satan for good measure. In an October 2010 speech that amounted to a virtual declaration of war against the United States, Badie railed against "Zionist-American tyranny" and predicted triumphantly that the United States was "heading towards its demise." Two months later, the so-called Arab Spring began, with the U.S. government enthusiastically backing—you guessed it—none other than Mohammed Badie's Muslim Brotherhood and its satellites across the Middle East and North Africa.

Understand that Badie's statements about America and Israel are not the ravings of a low-level, fringe cleric in some back-alley Suez mosque. He and Morsi are arguably the two most influential and powerful Muslim Brothers *in the world*. Their influence may only be topped by that of the movement's Spiritual Guide, Yusuf al-Qaradawi—the third person in what is essentially an Ikhwan Unholy Trinity.

In 1999, al-Qaradawi, an Egyptian native now based in Qatar, was banned from entering the United States because of his terror ties.[35] Nevertheless, the octogenarian preacher remains the equivalent of a jihadi rock star in the Muslim world. He hosts a top-rated weekly television show, called *Sharia and Life*, on Al-Jazeera television that is seen by tens of millions of Muslims across the Middle East. He also runs a heavily trafficked website called IslamOnline.

Islam may not have the equivalent of a pope, but al-Qaradawi, whom the Anti-Defamation League calls a "Theologian of Terror,"[36] is just about the closest thing to a galvanizing religious authority in the Sunni Muslim world. And he's Brotherhood, through and through. Indeed, he has been offered the position of MB Supreme Guide (the overall global leadership role Badie currently fills) on at least two occasions, but turned it down because he felt he could have more impact for the movement in other capacities.[37] Given his massive, multi-media global presence, it's hard to argue with al-Qaradawi's decision.

"Sheikh Yusuf al-Qaradawi is more than just an ideologue," Middle East expert Walid Phares told me in a 2012 interview. "He is also a strategist. We're talking about a Lenin here—a jihadi Lenin who controls the flow of the ideology but also gives the nod with regards to general strategic direction. He's the mentor today for the Muslim Brotherhood."[38]

Al-Qaradawi has used his position as the Brotherhood's chief Islamic jurist to sanction suicide bombings against American troops, as well as against Israeli women and children, and to praise Hitler as a divine instrument of Allah who put the Jews "in their place."[39] Yet in late 2011, reports surfaced that the Obama administration was using him as a key mediator in peace talks with the Taliban.[40]

During a 2009 speech on Al-Jazeera, al-Qaradawi openly fantasized about doing some Jew-killing of his own:

> I'd like to say that the only thing I hope for is that as my life approaches its end, Allah will give me an opportunity to go to the land of Jihad and resistance, even if in a wheelchair. I will shoot Allah's enemies, the Jews, and they will throw a bomb at me, and thus, I will seal my life with martyrdom. Praise be to Allah, Lord of the Worlds.[41]

This is nothing less than incitement to genocide, broadcast far and wide across the Muslim world via satellite. Yet every Muslim Brotherhood–linked figure I've interviewed can agree on one thing: they absolutely revere Sheikh Yusuf al-Qaradawi. Indeed, his views on Jews and Israel are par for the course within the Ikhwan movement. The destruction of Israel is a key, foundational principle for the Brotherhood on which the movement will never compromise, no matter how much extortion money the U.S. government coughs up.

———

Thanks to Mohammed Morsi's rise, Egypt's peace treaty with Israel, forged in 1979, will eventually be history. It's not a matter of if, but when. In their guts, Israeli leaders know this. They also know that what was almost unthinkable as recently as 2010—a military confrontation of some kind with their populous, heavily-armed southern neighbor and historical nemesis—is a distinct possibility sometime in the next few years.

The Muslim Brotherhood's hatred of the Jews is implacable, and fighting a war against Israel would help Morsi deflect public attention from food shortages, high levels of unemployment, and sectarian strife at home.

A 2012 poll by The Israel Project, a Washington, D.C.–based advocacy group, found that 77 percent of Egyptians agreed that, "The peace treaty with Israel is no longer useful and should be dissolved."[42]

Already, in the wake of Mubarak's ouster, Egypt's Sinai Peninsula has become a launching pad for terror attacks and rockets against Israeli soldiers and civilians.

When I arrived in Israel in August 2011 to co-host some of Glenn Beck's "Restoring Courage" live events, I was greeted with news of one such attack that had occurred only minutes before. Jihadists striking out of Sinai had fired on tour buses near the Israeli resort town of Eilat, killing eight Israeli civilians and wounding several more. Returning fire on the terrorists, Israel Defense Forces unintentionally killed six Egyptian soldiers.

Despite an immediate Israeli apology, Egypt's Brotherhood pounced, blaming the incident on Israel. One top MB leader hinted at military retaliation for the Egyptian soldiers' accidental deaths, warning that, "Zionists should realize that Egyptian blood now has a price, and it's a very high price after the success of our blessed revolution."[43] A year later, the Brotherhood—always game to market wild anti-Semitic conspiracy theories—publicly accused Israel's Mossad intelligence service of orchestrating yet another Sinai flare-up that saw jihadists storm an Egyptian police compound and kill sixteen policemen.[44]

Yes, the "blessed revolution" has done wonders for Egypt, Sinai in particular. The area has always been a sort of lawless zone where thieves, bandits, smugglers, and traffickers have plied their various illegal trades. Today, however, Sinai is taking on a much more sinister shape. Under Morsi's stewardship, it has become an Islamic terror base—including for al-Qaeda—and a front in the global jihad on Israel's southern border.

"What we see [in Sinai] today is a kind of coalition between the Salafis, some of them coming from Yemen, from Saudi Arabia, Palestinians and Bedouins," Israeli terrorism expert Dr. Ely Karmon told me in late 2012.[45] Incidentally, Israel controlled Sinai from 1967 until it withdrew from the area altogether in 1982 as part of the Camp David Accords. Ah, the endless benefits of "land for peace."

In the end, Sinai could prove to be the flashpoint that sparks a future war between Egypt and Israel. In that next engagement, whenever it comes (and it's coming), the Israelis will surely be comforted to know that Egypt's army will be fighting with high-tech American weaponry. As of this writing, the Obama administration was on schedule to deliver to Egypt in 2013 no less than twenty F-16 fighter jets and two hundred Abrams tanks.[46]

The shipments are part of a billion dollar deal struck with the government of Hosni Mubarak—a longtime U.S. ally, remember—in 2010, before the onset of the so-called Arab Spring that brought Morsi to power.[47] Instead of canceling the deal and telling Morsi and the Brotherhood to go pound Sahara sand, the Obama administration is helping to arm an avowed enemy of the United States and Israel.

Mind you, President Obama had already pledged a staggering $1 billion in aid back in May 2011 to support Egypt's revolution (what's a record-setting deficit when you can help fund hostile Egyptian Islamists?). A dogged, pro-Obama optimist might point out that this hefty aid package was necessary to ensure that the revolution worked out in America's best interests and solidified Egypt's peace treaty with Israel, except the exact opposite has happened on both counts, and in humiliating fashion. So how to explain the Obama administration's ongoing weapons shipments to the Morsi regime? And what about the reported delivery of 140,000 teargas canisters from the U.S. government to Egypt's Interior Ministry in April 2013?[48] What kind of message does that send from the Obama administration to the Brotherhood's secular, domestic opposition—the obvious target of said teargas?

It was the same kind of message Secretary of State John Kerry's March 2013 announcement—complete with Cairo photo-op alongside Morsi—of an additional $250 million in U.S. aid to Egypt sent to the Brotherhood and the world: *come hell or high water, we're with the Ikhwan.*

The State Department, by the way, had been pushing to provide hundreds of millions of dollars in additional funds to Morsi's government but was blocked from doing so by Congress.[49]

———

The F-16s. The Abrams tanks. The teargas. The $250 million. All of it came *after* the Islamist die had already been cast in Egypt. By then, the

Obama administration knew full well what it was dealing with in the form of Morsi and the Brotherhood. Video had emerged of Morsi calling Jews "blood-suckers" and "the descendants of apes and pigs," railing against "American enemies," and calling for a Muslim boycott of U.S. goods.[50] Any illusion of a moderate Brotherhood should have long since vanished.

So why does the Obama administration continue to embrace and empower the Brothers? As we'll see, the hard-left, morally relativist ideology of President Obama and his team is certainly one major factor. Another is ignorance about the nature of the enemy. Here's an analysis from a November 2012 piece in Britain's *Daily Telegraph*:

> Western governments have been pleasantly surprised by what they have seen from the Muslim Brotherhood.... The relationships are not yet deep, but the first impression of many Westerners is that the articulate, suited and often US-educated businessmen they meet are easier to talk to than many expected. This honeymoon has been sweetened by the discovery that the leaders of Egypt's Muslim Brotherhood seem largely centre-Right on the economy. While they have a different religious and political worldview, they want Western investment, trade and expertise; they don't want to become isolated like post-revolution Iran.[51]

That perfectly encapsulates the prevailing view of the Muslim Brotherhood among Western governments. *No robes, no bombs, nice suits, welcoming smiles, and fluent English—we can work with these guys.* The problem with this insane narrative of the Ikhwan as the "anti-al-Qaeda" is that al-Qaeda would not exist without the Brotherhood. The MB birthed AQ and although the two organizations have clear tactical differences today, they both share the exact same ideology and goals.

The teachings of Brotherhood ideologues like Hassan al-Banna and Sayyid Qutb inspired the entire modern Islamic terrorist enterprise—including al-Qaeda, Hamas, and, in many ways, the Shia revolutionaries in Iran. Those teachings perfectly supplement Islam's core texts, the Koran and Sunnah, which are littered throughout with calls for conquest and violence against non-Muslims. Combine the two—revolutionary ideology and extreme theology—and you have a lethal mix. Essentially, the Muslim Brotherhood is a totalitarian political movement with theological underpinnings. Nazis sought a thousand-year Reich founded on racial superiority; the Soviets wanted a global communist system; the Muslim Brotherhood and its offshoots like al-Qaeda, as well as the Shia jihadist axis of Iran and Hezbollah, all seek a global caliphate governed by sharia law. It's a seamless transition, from one great American enemy to the next.

The rise of the Muslim Brotherhood and the global Sunni Islamist movement does indeed represent the rise of America's next great enemy. China might be a great enemy in the future, and a declining (but still militarily formidable) Russia might be our enemy of the past, but the revolutionary Islamism epitomized by the Muslim Brotherhood is rapidly emerging as our great enemy of today. Yes, Iran is, as I write this, on the verge of acquiring nuclear weapons that would change the world landscape in horrific ways and pose an existential threat to the United States. But I believe, based on years of conversations with Israeli officials, that Israel will never allow Iran to acquire a nuclear weapon and will instead, at some point, conduct a preemptive strike against Iran's nuclear weapons facilities. If that happens, the Iranian regime will go from aspiring to lead the Islamic world to being a vengeful, weakened terrorist sponsor. And despite current differences (seen most clearly in the Syrian civil war, where Iran and Hezbollah are battling the Brotherhood and al-Qaeda as I write), I see Shia Iran eventually working closely with the Brotherhood-led Sunni Islamist movement toward the common goals of destroying Israel and taking on the West. The only question is whether Tehran will accept being a subsidiary or still angle to be top dog.

The wild card in this conversation, of course, is North Korea. Little is known about Kim Jong-un other than his fondness for Dennis Rodman and garish haircuts. He seems the type who tortured kittens and immersed himself in violent video games and films while growing up a spoiled child in his equally depraved father's palace in Pyongyang. Now this chubby sociopath is in control of a growing nuclear arsenal and his regime is vowing to blow U.S. cities off the map. In order to one day accomplish that feat, North Korea, like Iran, is actively working on intercontinental ballistic missiles that can reach the United States.

Also like Iran, Kim's regime has worked on electromagnetic pulse (or EMP) technology that could destroy America's electrical grid and send us back into the nineteenth century. All it would take is one nuclear missile, mounted on a Scud and fired from the deck of, say, an unmarked freighter a few hundred miles off of America's coast. Once that missile is detonated in the atmosphere above the United States, frying everything below, life as we know it ends, and the country collapses into chaos. Then we're talking about America's *last* great enemy.

The flip side is that the North Korean regime is eminently beatable and isolated and—minus its acquiring intercontinental ballistic missiles or EMP capabilities—can be erased overnight by the United States if a military engagement were to break out (and if the Obama administration were willing to use the appropriate force—a big if). At the end of the day, the North Korean regime just doesn't have the staying power, global reach, or numbers to be a long-term, existential threat.

Islamism, on the other hand, has an established track record of 1,400 years and counting of expansionist, jihadist carnage, not to mention tens if not hundreds of millions of fanatical adherents. Yet even a small number of Islamists can go a long way. Nineteen hijackers changed the course of American and world history on 9/11. Two young Islamic terrorists in

Boston were able to kill three people, wound 264 more, and shut down a major American city. Even failed attacks, like we saw with the attempted "Underwear Bombing" on Christmas Day 2009, chip away at the foundations of our country, changing the way we live and diminishing our freedoms.

The so-called Arab Spring—in reality, an Islamist Winter—has encouraged Islamist forces, led by the Muslim Brotherhood, to gain confidence that their ultimate goal is in sight: the reestablishment of a global Islamic caliphate that would see the entire Muslim world unite politically, economically, and militarily to aggressively take on the West and Israel in all spheres, while at the same time controlling a sizable chunk of the world's oil supplies and speaking with one powerful, influential voice at the UN.

Without the spread of the Muslim Brotherhood's destructive influence, there would be no al-Qaeda, there would be no Hamas, there would have been no 9/11, no War on Terror—heck, you'd even be able to leave your shoes on at the airport. This is not a group the United States government should be in the business of embracing—it's a group that should be weakened, marginalized, discredited, and defeated at every turn, along with the Islamist ideology it espouses. That includes here at home, where Muslim Brotherhood–linked organizations are securing positions in sensitive areas of the U.S. government thanks to the Obama administration's warm embrace of what it considers the MB's "moderate" brand of Islam. In this book, I'll show how the Muslim Brotherhood and their Sunni Islamist allies (working, when their interests intersect, with Shia jihadists), are rapidly positioning themselves as America's greatest scourge—and what we need to do about it.

An Islamist Winter is not just coming: it's already upon us. America's next great enemy is not just ascendant in the Middle East, it has set up shop inside the United States. Our government is not just ignorant of the enemy's ideology and goals, it is aiding and abetting their advance at every turn. The current Muslim Brotherhood–driven Islamist offensive can be defeated, just as other great waves of jihadist conquest have been driven back through the centuries. But to achieve victory we must first know our enemy. If the government will not take up that charge, the people must. Read on to find out what America is facing and how we can turn the tide.

CHAPTER TWO

HOW THEY'RE WINNING (AND HOW WE'RE HELPING)

"**T**his can't be the place. Can it?"

My cameraman Ian and I were standing in front of a non-descript building on a Brussels side street, trying to locate the headquarters of an organization that's been called "an umbrella group that comprises the global Muslim Brotherhood in Europe."[1]

"I'm pretty sure it's the place," Ian answered me. "See that little piece of paper right there in the slot next to the doorbell? It says 'Federation of Islamic Organisations in Europe.'"

It dawned on me that I should not have been surprised at all. It was just like the Muslim Brotherhood to stealthily tuck away one of its more important purported assets.

FIOE boasts some twenty-eight member organizations that hail from across the European Union, as well as from Russia and Turkey.[2]

FIOE representatives meet with officials from the EU and other political bodies to lobby on Islamic issues and—in classic Western Brotherhood fashion—present FIOE as Europe's only credible Muslim dialogue partner.

After ringing the doorbell of the organization's Brussels base repeatedly with no answer, I walked around the side of the building to investigate further and was met by a short, fifty-something Arab man in a work shirt and paint-splattered jeans. In broken English, he explained that he commuted in from France every day to do maintenance work on the building. He didn't seem to understand what "FIOE" meant. All he knew was that he was making a living.

As we were talking, another Arab man who looked barely out of his teens walked up to us and asked who we were looking for. His behavior seemed suspicious from the outset.

"No one is here," he said at first. Then, after a few minutes of chatting with us about why we were in Brussels, he changed his tune.

"I'll go in and check if anyone is upstairs," he said, disappearing into the building.

A few minutes later, he emerged. "No one is here," he said, looking as if he were concealing a smile. "But I will take down your information and they will call you when they get back."

As I wrote down my phone number and email address, two young Arab women in hijabs walked past us and into the building. Yes, the place was just stone empty.

In my travels around Brussels, I found that it represented a sort of microcosm of the Islamist project in the West. Before our stop at FIOE headquarters, we spent time at the Great Mosque of Brussels, a large structure built with Saudi funding that lies just a block from European Union buildings. Anti-Semitic attacks are on the rise in the city, a phenomenon many locals I spoke to attributed to a growing Muslim presence that now makes up some 30 percent of Brussels's overall population.

Women covered in hijabs and niqabs and men in Islamic garb are common sights, and Muslim Brotherhood front organizations like FIOE abound, always ready to make their case to officials based in the European Union's headquarters.

Other than EU officials, no one I spoke to, particularly local Jews, held much optimism about Brussels's future. Aggressive Islamization, they believed, would continue apace, which meant culture clashes were inevitable—in Belgium and other European countries—because Europe, with its open borders immigration polices, aging indigenous populations, collapsing economies, and wholesale abandonment of its once-strong Judeo-Christian heritage and identity, has placed itself in an extremely precarious position. Its boisterous, confident Muslim minority—which now numbers some 20 million overall in European Union countries, not counting illegal arrivals—smells weakness and complacency in its hedonistic hosts. News of Islamic terrorism-related arrests is now a part of daily life in Europe, and sharia enclaves are not just on the horizon: they're already present in Great Britain, the Netherlands, Sweden, France, Germany, and elsewhere. Confrontation is coming—and it won't be pretty. Walk around some of Europe's more hardcore Muslim neighborhoods, as I have, and you can almost feel it in your bones.

Unfortunately, America seems determined to duplicate Europe's mistakes in nearly every way.

———

Although it has reached new and dangerous heights under the Obama administration, the U.S. government's courtship of the Muslim Brotherhood actually dates back to the early 1950s under President Dwight D. Eisenhower, when the CIA backed Said Ramadan, son-in-law of MB founder Hassan al-Banna and father of Islamist provocateur Tariq Ramadan.[3] Then, as now, American decision-makers believed the Brotherhood could prove an invaluable asset against an implacable foe. During

Eisenhower's day, it was the Soviet Union, which had gobbled up Muslim Central Asia and was flexing its muscle throughout the Middle East—and whose atheism the Brothers despised. Today, the great enemy is seen as al-Qaeda and affiliated hardcore Salafi jihadi groups, whose violent agenda the Brotherhood supposedly opposes (when in reality the Brotherhood opposes only the timing of al-Qaeda's jihad, not its endgame).

Likewise, today, as in Eisenhower's day, policymakers are seeking a Muslim voice that has credibility—both theologically and on the all-important Arab street—and has the numbers, influence, and reach to speak to a broad tract of the Islamic world in ways favorable to the West. The Ikhwan was—and is—that voice, or so the wishful thinking has gone inside the Washington Beltway. During the Cold War, the United States wanted the Brothers to denounce atheistic communism to the Muslim masses. Today, U.S. policymakers assume the Brotherhood can be the crucial force that turns Muslims away from jihad and toward a moderate, non-violent form of Islamism. Unfortunately, that's not going to happen, because surface appearances aside, the Muslim Brothers are hardly moderates. As respected Middle East expert Daniel Pipes explains:

> All Islamists are one; a moderate Islamist is as fantastical a notion as a moderate Nazi. Every member of this barbaric movement is a potential totalitarian thug. Western governments should neither accept nor work with the one or the other.[4]

Yet for the better part of the last two decades, particularly since 9/11, the U.S. government—under both Republican and Democrat administrations—has done exactly that, investing in the Muslim Brotherhood as a "moderate" counterweight to violent jihadists. The Brotherhood, of course, has willingly taken all of the funding, support, and legitimacy that a U.S. seal of approval brings and used it to its own devious ends.

During the Cold War, the damage caused by America's romance with the Brotherhood was limited, though Osama bin Laden and other MB-linked terrorists indirectly benefited from American support for the Afghan *mujahideen* against the Soviets. Today, however, when America's next great enemy is revolutionary Sunni Islamism, aid to the Muslim Brotherhood means supporting a group devoted to establishing a caliphate ruled by sharia law—not to mention, a group that has America squarely in its crosshairs. How's that for realpolitik?

Whereas al-Qaeda seeks to bring about sharia states rapidly through violence, the Muslim Brothers favor a gradual, termite-like approach, burrowing deeply into a host society and eating away at it slowly from within. They'll acquire positions of influence, often behind the scenes, in government, academia, and the media. They'll start Islamic organizations at the grassroots level and build (or slowly absorb) mosques and Islamic schools. They'll even hold their nose and work with ideologically divergent factions, namely the Left, to advance their ultimate goals. Then, when they have the numbers and the influence, and the situation is deemed ideal, the final phase can begin. It could consist of violent jihad, depending on the favorability of conditions on the ground in a given country. But jihad may not be necessary—exploiting domestic instability to peacefully seize power has been the Brotherhood's model thus far for the Middle East and North Africa during the so-called Arab Spring. And the results have been impressive.

■ In Egypt and Tunisia, Muslim Brotherhood parties are now in control following electoral victories.

■ In Morocco, an Islamist named Abdelilah Benkirane was elected prime minister in 2011. He's a member of the Justice and Development Party, the MB's Moroccan offshoot, which won a plurality of seats in the country's 2011 parliamentary elections.

■ Although the Brotherhood's Libyan affiliate, the Justice and Construction Party, finished a distant second in national elections in July 2012 (after being favored to win), the party has quickly regrouped, and conditions on the ground favor the Brothers' eventual dominance.

Post-Gaddafi Libya remains a frighteningly unstable place. Its second largest city, Benghazi, is a jihadist hotbed where Westerners dare not tread (as America so painfully learned with the consulate attack of September 11, 2012).

■ In Jordan, the Brotherhood's Islamic Action Front, the main opposition force to King Abdullah II, is gaining ground fast on the heels of the Islamist Winter revolutions and has helped lead regular demonstrations against the monarchy. Abdullah is well aware of the gathering Ikhwan threat, a view he shared in an expansive, 2013 interview with Jeffrey Goldberg of *The Atlantic*:

> ...[Abdullah] believes his Western allies are naive about the Brotherhood's intentions. "When you go to the State Department and talk about this, they're like, 'This is just the liberals talking, this is the monarch saying that the Muslim Brotherhood is deep-rooted and sinister.'" Some of his Western interlocutors, [Abdullah] told me, argue that "the only way you can have democracy is through the Muslim Brotherhood." His job, he says, is to point out that the Brotherhood is run by "wolves in sheep's clothing" and wants to impose its retrograde vision of society and its anti-Western politics on the Muslim Middle East. This, he said, is "our major fight"—to prevent the Muslim Brothers from conniving their way into power across the region.... The king argues that a new, radical alliance is emerging—one that both complements and rivals the Iranian-led Shia crescent. "I see a Muslim Brotherhood crescent developing in Egypt and Turkey," he told me. "The Arab Spring highlighted a new crescent in the process of development."[5]

■ Events unfolding in Jordan's next door neighbor, Syria, may go a long way toward determining King Abdullah's fate. Already, over half a million Syrian refugees have crossed into Jordan as a result of Syria's brutal civil war.[6] As I write this, the "victor" in that bloody conflict has yet to be determined, even after some eighty thousand civilians (and counting) have been killed. One thing, however, seems certain: sharia will rule in Syria if dictator Bashar al-Assad is toppled. According to the *New York Times*:

> In Syria's largest city, Aleppo, rebels aligned with Al Qaeda control the power plant, run the bakeries and head a court that applies Islamic law. Elsewhere, they have seized government oil fields, put employees back to work and now profit from the crude they produce.
>
> Across Syria, rebel-held areas are dotted with Islamic courts staffed by lawyers and clerics, and by fighting brigades led by extremists. Even the Supreme Military Council, the umbrella rebel organization whose formation the West had hoped would sideline radical groups, is stocked with commanders who want to infuse Islamic law into a future Syrian government.
>
> Nowhere in rebel-controlled Syria is there a secular fighting force to speak of.[7]

■ Like its fellow monarchy in Jordan, the Saudi Royal Family is alarmed by the Muslim Brotherhood's growing clout. The Saudis know the Brotherhood well. For decades the Saudi regime worked closely with the Brotherhood to spread Islamism worldwide. But the relationship has become strained, with the Saudi Royals feeling threatened by an "Arab Spring" that brought the MB to dominance through democratic means, undercutting the legitimacy of the Saudi monarchy.

In an April 2013 interview on Arab television, Saudi Prince Alwaleed Bin Talal said of the revolutions sweeping the region, "I don't refer to it as 'the Arab Spring,' but rather as 'the so-called Arab Spring.' I call it 'the Arab destruction.'" He continued, "If any ruler thinks he is immune, he is making a grave mistake. Nobody is immune.... Whoever thinks that this flame will not reach his country is mistaken." Alwaleed added that in his own country "several Saudi sheikhs reek of Muslim Brotherhood. This is known to all. I won't mention names, but this is clear.... We should meet more of the people's demands, to avoid giving the [Brotherhood] the opportunity to take advantage of the poverty, the housing problems, or the cost of living."[8] The Brotherhood, in other words, is a revolutionary problem, not a solution.

■ Saudi Arabia's neighbors in the Persian Gulf region are experiencing similar Brotherhood surges. In the case of Qatar, its relations with the Ikhwan are by choice. The wealthy kingdom, riding the regional Islamist wave, is rapidly replacing Saudi Arabia as the MB's main global bankroller, pledging billions, for example, to help prop up the Mohammed Morsi regime in Egypt.

In the United Arab Emirates, however, ninety-four people were arrested in early 2013 and charged with participating in an alleged Muslim Brotherhood plot to overthrow the government.[9] Kuwait worked with the UAE to break up the accused MB cell.[10] Dubai's police chief has warned repeatedly about the Brotherhood's noxious influence in the Emirates, and has wondered aloud why the West "sympathizes, adopts and supports" the Ikhwan.[11]

———

The Brothers believe that in the long run, they'll win, not only in the Arab world, but in the West, where they make a show of publicly condemning terrorist acts their own poisonous ideology has helped inspire.

For instance, the mainstream media showed little interest in the fact that the Tsarnaev brothers attended the Islamic Society of Boston (ISB) mosque in Cambridge before carrying out their deadly attack on the Boston Marathon in April 2013. ISB is owned and operated by the Muslim American Society, which federal prosecutors have described as an "overt arm of the Muslim Brotherhood in America."[12] So what did the Tsarnaevs learn at ISB? Did the mosque's teachings play a part in their radicalization process? We may never know, and the media isn't exactly breaking down the mosque's doors to inquire.

We do know, however, that the Tsarnaevs were not the only terrorists who have attended ISB. Former worshippers include Aafia Siddiqui, a convicted al-Qaeda terrorist; Tarek Mehanna, who was sentenced to seventeen years in prison in 2012 for conspiring to aid al-Qaeda; and Abdulrahman Alamoudi, the mosque's first president and an al-Qaeda financier, who was convicted in federal court in 2004 for his role in an assassination plot against then-Saudi Crown Prince Abdullah.[13] Alamoudi, incidentally, was an "outreach partner" for the Bill Clinton and George W. Bush administrations.[14]

In 1996, Alamoudi spoke at an Islamic conference where he summarized the Brotherhood's strategy in the United States:

> I have no doubt in my mind, Muslims sooner or later will be the moral leadership of America. It depends on me and you, either we do it now or we do it after a hundred years, but this country will become a Muslim country. And I (think) if we are outside this country we can say 'oh, Allah destroy America', but once we are here, our mission in this country is to change it.... There is nowhere for Muslims to be violent in America, nowhere at all. We have other means to do it. You can be violent anywhere else but in America.[15]

Got that? Muslims can kill and maim unbelievers anywhere they want, but in America the name of the game is to be an Islamist in sheep's clothing. Alamoudi's declaration is hardly surprising since he was merely repeating themes laid out in the Brotherhood's own documents years before.

THE PROJECT

In late September 2012, I appeared in a two-part documentary series produced by TheBlaze TV detailing one of the most important documents you've probably never heard of. Don't be offended—the vast majority of our intelligence community has never heard of it either.

The documentary featured a host of leading terrorism analysts and Islamism experts, as well as former and current U.S. lawmakers and intelligence officials, breaking down a Muslim Brotherhood manifesto that has become known simply as, "The Project." The existence of the fourteen-page document was first revealed in a 2005 book, published in France, by Swiss journalist Sylvain Besson.[16] According to Besson, The Project was recovered when Swiss authorities raided the lakeside villa of longtime Muslim Brotherhood "foreign minister" Youssef Nada shortly after the 9/11 attacks.

Dated December 1, 1982, it outlines a twelve-point strategy for the Muslim Brotherhood to "establish an Islamic government on earth." Nada reportedly told Swiss authorities that the strategic plan had been drafted by "Islamic researchers" affiliated with the Brotherhood, but he also downplayed The Project as an insignificant document (in his authorized biography, he says it was actually found in a Brotherhood colleague's home down the street, not his).[17]

Not surprisingly, it's much more important than Nada has let on. Some have speculated that Yusuf al-Qaradawi, the Brotherhood's

Spiritual Guide, had a hand in drafting The Project.[18] He certainly echoed it in his 1990 book, *Priorities of the Islamic Movement in the Coming Phase*. According to Middle East expert Olivier Guitta:

> "The Project" is a roadmap for achieving the installation of Islamic regimes in the West via propaganda, preaching, and, if necessary, war. It's the same idea expressed by Sheikh Qaradawi in 1995 when he said, "We will conquer Europe, we will conquer America, not by the sword but by our Dawa [proselytizing]."[19]

One intelligence official told Besson that The Project signifies "a totalitarian ideology of infiltration which represents, in the end, the greatest danger for European societies."[20] Juan Zarate, President George W. Bush's counterterrorism czar, told the Swiss author that the document represents the Brothers' blueprint for "spreading their political ideology." Zarate added, "The Muslim Brotherhood is a group that worries us not because it deals with philosophical or ideological ideas but because it defends the use of violence against civilians."[21]

My friend and colleague Patrick Poole, who was the first U.S.-based journalist to report on The Project, summarized the tactics, techniques, and goals it set for the Brotherhood:

- Develop a comprehensive hundred-year plan to advance Islamist ideology throughout the world
- Network and coordinate actions between like-minded Islamist organizations
- Avoid open alliances with known terrorist organizations and individuals to display the appearance of "moderation"

- Infiltrate Muslim organizations to realign them to meet Muslim Brotherhood goals
- Establish financial networks to fund work of converting the West
- Conduct surveillance, obtain data, and establish databases to store such information
- Establish a media watchdog system to warn Muslims of "international plots fomented against them"
- Build extensive social networks of schools, hospitals, and charitable organizations dedicated to Islamist ideals
- Engage committed Muslims in all Western institutions, including in government, NGOs, private organizations, and labor unions
- Create autonomous "security forces" to protect Muslims in the West
- Keep Muslims living in the West "in a *jihad* frame of mind"
- Support jihadist movements throughout the Muslim world through preaching, propaganda, personnel, funding, and technical and operational support
- Make the Palestinian cause a wedge issue for Muslims
- Instigate hate campaigns against Jews and reject any discussion of conciliation or coexistence with them
- Create jihad terror cells within Palestine
- Link the terrorist activities in Palestine with the global terror movement[22]

In short, more than thirty years ago the Brotherhood laid out a strategy to put up a false front of peace, coexistence, and cooperation to the Western world, while acting covertly to subvert those same ideals—

and to a large degree they have succeeded. In 2004, for instance, the Dutch Secret Service observed how the MB worked in the Netherlands:

> Radical branches of the Muslim Brotherhood employ covert Dawa strategies. Rather than confronting the state power with direct violence, this strategy seeks to gradually undermine it by infiltrating and eventually taking over the civil service, the judicature, schools, local administrations, et cetera. Apart from clandestine infiltration, covert Dawa may also be aimed at inciting Muslim minorities to civil disobedience, promoting parallel power structures or even inciting Muslim masses to a revolt.[23]

As Poole notes, The Project lays out the global strategy the Muslim Brotherhood has followed for decades, yet it has been ignored by the media:

> One might be led to think that if international law enforcement authorities and Western intelligence agencies had discovered a...document revealing a top-secret plan developed by the oldest Islamist organization with one of the most extensive terror networks in the world to launch a program of "cultural invasion" and eventual conquest of the West that virtually mirrors the tactics used by Islamists for more than two decades, that such news would scream from headlines published on the front pages and above the fold of the *New York Times*, *Washington Post*, *London Times*, *Le Monde*, *Bild*, and *La Repubblica*. If that's what you might think, you would be wrong.[24]

And it gets worse.

CIVILIZATION JIHAD

Suppose, during a previous era, that U.S. authorities were able to obtain documents containing a comprehensive list of Soviet front organizations operating inside the United States. Suppose these documents not only provided a list of all the major players seeking to destroy America from within and subvert it to communism, but also laid out specifics on how they would go about doing so. Imagine striking this mother lode in 1948, as the Cold War was heating up, or finding a similar treasure trove on Nazi infiltration as Hitler's war machine was beginning its catastrophic march in 1939. This would have been a landmark intelligence breakthrough, heralded by the U.S. government as a game changer that would, in the long run, help preserve American freedom and liberty, not to mention an untold number of American lives.

What if I told you the U.S. government has such documents in its possession today? Except these documents don't concern great enemies of the past, like the Soviets or the Nazis. Rather, they expose the nefarious activities on U.S. soil of America's next great enemy: the Muslim Brotherhood. Wouldn't you want the government to take decisive action against the organizations named in these documents and inform the American people?

Well, brace yourself. The government does indeed have such documents in its possession. But rather than shutting down the groups named within and prosecuting their leaders for sedition, it has rushed headlong to embrace them.

The man behind the most revealing of these documents is Mohamed Akram Adlouni, a former top U.S. Muslim Brotherhood leader connected to the Hamas network who has worked out of Lebanon in recent years. Akram's name appeared in multiple exhibits presented as government evidence in the landmark Holy Land Foundation terrorism trial (which saw several American Brotherhood operatives convicted for funding Hamas).

According to court documents, Akram was the head of planning for the senior Muslim Brotherhood network in America and held other key positions within the organization, including a place on the U.S. Ikhwan's Shura Council.[25] In short, he's no mere bit player on the fringes of the MB universe; rather, he was a very important cog in the American Brotherhood before returning to work for the movement in his native Middle East, where he remains a key Ikhwani today.

One of the exhibits showcased by prosecutors in the Holy Land Foundation trial was a document authored by Akram in May 1991. Called, "An Explanatory Memorandum on the General Strategic Goal for the Group in North America," it was directed to Akram's fellow MB leaders and played a decisive role in forging the long-term vision of the organization in North America.[26]

The memo lays out a multi-pronged plan to wage a new kind of warfare from within the United States—not one waged with bombs or bullets in classic terrorist style, but a covert war of deception fought in the media, in the courtrooms and classrooms, in our political institutions, and throughout our civic life.[27]

In the introduction to the memo, Akram expands on principles previously agreed upon by Brotherhood leaders in 1987. He outlines a plan of "settlement" whereby the Muslim Brotherhood would infiltrate American society. Akram urges that "the Movement must plan and struggle to obtain 'the keys' and the tools of this process in carrying out this grand mission as a 'Civilizational-Jihadist' responsibility which lies on the shoulders of Muslims and—on top of them—the Muslim Brotherhood in this country."[28]

Surely, by "Jihadist" Akram means someone engaged in a spiritual struggle to become a better person. Or not. He explains that Muslims'

"Civilizational-Jihadist responsibility" involves nothing less than waging a covert war from within:

> The process of settlement is a "Civilization-Jihadist" process with all the word means. The Ikhwan must understand that all their work in America is a kind of grand Jihad in eliminating and destroying the Western civilization from within and "sabotaging" its miserable house by their hands and the hands of the believers so that it is eliminated and God's religion is made victorious over all religions. Without this level of understanding, we are not up to this challenge and have not prepared ourselves for Jihad yet. It is a Muslim's destiny to perform Jihad and work wherever he is and wherever he lands until the final hour comes, and there is no escape from that destiny except for those who chose to slack.[29]

Never fear, Islamists: when it comes to jihad, Akram and the Brothers are anything but slacking. Akram goes on to say that the most important elements in waging this "grand jihad" against Western Civilization will include, "a mastery of the art of 'coalitions', the art of 'absorption' and the principles of 'cooperation.'"[30] Meaning that this war from within will not be primarily conducted through violent means—although terrorism is always an option—but that the Brotherhood intends to destroy our civilization from the inside incrementally.

The Brothers' stealth strategy includes gaining and exercising influence in the media, government, and educational circles; building mosques across a wide geographical area and establishing self-segregating Islamic enclaves; forging alliances with the political Left; and engaging in a mass media blitz to reshape the national conversation (and public policy) when it comes to Islam, Israel, and the broader Middle East.

This methodical strategy of infiltration, co-optation, and deception had already been articulated in The Project and adopted by the international Muslim Brotherhood leadership in the early 1980s. The reason Akram's strategic memo is so significant is that it expands upon The Project to detail how the Brotherhood's gradualist plan would be implemented in the United States.

Perhaps even more important, the Explanatory Memorandum included a comprehensive list of twenty-nine American-Muslim organizations that Akram enthusiastically identifies as the Brotherhood's allies in this "Grand Jihad":

> A list of our organizations and the organizations of our friends [Imagine if they all march according to one plan!!!]
>
> 1- ISNA = ISLAMIC SOCIETY OF NORTH AMERICA
>
> 2- MSA = MUSLIM STUDENTS' ASSOCIATION
>
> 3- MCA = THE MUSLIM COMMUNITIES ASSOCIATION
>
> 4- AMSS = THE ASSOCIATION OF MUSLIM SOCIAL SCIENTISTS
>
> 5- AMSE = THE ASSOCIATION OF MUSLIM SCIENTISTS AND ENGINEERS
>
> 6- IMA = ISLAMIC MEDICAL ASSOCIATION
>
> 7- ITC = ISLAMIC TEACHING CENTER
>
> 8- NAIT = NORTH AMERICAN ISLAMIC TRUST

9- FID = FOUNDATION FOR INTERNATIONAL DEVEL-
OPMENT

10- IHC = ISLAMIC HOUSING COOPERATIVE

11- ICD = ISLAMIC CENTERS DIVISION

12- ATP = AMERICAN TRUST PUBLICATIONS

13- AVC = AUDIO-VISUAL CENTER

14- IBS = ISLAMIC BOOK SERVICE

15- MBA = MUSLIM BUSINESSMEN ASSOCIATION

16- MYNA = MUSLIM YOUTH OF NORTH AMERICA

17- IFC = ISNA FIQH COMMITTEE

18- IPAC = ISNA POLITICAL AWARENESS COMMITTEE

19- IED = ISLAMIC EDUCATION DEPARTMENT

20- MAYA = MUSLIM ARAB YOUTH ASSOCIATION

21- MISG = MALASIAN [sic] ISLAMIC STUDY GROUP

22- IAP = ISLAMIC ASSOCIATION FOR PALESTINE

23- UASR = UNITED ASSOCIATION FOR STUDIES AND
RESEARCH

24- OLF = OCCUPIED LAND FUND

25- MIA = MERCY INTERNATIONAL ASSOCIATION

26- ISNA = ISLAMIC CIRCLE OF NORTH AMERICA

27- BMI = BAITUL MAL INC

28- IIIT = INTERNATIONAL INSTITUTE FOR ISLAMIC THOUGHT

29- IIC = ISLAMIC INFORMATION CENTER[31]

Representatives from at least one of these groups, ISNA, advise the FBI and have strolled the halls of the White House. Indeed, Akram's lengthy list of Muslim Brotherhood fronts and associates includes virtually every leading American-Muslim organization except Obama administration favorites the Council on American-Islamic Relations (CAIR), the Muslim American Society (MAS), and the Muslim Public Affairs Council (MPAC)—all of which were created a few years *after* Akram wrote the Explanatory Memorandum. These groups have aggressively muscled their way to the front of the pack of American Islam and, with help from the U.S. government and the mainstream media, have seized a virtual monopoly over any discourse emanating from the U.S. Muslim community. Which means a large chunk of the media-appointed, "moderate" Muslim spokespeople that you see flashing across your television screen each day are little more than pawns of the Ikhwan.

Again: the U.S. government has had the Explanatory Memorandum in its possession for nearly a decade. It obtained it in 2004, when federal agents raided the Annandale, Virginia, home of MB/Hamas operative Ismail Elbarasse. It was there, just a few miles from the White House, that agents uncovered a secret sub-basement containing hundreds of official Muslim Brotherhood documents. According to a *Washington Post* account of the raid:

> At Elbarasse's home on Whistler Court, agents seized computer disks, bank records and Arabic documents, including one document titled "For Your Eyes Only—How to Propagate Islam."
>
> Also seized, according to court records, were copies of checks from the Dar Al-Hijra mosque in Falls Church; an Arabic CD with an "evaluation of the Jihad movement"; a piece of paper containing the address of the Norfolk Naval Station; Israeli travel documents; various "anti-Israel materials"; and documents concerning the Muslim Brotherhood, a secretive movement of political activists dedicated to restoring Islamic rule in secular Arab societies.
>
> In addition, agents seized a document called an "anarchist cookbook" and an item referred to in court records as "Spreadsheet of trained pilots 'Law Enforcement Only.'"[32]

Akram's Explanatory Memorandum was one of the documents agents seized. While the memo's contents became public during the Holy Land Foundation trial, box upon box of additional documents uncovered in the raid of Elbarasse's well-kept suburban home have yet to be released by the U.S. government, despite repeated requests by various national security-focused organizations and members of Congress.

The Explanatory Memorandum alone was a massive game changer in understanding the Brotherhood's network and intentions inside the United States. How many more documents like it were found in Elbarasse's home? And why would this Hamas operative be in possession of a "Spreadsheet of trained pilots"? The Obama administration—like the Bush administration before it—has yet to answer any of these questions. For all we know, the rest of the documents are locked away in some dusty basement, discarded and forgotten. And based on the Obama administration's close alliance with various U.S. Muslim Brotherhood–tied organizations and individuals, those docs won't see the light of day anytime soon. Here are just a few examples of the MB's influence on the Obama White House:

■ A December 2012 piece in Egypt's *Rose El-Youssef* magazine alleged that six American Islamists who work closely with the Obama administration in various capacities are, in fact, operatives of the Muslim Brotherhood.[33] The Investigative Project on Terrorism, which translated the *Rose El-Youssef* article into English, described its troubling contents:

> The...story...suggests the six turned the White House "from a position hostile to Islamic groups and organizations in the world to the largest and most important supporter of the Muslim Brotherhood."
>
> The story is largely unsourced, but its publication is considered significant in raising the issue to Egyptian readers.
>
> The six named people include: Arif Alikhan, assistant secretary of Homeland Security for policy development; Mohammed Elibiary, a member of the Homeland Security Advisory Council; Rashad Hussain, the U.S. special envoy to the Organization of the Islamic Conference; Salam al-Marayati, co-founder of the Muslim Public Affairs Council (MPAC); Imam Mohamed Magid, president of the Islamic Society of North America (ISNA); and Eboo Patel, a member of President Obama's Advisory Council on Faith-Based Neighborhood Partnerships.[34]

■ A year-long investigation, culminating in October 2012, also conducted by the Investigative Project on Terrorism (IPT), found that radical Islamists conducted hundreds of visits to the Obama White House during the president's first term and met with top administration officials.[35] For instance, after scouring through millions of White House visitor log entries, IPT found that individuals from the Hamas-linked Council on American-Islamic Relations (CAIR) were among the administration's guests at 1600 Pennsylvania Avenue. This despite the fact that the FBI supposedly cut ties with CAIR after the Islamist outfit was named an unindicted co-conspirator in the largest terrorism financing trial in American history.[36]

■ In February 2012, after meetings between FBI Director Robert Mueller and representatives from several American-Islamist organizations—including the Brotherhood-linked Islamic Society of North America and Muslim Public Affairs Council—it was announced that the FBI had purged hundreds of counterterrorism training documents that were used to educate federal agents about the Islamist threat.

The FBI's Islamist friends were permitted to review the materials and helped deem that more than seven hundred documents and three hundred presentations should be eliminated due to "anti-Muslim" language.[37] Even before the purge, the Obama administration had already handed down edicts that terms like "Islamic terrorism," "radical Islamist," and "jihadist" could not be used by government agencies. So I suppose the FBI's capitulation was the natural, and pathetic, next step. Nothing like letting your enemies review and censor the very materials that could lead to their exposure.

When details emerged that FBI agents had actually interviewed Tamerlan Tsarnaev in 2011—*two years* before he and his younger brother carried out the deadly terror attack at the Boston Marathon—but had found no cause for suspicion (even after Russian authorities warned that Tsarnaev was a radical Islamist), I was angered but not surprised.[38] After all, the same thing happened in 2009 when Muslim convert Abdulhakim Muhammad was subject to a preliminary investigation by the FBI's joint counterterrorism task force prior to his jihadist attack on a military recruiting station in Little Rock, Arkansas, that left one American soldier dead and another seriously injured.[39]

How much of the FBI's inaction in these two cases can be traced back to a culture of rampant political correctness enforced at the very top of the bureau? And worse still, to the ideology of the man who currently sits in the Oval Office?

———

President Obama is not a Muslim, but he is quite fond of Islam. This is clearly due in large part to his family lineage (for starters, his father and stepfather were both Muslims) and to the fact that he spent four formative years as a boy in Indonesia, a Muslim nation where he attended an Islamic *madrassah* for a time. Obama believes that he understands "the real Islam" based on his personal experiences, which include close friendships with a Pakistani roommate and other Pakistani Muslims during his stint at Occidental College in the late 1970s and early 80s. Obama traveled to Pakistan with one of those friends and spent three weeks there in 1981. During the 2008 presidential campaign, he even said the trip bolstered his credibility on foreign policy.[40] Maybe he could see Karachi from his window.

Obama thinks he "gets" Islam and, by extension, understands the Muslim Brotherhood and other Islamists and what makes them tick, including their many grievances—some of which he shares. At the top of that list is Western "imperialism" against oppressed, Third World (often Muslim) peoples, with the chief violators being the United States, Great Britain, and Israel. The fact that most of the so-called oppressed are not white and the "oppressors" are only adds fuel to Obama's progressive fire. To him, the Muslim Brotherhood is not a dangerous Islamist organization but a revolutionary liberation movement that opposes corrupt, U.S.-supported dictatorships (like Mubarak's) and Western imperialism and stands for authentic, true Islam. To President Obama, the "Muslim" in the Muslim Brotherhood is secondary, even insignificant. It's the MB's struggle against the existing and inherently unfair global order—one set up by greedy, imperialistic, capitalistic Western powers—that really matters and must be supported.

And support it the president has, time and time again—whether it's publicly castigating and isolating Israel, assisting Ikhwan-centric regimes throughout the Muslim world, or working with Brotherhood-linked Islamists in the United States. As far back as 2007, then-candidate Obama was dropping hints that he would embark on this Islamist-friendly course as president—that he, the worldly, charismatic "great healer," the veteran of an Indonesian madrassah and a few weeks in Pakistan—would bridge the gap between the Muslim world and the West. Believing himself the right man, with the right name and the right background to placate the seething Muslim masses, he has never missed a chance to showcase his supposed brilliance in Muslim relations. The results have been disastrous for U.S. national security and an Allah-send for the Muslim Brotherhood. A few examples:

■ In 2007, then-Senator Barack Obama, never lacking confidence in his own transcendent brilliance and magnetism, told New Hampshire Public Radio:

> I truly believe that the day I'm inaugurated [as president], not only does the country look at itself differently, but the world looks at America differently.... If I'm reaching out to the Muslim world they understand that I've lived in a Muslim country and I may be a Christian, but I also understand their point of view.... My sister is half-Indonesian. I traveled there all the way through my college years. And so I'm intimately concerned with what happens in these countries and the cultures and perspective these folks have. And those are powerful

tools for us to be able to reach out to the world…then I think the world will have confidence that I am listening to them and that our future and our security is tied up with our ability to work with other countries in the world that will ultimately make us safer.[41]

I'm sure the al-Qaeda–linked terrorists who stormed the U.S. consulate in Benghazi and slaughtered four Americans were given pause by the fact that Barack Obama has a sister who is half-Indonesian. Ditto for Fort Hood shooter Nidal Hasan, the Boston bombers, and the Taliban jihadists who are killing U.S. troops in Afghanistan.

■ 2007 was also the year that *New York Times* columnist Nicholas Kristof wrote a fawning profile of the future president called "Obama: Man of the World." In one passage from the piece, the smitten Kristof managed—unknowingly—to capture everything that is wrong with Obama's approach to the Muslim world:

> He once got in trouble for making faces during Koran study classes in his elementary school, but a president is less likely to stereotype Muslims as fanatics—and more likely to be aware of their nationalism—if he once studied the Koran with them.
>
> Mr. Obama recalled the opening lines of the Arabic call to prayer, reciting them with a first-rate accent. In a remark that seemed delightfully uncalculated (it'll give Alabama voters heart attacks), Mr. Obama described the call to prayer as "one of the prettiest sounds on Earth at sunset."[42]

It's all there: Obama's reverence for Islamic culture, his determination to prove his Islamophile bona fides ("Hey, I love the Arabic call to prayer! And guess what? My sister is half-Indonesian!"), and his—and Kristof's—

assumption that Koran classes taken as a small boy in Indonesia some forty years ago left Obama uniquely equipped to improve relations with the Muslim world.

Don't you see, Muslims? Your friend Barry *gets it*. He gets *you*! Why, just look at his close relationship with Rashad Hussain.[43] In 2010, on naming Hussain as "special envoy" to the Organisation of the Islamic Conference (OIC), Obama gushed that Hussain was "a hafiz of the Qur'an."[44] Which means Hussain can recite the entire Koran from memory. Obama neglected to mention Hussain's troubling links to groups affiliated with the Muslim Brotherhood.[45]

■ In January 2009, Obama chose to give the Arabic-language network Al-Arabiya the first formal interview of his presidency as part of his stated effort to improve America's image in the Muslim world. It was the beginning of the Obama Global Apology Tour. During the interview, he again stressed his family ties to Islam and criticized America: "all too often the United States starts by dictating—in the past on some of these issues—and we don't always know all the factors that are involved," said the Apologist-in-Chief. "[T]he language [Americans] use has to be a language of respect. I have Muslim members of my family. I have lived in Muslim countries."[46] The result of Obama's pandering? Polls show that the United States is more unpopular than ever in the Muslim world.[47]

■ In April 2009 at the G-20 Summit in London, President Obama bowed to King Abdullah of Saudi Arabia as other Western leaders looked on in shock. Heck, even Abdullah looked surprised. This was an act of full on, he-must-have-lost-a-contact lens prostration by an American president to an Islamist despot whose government has spent billions spreading radical Islamism around the world. As I wrote of "The Bow" in my 2011 book, *The Terrorist Next Door*:

> Obama's shameless act of groveling, performed in one of his
> first forays onto the international stage, signaled that debasing

America and exalting Islam would be key elements in achieving his oft-stated goal of improving America's image in the
Muslim world.

... From Riyadh to London to Jakarta and beyond,
Islamists saw Obama's bow to Abdullah and smiled broadly.
To them, The Bow—and the steady stream of pandering, pro-
Islamic policies that have followed from the Obama White
House—represented a green light to further expand their
tentacles into the United States....

No Islamist entity has seized upon the message sent by The
Bow more than the Muslim Brotherhood.[48]

Indeed.

■ In June 2009, President Obama delivered his now-infamous Cairo
speech, in which he, once again, apologized for America's behavior
toward the Muslim world and sought "a new beginning" between the
U.S. and the Religion of Peace. The Obama administration reportedly
"insisted" that at least ten Muslim Brothers (who were then in opposition
to the Mubarak regime) be allowed to attend the speech at Cairo University.[49] Why would the Obama administration be so adamant that
members of an openly anti-American, anti-Semitic Islamist organization
be permitted to attend the event? Because the administration views the
Brotherhood as authentic "moderate" Islam, even though the Ikhwan's
so-called "moderation" is a confessed front, a mere tactic.

During his Cairo address, the president also uttered this jaw-dropper:
"I consider it part of my responsibility as President of the United States
to fight against negative stereotypes of Islam wherever they appear."[50]
I'm pretty sure that's not what the Founders had in mind.

If only Obama, who has said—with a straight face—that "Muslims
have suffered the most at the hands of extremism"[51] would be so passionate about the Christian minorities that the Muslim Brotherhood and

its offshoots are harassing, torturing, and murdering throughout the Muslim world. As it stands, he and his allies in the mainstream media have been missing in action on one of the most pressing issues of our time: the wholesale emptying of Christians from the Middle East—the birthplace of Christianity—due to relentless Islamist persecution.

It is a phenomenon that has been sped up immeasurably by the so-called Arab Spring that the Obama administration has so steadfastly supported. In Egypt, in the post-Mubarak era, Christian churches are frequent targets of arson. In October 2011, a group of Cairo Coptic Christians protested the burning of one such church and were attacked by Egyptian security forces. More than a dozen Copts were killed. Video footage showed the Christian protestors not only being shot but even run over by armored personnel carriers.[52] President Obama's risible response to the anti-Christian carnage was to issue a statement urging "restraint on all sides."[53] Point taken. The next time Egypt's Christians are dodging Islamist bullets or being crushed to death by Muslim security forces, I'm sure they'll remember to exercise the proper "restraint."

■ During a visit to India in 2010, Imam Obama issued one of his more memorable fatwas. While meeting with a group of university students in Mumbai, the president was asked his opinion on jihad, or Islamic holy war. Obama's answer flew in the face of fifteen hundred years of carnage and conquest carried out by self-proclaimed jihadists. "The phrase jihad has a lot of meanings within Islam and is subject to a lot of different interpretations," Imam Obama intoned.

"I think all of us recognize that this great religion in the hands of a few extremists has been distorted to justify violence towards innocent people that is never justified. And so, I think, one of the challenges that we face is, how do we isolate those who have these distorted notions of religious war."[54] Oh, like the Muslim Brotherhood? The Brothers are the modern-day godfathers of those "distorted notions of religious war" the president mentions, yet are still invited to the White House and receive hundreds of millions in U.S. aid.

What the president left out of his comments in Mumbai was the bedrock belief that drives the Obama administration's entire "countering extremism" strategy: violent al-Qaeda jihadists bad, MB stealth jihadists good. As for jihad, its primary meaning since Islam roared out of the Arabian Peninsula in the seventh century to conquer a good chunk of the known world has been "holy war," not spiritual striving. Indeed, the people of India know jihad all too well. Untold millions of non-Muslim Indians died at the hands of Muslim jihadists between the seventh and twentieth centuries. More recently, in 2008, Mumbai—the city where Obama delivered his "jihad" remarks—was the scene of an Islamic terrorist rampage that left 164 people dead and the world's third largest city in utter chaos for days. Perhaps the president can bring along CIA Director John Brennan on his next trip to Mumbai. Brennan, who likes to refer to Jerusalem by its Arabic name, "Al-Quds," has called jihad, "a legitimate tenet of Islam." He's also extolled Islam as a faith of "peace and tolerance," of "goodness and beauty," that has "shaped [his] own worldview."[55]

How do you say, "we're in deep doo-doo," in Arabic?

What was perhaps the most shocking—and disastrous—of all President Obama's Islamo-panders occurred during his speech to the UN General Assembly on September 25, 2012. Just thirteen days after Islamic jihadists murdered four Americans in Benghazi, the president stood before the world's leaders and uttered the now-infamous line: *"The future must not belong to those who slander the prophet of Islam."*[56] It was the kind of exhortation that you'd hear from a Wahhabi imam during Friday prayers in Mecca. Yet it came from the mouth of a sitting President of the United States—the supposed Leader of the Free World.

At the time of his UN speech, Obama and his team were in the middle of a scandalous effort to portray the Benghazi attack as a spontaneous reaction by Libyan locals to a little-seen, low-budget YouTube video lampooning Islam's prophet (who must never be slandered). The video, called "The Innocence of Muslims" consisted of fourteen minutes of trailer clips put together by an Egyptian native living in California named Mark Basseley Youssef. The clips are so risibly produced, and the acting so remarkably bad, that it's hard to believe anyone would watch it for thirty seconds without bursting out laughing. But as the Ayatollah Khomeini once said, "there is no humor in Islam."

The clips were somehow discovered by the Muslim-world-at-large and sparked riots and protests from Pakistan to Gaza and beyond (it doesn't take much to rile the followers of what columnist Michelle Malkin has dubbed, "The Religion of Perpetual Outrage"). In the process, Youssef's video quickly became the Obama administration's go-to scapegoat for the Benghazi attack and the storming of American embassies in Egypt, Yemen, and Tunisia during the anniversary week of the 9/11 attacks.

For example, according to the father of Tyrone Woods, a former Navy SEAL who was killed in the Benghazi assault, then-Secretary of State Hillary Clinton, in offering her condolences, told him that the administration would "make sure that the person who made that film is arrested and prosecuted."[57] Not the jihadists that murdered Tyrone Woods. No, a chubby, ex-con pseudo-filmmaker was apparently the main focus of the Obama administration's post-Benghazi investigations. And they got their man: Youssef was promptly arrested, supposedly for unrelated probation violations, and sentenced to a year in federal prison.[58] That'll teach him not to slander the prophet of Islam.

It later emerged, of course, that the Benghazi incident was a well-coordinated jihadist assault that had nothing to do with any film (al-Qaeda training videos aside). Same with the other embassy attacks.

But in classic, never-let-a-crisis-go-to-waste fashion, the Obama administration saw an opening to advance a growing push by the Muslim Brotherhood and its allies to outlaw so-called "hate speech" about Islam worldwide. Indeed, on the heels of "The Innocence of Muslims" debacle, Mohammed Morsi, Yusuf al-Qaradawi, and other Brotherhood leaders called for global laws that would make it illegal to insult Islam's prophet Mohammed—including inside the United States. The Brotherhood bigwigs were echoed by American imams, including one in New Jersey who called for "limits and borders [on] free speech" when it comes to the Religion of Peace.[59]

These Islamist calls for global "hate speech" laws regarding supposed defamation of religion have been gathering steam in recent years at the United Nations, courtesy of an organization called the Organisation of Islamic Cooperation (OIC). The OIC consists of fifty-six Muslim-majority countries plus the Palestinian Authority, all speaking with one powerful and influential voice at the UN. In addition to leading the push to delegitimize Israel on the world stage, the OIC is also the driving force behind efforts to criminalize free speech about Islam. In his 2012 book, *Spring Fever: The Illusion of Islamic Democracy*, author Andrew McCarthy writes:

> Another Muslim Brotherhood brainchild made possible by Saudi funding, the OIC primarily seeks global recognition of the worldwide ummah as a single, supranational community, with the OIC as its sovereign and voice. It is well on the way to achieving that goal...the OIC's overarching aim is to Islamize societies through the gradual implementation of sharia standards. It would govern its subjects in accordance with classical sharia. It would also dramatically expand its domain beyond OIC countries by purporting to speak for Muslims *living in the West*.[60]

McCarthy calls the OIC, "a caliphate in the making." Interestingly enough, when I asked the alleged leader of Germany's Muslim Brotherhood, Ibrahim el-Zayat, about the possibility of reviving the caliphate, he answered, in part:

> ... if you look at the European Union now—you'll see that Catherine Ashton [the EU Foreign Affairs chief] is quite powerless. But at the same time it could be a quite powerful position. But a structured position based on an organic structure with an institutional setting. This is what should be the future of the world. To have the United Nations become more powerful, more working, to have other entities.

El-Zayat provided an intriguing window into what some Islamists might be thinking as they continue their global march. The OIC could very well be one of the "other entities" he mentions and a vehicle for establishing a de facto caliphate that does not identify itself as such—and with the veneer of UN legitimacy, to boot. The leader of the OIC, depending on who it is, could then potentially be seen as a caliph-type figure. And voila! The Brotherhood and its allies would have a twenty-first century caliphate without the world even realizing what hit it.

It's a safe bet, however, that the Obama administration won't be surprised. In December 2011, then-Secretary of State Hillary Clinton hosted a three-day, closed-door conference with OIC leaders to discuss the possibility of implementing a UN resolution that would essentially establish guidelines on free speech about Islam and outlaw "Islamophobia" around the world.[61]

It's no exaggeration to say that if the OIC—with the support of the Obama administration—has its way, books like the one you're holding right now will be banned. Any coverage of Islam-related issues and the

Middle East will be filtered through the Brotherhood—which means the truth about the MB and what it represents will never see the light of day.

CHAPTER THREE

A HISTORY OF VIOLENCE

The man they call "Islam's Savior" appeared in desperate need of one. Tariq Ramadan, darling of the European Left and arguably the West's most influential Islamist, had just been informed that eight minutes still remained in our interview, which was scheduled to run a full half hour. He looked at me with a nervous, almost pleading smile and checked his watch, seemingly counting the seconds until he could bolt out the door and back into the warm embrace of his effete leftist admirers at Oxford University, where he's comfortably ensconced as a professor of Contemporary Islamic Studies.

At that moment, I imagine Ramadan was wondering how in the name of Allah his handler at Oxford could have possibly scheduled our little sitdown. My line of questioning increasingly centered on his alleged ties to the Muslim Brotherhood, and while respectful, I kept probing. I had made the hour-plus trip from London to Oxford to learn more about the inner workings of the Brotherhood from Ramadan—a man who is literally heir to MB royalty—and I was determined to make my time with the notoriously evasive Islamo-spin-doctor worthwhile.

"I'm the grandson of the founder of the Muslim Brotherhood, which was a fact and is a fact and which is well known," Ramadan told me, barely masking his annoyance. "And even when I was invited [to the United States] by the State Department, this is the way they were introducing me. So, this is something which is known. I'm not a member [of the Muslim Brotherhood], I never was a member—so this is something also which is known."

Yet one needn't be a "member" or formally tied, say, to the Brotherhood's leadership in Egypt in order to promote the Ikhwan's agenda. As we'll see, that's not how the organization operates. For instance, the Brotherhood's former Supreme Guide, Mustafa Mashour, confirmed in a 1998 interview that belonging to the MB is about adhering to a specific ideology and way of thinking—no membership card required. He added that the work carried out by Tariq Ramadan and his brother, Hani Ramadan, "is totally in keeping with the purest traditions of the Muslim Brotherhood."[1] Likewise, French geopolitical analyst Olivier Guitta has written that, "Most European secret service agencies are convinced that, at the end of the 1980s, the Muslim Brotherhood chose Tariq Ramadan to be their European representative."[2]

When the Muslim Brotherhood's top global leader says you are marching to the beat of his organization, and European intelligence agencies reportedly agree, you should probably expect to answer a few questions about where your loyalties lie. Furthermore, Ramadan is indeed the grandson of none other than the Muslim Brotherhood's founder, Hassan al-Banna, and son of one of the most influential global operatives in MB history, Said Ramadan. The elder Ramadan helped establish the Ikhwan network in Europe and played a pivotal role in the founding of both

Switzerland's Islamic Center of Geneva and Germany's Islamic Center of Munich, two longtime Brotherhood hubs from which the group spread its tentacles throughout the West. But how dare I suggest the apple might not fall far from the tree when it comes to Tariq? The *New York Times* headline practically writes itself: "Right Wing Television Host, Long Accused of Islamophobia, Levels False Accusations at Muslim Scholar."

Ramadan's responses during our conversation were wordy and ambiguous. He seemed slightly irritated by some of my queries about the Brotherhood and perhaps a bit surprised at my level of knowledge about the extremist track record of Granpa al-Banna. This wasn't the BBC and I wasn't a clueless left-wing dupe of the sort Ramadan has spun like a top for years. Nevertheless, he remained composed, even as my questions became more pointed. This came as no surprise. French journalist Caroline Fourest has written an entire book devoted to exposing Ramadan as a master of obfuscation. *Brother Tariq: The Doublespeak of Tariq Ramadan* painstakingly examines Ramadan's history of radical associations and statements, concluding that he is a devout Islamic supremacist who has cannily pulled the wool over the eyes of Western elites with his talk of a supposed "Third Way" that would essentially see Europe's Muslims become integrated, but not quite assimilated, into their host countries.

You would think the whole lack of assimilation thing might pose a problem. But that would mean you are actually thinking, whereas our elites in the media, academia, and government, who have lavished praise upon Ramadan, most certainly are not, beyond, "Boy, this Tariq guy is handsome, a sharp dresser, and sounds perfectly reasonable—although I have no idea what he's talking about. Bingo! We've got ourselves a moderate Muslim!" Hence, Ramadan has scored roles as an advisor on Muslim issues for both the European Union and the British government under former Prime Minister Tony Blair. He has also been christened one of the "Top 100 Innovators of the 21st Century" (*Time* magazine) and "Top 100 Global Thinkers" (*Foreign Policy* magazine) and has received fawning profiles from the reliably dhimmified *New York Times*, among others.

Fourest, by the way, is no right-wing rabble-rouser. She is a liberal feminist who had become fed up after years of observing Ramadan's forked tongue at work in European circles, particularly his portrayal of sharia law as female-friendly and liberating. In *Brother Tariq*, she highlights a now infamous 2003 debate between Ramadan and former French President Nicolas Sarkozy—then France's Minister of the Interior—on French TV in which Ramadan refused to support a ban on the stoning of female adulterers, calling instead for a "moratorium" on the practice in the Muslim world. A visibly outraged Sarkozy responded, "A moratorium? Mr. Ramadan, are you serious? A moratorium, that is…we should, for a while, hold back from stoning women?"[3] The confrontation with Sarkozy came on the heels of an op-ed written by Ramadan's brother, Hani, which supported death by stoning as the proper punishment for adultery. Tariq and Hani are close; the two have both played prominent roles at Switzerland's Geneva Islamic Center, a longtime gathering place for Islamic radicals founded by their infamous father. Would it be a stretch to assume they hold similar views on stoning, just as they clearly do on other Islamic issues?

Ramadan's "moratorium" pronouncement, delivered before some six million French television viewers, would have been a career-killer for a man of lesser talents. Alas, much like the jihadist organization to which his father and grandfather devoted their lives, Ramadan has a Teflon-like quality: declared dead on several occasions only to come back stronger and more influential than before. Over the years, he's been banned from no fewer than eight countries—including Saudi Arabia and Mubarak's Egypt—due to his alleged ties to terrorists and, more than likely, his Ikhwan family heritage.

Ramadan was barred from entering France for six months in the mid-1990s for suspected links to Algeria's Armed Islamic Group (better known as GIA), which carried out a number of deadly attacks in France around that same time. Likewise, his visa was revoked in 2004 by the Bush administration just days before he was set to begin teaching at the University of Notre Dame. The U.S. ban came after it emerged that Ramadan had donated $1,300 to a French Muslim "charity" organization that, in turn, gave money to the terror group Hamas. Ramadan made the donations between 1998 and 2002. The organization was blacklisted by the U.S. Department of the Treasury in 2003.[4]

In explaining the decision to revoke Ramadan's visa, a Department of Homeland Security spokesman cited a clause in the Patriot Act that bars foreigners who "endorse or espouse terrorist activity or persuade others" to support terrorism.[5] When I spoke to Ramadan about it at Oxford, he remained indignant.

"At one point, in the name of the Patriot Act…my visa was revoked," he sniffed. "They used the Patriot Act because I was supporting a Palestinian organization."

Yes, one that was giving money to the Islamist terrorist group Hamas.

"And then it was a political thing," he continued. "I was critical of the Iraq invasion and American support for Israel…when Hillary Clinton took office and lifted the ban, it showed that it was not a legal thing, it was a political stand [by the Bush administration]."

The Obama administration, always eager to show the Brotherhood and its acolytes some love, lifted the ban on Ramadan in 2010, courtesy of a signed order by Secretary of State Hillary Clinton. He now travels freely within the United States, attending conferences and giving lectures before star-struck liberal audiences, his faux moderate act undoubtedly reassuring to their naïve Western ears. For instance, when I asked whether he believed Islamic sharia law was compatible with the U.S. Constitution and European law, Ramadan delivered a masterfully deceptive response.

"My position is to say 'look, sharia is a way. It's a path,'" he intoned. "So, for example, when I am based in Switzerland—my country—or in the West and the law of the country is saying that we are equal before law, I say 'This is my sharia.' So my understanding of sharia is that it is not a closed system. It's an open system...."

"It's not a provocation," he continued. "It's something that I want the people to understand deeply because this is what you feel at home—the sense of belonging that is important for living together...the very narrow understanding of sharia is problematic not only for the West but for Muslims themselves."

For a minute there, you might have thought we were talking about the rules for your local fantasy football league rather than Islamic sharia law—a barbaric system that promotes stonings, beheadings, and discrimination against women and religious minorities. Indeed, Ramadan, in keeping with the Brotherhood's tradition, is an expert in *taqiyya*, the practice of lying—especially to non-believers—to advance the cause of Islam. This has long been central to the Brotherhood's strategy, particularly in the West. And it works. How else could Ramadan, with his incendiary track record, acquire a position at Oxford University, one of the most famous and prestigious institutions of higher learning in the world? To an English-speaking audience, Ramadan presents himself as a beacon of interfaith harmony and progressive, "European Islam." But for Muslim audiences, his message, often delivered in Arabic, is far less benign.

He first gained rock star status during the 1990s for his fiery lectures to large crowds of predominantly young French Muslims in the city of Lyon. From there, audiotapes bearing Ramadan's message of "Islamizing modernity, rather than modernizing Islam" spread throughout France's gritty Muslim suburbs, with destructive consequences. In 2003, a French court found that language used by Islamist preachers like Ramadan "can influence young Muslims and can serve as a factor inciting them to join up with those engaged in violent acts."[6] It comes as no surprise, then, that a Spanish judge has alleged that Ahmed Brahim—a convicted al-Qaeda member from Algeria—had "routine contacts" with Ramadan. Or that the leader of a jihadist group accused of planning an attack on the U.S. Embassy in Paris said during his 2001 trial that he had studied with Brother Tariq.[7] There have also been longstanding rumors—never confirmed—that Swiss authorities believe Tariq and his brother, Hani, helped organize a meeting attended by al-Qaeda leader Ayman al-Zawahiri and the notorious "Blind Sheikh," Omar Abdel-Rahman, in Geneva in 1991.[8]

Ramadan, of course, denies it all. And his leftist admirers, enthralled by his harangues against capitalism and Western imperialism, are all too happy to tar his critics as bigoted Islamophobes. When Ramadan assures non-Muslim audiences that the Muslim Brotherhood has eschewed violence and that his grandfather, Hassan al-Banna, was a peaceful reformer, his words are usually taken at face value. "I have studied Hassan al-Banna's ideas with great care and there is nothing in this heritage that I reject," Ramadan once told a French interviewer. "His relation to God, his spiritualism, his mysticism, his personality, as well as his critical reflections on law, politics, society and pluralism, testify for me to his qualities of heart and mind. His commitment also is a continuing reason for my respect and admiration."[9] What Ramadan neglected to mention in this loving ode to his grandfather was al-Banna's unwavering "commitment" to violent jihad. As we'll see shortly, al-Banna was a jihadist to his very core who longed for an Islamic caliphate—established by force, if necessary.

"You say al-Banna was against violence," I pressed Ramadan. "But he did talk about jihad often and I don't think he meant defensive jihad."

"We have no proof of [al-Banna] asking anyone to act violently in Egypt," Ramadan answered. "And the only thing he said and is written [approving violence] is in Palestine—against [Jewish paramilitary groups] and the people who were trying to colonize the country—[violence] was legitimate. But in Egypt, it was not."

In other words, killing Jews who were resettling their ancient homeland, Israel, was a noble pursuit in al-Banna's (and, presumably, Tariq's)
eyes. In fact, Ramadan's father Said personally led the Brotherhood's
jihad against the fledgling state of Israel in 1948. Hatred for Jews runs
in the family (which may explain Tariq Ramadan's frequent attacks on
"Jewish intellectuals").[10]

As for Ramadan's suggestion that al-Banna opposed violence within
Egypt, the facts laid out in this chapter scream otherwise. But Tariq
Ramadan is not one to let facts get in the way of some good taqiyya.

Besides, to his relief, our thirty minutes were up and it was time for
him to rush off to his next appointment. The scion of Muslim Brotherhood royalty is in high demand: there is a boundless supply of Islamists
to rile and infidels to beguile. In Brother Tariq's world, an alleged right-
wing hater like me—bearing probing questions and Zionist inclinations—
doesn't deserve thirty seconds, let alone thirty minutes. After a cursory
goodbye he was off, carrying eighty-four years of Muslim Brotherhood
ideology in his bloodstream.

"What did you think? " I asked my cameraman as we packed up.

"I don't think he liked you very much," he replied with a grin.

———

Perhaps better than anyone else alive today, Tariq Ramadan knows
and fully grasps the violent legacy of his grandfather. He simply chooses
to lie about it—and it works, time and time again. The reason he's able
to get away with it is simple. The vast majority of today's Western leaders that Ramadan and other slick Islamist spokesmen spend their days
hoodwinking flat-out ignore the first rule of war: know your enemy. If
you don't believe me, take a poll of both houses of the U.S. Congress and
ask members a) Who Hassan al-Banna was and b) What Hassan al-Banna
believed and you'll mostly be greeted by blank stares as annoyed Hill
staffers try to shoo you away. I've spent a decade in Washington, D.C.,

and interviewed dozens of lawmakers from states across the Republic. I'd estimate that out of the 535 members of Congress, maybe forty could pass the hypothetical al-Banna poll. In my experience, Democrats are the most egregiously uninformed, but most Republicans don't know enough about our Islamist enemies either. Plus, both sides are crippled by political correctness and a refusal to link Islamic terrorism with the Islamist ideology that inspires it. Because that would require, heaven forbid, a serious examination of the Koran and hadiths—the texts the terrorists themselves cite, time and time again—and how they encourage violence. And we just can't have that, because we all know that Islam is a religion of peace and beyond reproach.

In the House, some of the better informed members are Michele Bachmann, Trent Franks, Louie Gohmert, and Peter King. The Senate, on the other hand, is a wasteland. John McCain and Lindsey Graham are the Senate's most vocal members on national security, but both are also die-hard interventionists whose policy prescriptions for the Middle East— arming rebel factions and hoping that an acceptable Islamo-democracy emerges—inadvertently help the Brotherhood and other hostile Islamists. Witness McCain's bizarre visit to the notorious jihadist hotbed of Benghazi, Libya, in April 2011. Reports were rampant then that the rebel forces working to overthrow Gaddafi were riddled with al-Qaeda types, including some who had fought against American troops in Iraq. McCain, undaunted, encouraged the U.S. government to arm these same Libyan mujahideen, whom he called his "heroes."[11] Despite McCain's giddy endorsement, our dalliance with Benghazi's Islamists hasn't worked out so well, if the September 2012 sacking of our consulate and subsequent murder of four Americans there, including Ambassador Chris Stevens, is any indication.

In an age when America is waging war—militarily and ideologically—against Islamic fundamentalists, the pervasive ignorance in Congress about the Muslim Brotherhood and its ilk is not just

unacceptable, it's downright disgraceful. You cannot begin to understand al-Qaeda, for instance, without first understanding the history
and ideology of the Muslim Brotherhood, the organization that spawned
AQ and so many other Islamist movements bent on the destruction of
the United States.

Which brings us back to Hassan al-Banna. Ever wonder where
al-Qaeda, Hamas, and other Islamikaze suicide bombers got their inspiration? In his book, *Jihad and Jew Hatred: Islamism, Nazism and the
Roots of 9/11*, German author Matthias Küentzel recounts the Brotherhood founder's morbid glorification of jihadi martyrdom, or what al-
Banna called "the Art of Death." Küentzel writes:

> In 1938, in a leading article entitled "Industry of Death,"
> which was to become famous, Hassan al-Banna explained to
> a wider public his concept of jihad—a concept in which the
> term Industry of Death denotes not something horrible but an
> ideal. He wrote, "To a nation that perfects the industry of
> death and which knows how to die nobly, God gives proud
> life in this world and eternal grace in the life to come."
>
> According to al-Banna, the Koran enjoins believers to love
> death more than life. Unfortunately, he argues, Muslims are
> in thrall to a "love of life." "The illusion which had humiliated
> us is no more than the love of worldly life and the hatred of
> death." As long as the Muslims do not replace their love of
> life with the love of death as required by the Koran, their
> future is hopeless. Only those who become proficient in the
> "art of death" can prevail. "So, prepare yourself to do a great
> deed. Be keen on dying and life will be granted to you, so work
> towards a noble death and you will find complete happiness,"
> he writes in the same essay, republished in 1946 under the
> title, "The Art of Death."[12]

In 2001, shortly after the 9/11 attacks, a Taliban fighter famously proclaimed, "The Americans lead lavish lives and they are afraid of death. We are not afraid of death. The Americans love Pepsi Cola, but we love death."[13] Clearly, thi s reasonable chap had embraced al-Banna's "Art of Death" concept. Repeatedly over the past three decades, Osama bin Laden, Ayman al-Zawahiri, Ayatollahs Khomeini and Khamenei, and Hezbollah's Sheikh Hassan Nasrallah have espoused this theme. So have the 9/11 hijackers, the London and Madrid mass transit bombers, and the Brotherhood's Palestinian branch, Hamas. For example, as Israel conducted Operation Pillar of Defense against Hamas terrorists in Gaza in November 2012, Hamas's military wing, the al-Qassam Brigades, released a video declaring that their fighters "love death more than [Israelis] love life."[14] This kind of fanatical mentality, popularized in the modern age by al-Banna, has brought us the grotesque ritual of Palestinian mothers eagerly sending their sons to conduct suicide attacks that murder and maim Israeli women and children.

Every last modern-day jihadist—whether Palestinian, Pakistani, or Parisian—owes a depraved debt, in some form or fashion, to the Muslim Brotherhood. The virtual death cult festering today across the Islamic world can clearly be traced back to the teachings of al-Banna, Sayyid Qutb, and their Brotherhood acolytes. But the Ikhwan didn't create it all out of thin air. The Muslim glorification of martyrdom is as old as Islam itself and comes directly from the Koran and hadiths. A few examples:

- "Let those who fight in the Cause of Allah sell the life of this world for the hereafter. To him who fights in the Cause of Allah, whether he is slain or gets victory—soon shall We give him a great reward." (Qur'an: 4:74)
- "If you are slain, or die, in Allah's Cause [as a martyr], pardon from Allah and mercy are far better than all they could amass." (Qur'an: 3:156)

- "Think not of those who are slain in Allah's Cause as dead. Nay, they live, finding their provision from their Lord. Jubilant in the bounty provided by Allah: and with regard to those left behind, who have not yet joined them, the Martyrs glory in the fact that on them is no fear, nor have they cause to grieve. Allah will not waste the reward of the believers." (Qur'an: 3:169)

- "The Prophet said, 'Nobody who dies and finds Paradise would wish to come back to this life even if he were given the whole world and whatever is in it, except the martyr who, on seeing the superiority of martyrdom, would like to come back to get killed again in Allah's Cause.'" (Bukhari: V4B52N53)

- "I heard Allah's Apostle saying, 'Allah guarantees that He will admit the Muslim fighter into Paradise if he is killed, otherwise He will return him to his home safely with rewards and booty.'" (Bukhari: V4B52N46)

That is but a very small taste of what generation after generation of Muslims have ingested for some 1,400 years from their holy books. Hassan al-Banna's genius was to take the "Art of Death" message taught throughout Islam's core texts and package it into an easily digestible, modern form that would resonate with contemporary Islamists enraged by Western imperialism and the re-birth of Israel. Not surprisingly, al-Banna's emphasis on the glories of martyrdom had a powerful and immediate impact on his followers, as Küentzel recounts:

These notions struck a deep chord, at least with the "troops of God," as the Muslim Brothers liked to be known. When-ever their cohorts marched in close formation through the streets of Cairo, their voices rang out with this song: "We are afraid not of death but we desire it.... How wonderful death is.... Let us die in redemption for Muslims" followed by the chorus; "jihad is our course of action.... And death in the cause of God our most precious wish."[15]

Contrary to his grandson Tariq Ramadan's silver-tongued spin, violent jihad and "death for the sake of Allah," as alluded to in the Brotherhood's founding motto, were the foremost pillars of Hassan al-Banna's world-view. The MB architect expounded further on his Art of Death teachings in a long essay called "On Jihad." It contained al-Banna's most authoritative comments on the topic, and he made his stance abundantly clear throughout, beginning with the title of the preface: "All Muslims Must Make Jihad."

> Jihad is an obligation from Allah on every Muslim and cannot be ignored nor evaded. Allah has ascribed great importance to jihad and has made the reward of the martyrs and the fighters in His way a splendid one. Only those who have acted similarly and who have modelled themselves upon the martyrs in their performance of jihad can join them in this reward. Furthermore, Allah has specifically honoured the Mujahideen with certain exceptional qualities, both spiritual and practical, to benefit them in this world and the next. Their pure blood is a symbol of victory in this world and the mark of success and felicity in the world to come.
>
> Those who can only find excuses, however, have been warned of extremely dreadful punishments and Allah has described them with the most unfortunate of names. He has reprimanded them for their cowardice and lack of spirit, and castigated them for their weakness and truancy. In this world,

they will be surrounded by dishonour and in the next they will be surrounded by the fire from which they shall not escape though they may possess much wealth. The weaknesses of abstention and evasion of jihad are regarded by Allah as one of the major sins, and one of the seven sins that guarantee failure.

Islam is concerned with the question of jihad and the drafting and the mobilisation of the entire Umma into one body to defend the right cause with all its strength than any other ancient or modern system of living, whether religious or civil. The verses of the Qur'an and the Sunnah of Muhammad (PBUH) are overflowing with all these noble ideals and they summon people in general (with the most eloquent expression and the clearest exposition) to jihad, to warfare, to the armed forces, and all means of land and sea fighting.[16]

No gray areas there. Al-Banna's message is clear, unambiguous and direct: jihad against the infidel is not only glorious; it is a virtual E-ZPass to heaven and absolutely mandatory for each and every Muslim. He goes on to cite numerous Koranic verses and hadiths that support his glowing view of jihad and martyrdom, as well as quotes from various Muslim scholars. And in case you thought that by "jihad" he meant spiritual striving or internal cleansing—as the Tariq Ramadans of the world would have us believe today—al-Banna makes clear in "On Jihad" that he disagrees with that notion completely, referring to it as "unsound teaching." He then closes the essay with a rousing call to arms:

> My brothers! The ummah that knows how to die a noble and honourable death is granted an exalted life in this world and eternal felicity in the next. Degradation and dishonour are the results of the love of this world and the fear of death. Therefore prepare for jihad and be the lovers of death.

Life itself shall come searching after you.... You should yearn for an honourable death and you will gain perfect happiness. May Allah grant myself and yours the honour of martyrdom in His way![17]

Hassan al-Banna: jihadist. Not a moderate. Not a pragmatist. Not a reformer, unless you count reform as returning to the bloody norms of the seventh century Arabian desert. Not misunderstood or misinterpreted. Not an anti-colonialist freedom fighter defending oppressed Muslims and not a man of peace, as some of his modern apologists, both Islamist and leftist, would have us believe. The real Hassan al-Banna was essentially an old-fashioned Islamic jihadist, only better educated, more eloquent, and dressed up in modern clothes. He was no scholar in any realistic sense of the word and, like the founders of other totalitarian movements, was a visionary solely for the new and diabolical methods he used to spread his message, build his organization, and gain power. Al-Banna's main accomplishment was updating and repackaging the time-tested Islamic supremacist ideology of jihad and conquest for the restless Muslim masses of his day, much to the continuing detriment of all mankind. The heritage of the organization he conceived and its various terrorist offshoots tell the story. Memo to the Obama administration: there is really no nuance here. It is very black and white. The Muslim Brotherhood has never disavowed its jihadist founder and continues to subscribe to his violent teachings today; they remain the bedrock upon which the organization functions and the reason for its very existence. And from the beginning, no one has borne the brunt of al-Banna's devilish legacy more than Israel and the Jews.

There was a time, not very long ago, that Jews made up a sizable minority in Egypt. This sounds hard to believe today; Israel and Egypt spent a good portion of the last sixty-five years as mortal enemies and may be heading there again thanks to the ascendance of the Muslim Brotherhood. Today, fewer than one hundred Jews remain in Egypt, most of them elderly, and they live in fear. But in 1933, up to eighty thousand Jews lived in the country, based mainly in Cairo and Alexandria, enjoying a brief period of relative tolerance under the reign of King Fuad I. Fuad allowed Jews to serve in parliament. Under his reign, the anti-Jewish oppression, pogroms, and dhimmitude of previous centuries seemed to be fading. His government even permitted a thousand Jewish immigrants to land in Port Said on their way to Palestine in 1933.[18] To be fair, Fuad's Egypt was far from a paradise for Jews: despite some advances, they were still looked upon as second-class citizens forever cursed by Allah in the Koran as "the sons of apes and pigs." But the focus of most Egyptians' ire was not on Jews and the fledgling Zionist movement but rather on the hated British occupiers. That all changed in the mid-1930s, thanks to an unholy alliance between the German Nazi Party and Hassan al-Banna's Muslim Brotherhood.

The swift and harsh nature of Egypt's turn against the Jews is particularly chilling given that in 1933 there were actually large anti-Nazi demonstrations held in Cairo.[19] Beneath the surface, however, something nasty was brewing. The Nazi Party was making inroads in Egypt and it had a fervent and influential admirer on the ground in Hassan al-Banna. While the Muslim Brotherhood founder did not embrace the Nazi ideology of Aryan superiority, he was fully on board with Hitler's despotic, anti-democratic ideals and most of all, with Der Fuhrer's rabid Jew hatred. It wasn't long before Nazi agents were funding al-Banna and his growing Islamist movement. Nazi money even helped finance the creation of the Brotherhood's "Secret Apparatus"—a paramilitary terrorist wing that went on to carry out assassinations and other violent mayhem on Egyptian soil and beyond.[20] The Obama administration and the

Brotherhood's assorted Western admirers may be shocked to learn that to this day the organization has never formally abolished this terror cell. In fact, if the Brothers' violent tactics and jihadist-outreach in Egypt these past two years are any indication, they seem bent on revamping the Special Apparatus in a major way.

The Ikhwan thanked the Nazis for their support by translating Hitler's *Mein Kampf* and *The Protocols of the Elders of Zion* into Arabic and publishing the kind of crude, anti-Semitic caricatures common in pro-Nazi newspapers. But al-Banna's activities against the Jews weren't limited to mere propaganda. The Brotherhood went into action around 1937, collecting money for Arab fighters in Palestine and attacking Jewish-owned shops in Cairo.[21] The Secret Apparatus also played a role in a bloody Arab revolt in Palestine against British forces and Jews. Armed bands of Hassan al-Banna's jihadists hunted down Jewish immigrants, many of whom had only recently escaped the horrors of the Holocaust. As al-Banna's grandson, Tariq Ramadan, has proudly recounted:

> Al Banna provided assistance to the Palestinians by sending them an advisor and a specialist in military training, raising funds to buy weapons, and setting up training camps that he ran jointly with members of the Special Organization. Volunteers came to Palestine in groups to support the resistance.[22]

In 1936, the Egyptian Brotherhood had only eight hundred members. By 1938, when it had fully committed itself to the Nazis' anti-Semitic agenda and jihad against the Jews—both in Egypt and abroad—the group's membership had exploded (no pun intended) to two hundred thousand, with branches emerging throughout the Middle East and North Africa. The Secret Apparatus alone boasted forty thousand committed jihadists.[23] As with his glorification of martyrdom and jihad, al-Banna could draw on endless material from the Koran and hadiths as theological justification for his anti-Jewish offensive. Some examples:

- "Ignominy shall be [the Jews'] portion wheresoever they are found.... They have incurred anger from their Lord, and wretchedness is laid upon them... because they disbelieve the revelations of Allah and slew the Prophets wrongfully... because they were rebellious and used to transgress." (Surah 111, v. 112)
- "[The Jews] are the heirs of Hell.... They will spare no pains to corrupt you. They desire nothing but your ruin. Their hatred is clear from what they say.... When evil befalls you they rejoice." (Surah 111, v. 117–20)
- "Because of the wrongdoing of the Jews.... And of their taking usury... and of their devouring people's wealth by false pretenses. We have prepared for those of them who disbelieve a painful doom." (Surah IV, v. 160–61)
- "Allah hath cursed [the Jews] for their disbelief." (Surah IV, v. 46)
- "O ye who believe! Take not the Jews and Christians for friends." (Surah V, v. 51)
- "And thou wilt find them [the Jews] the greediest of mankind." (Surah 11, v. 96)
- "Allah fighteth against [the Jews]. How perverse they are!" (Surah IX, v. 30)
- "[The Jews] spread evil in the land." (Surah V, vs. 62–66)
- "The last hour would not come unless the Muslims will fight against the Jews and the Muslims would kill them until the Jews would hide themselves behind a stone or a tree and a stone or a tree would say: Muslim, or servant

of Allah, there is a Jew behind me; come and kill him."
(41:6985)

In addition, the Koran refers to the Jews in the context of "apes and pigs" multiple times. Egypt's Muslims were well acquainted with the idea of Jews as sub-humans, and they knew Islam's prophet, Mohammed, had carried out numerous massacres of Arabian Jewish tribes. Al-Banna and his Nazi partners simply tapped this anti-Jewish legacy.

While ridding the region of Western, particularly British, influence and reestablishing a caliphate governed by sharia law were paramount goals, by 1948 the Brothers' immediate mission was to prevent the reestablishment of the Jewish state of Israel by any means necessary. Al-Banna had spent the previous decade engineering Ikhwan attacks on Jewish-owned businesses and synagogues in Egypt, sending fighters to Palestine, and solidifying his relationships with German Nazis (Egypt had become a refuge for Nazi fugitives in the aftermath of World War II). Now the moment of truth had arrived. The rebirth of Israel was imminent and al-Banna's close associate, Haj Amin al-Husseini, the infamous Grand Mufti of Jerusalem, turned to the Brotherhood for help in pushing the Jews into the sea.

The Mufti had lived in Berlin as an honored guest of the Nazis during World War II, meeting with Adolf Hitler and personally visiting Nazi death camps. He encouraged Hitler and his minions to extend the Final Solution to the Jews living in the Arab world and even helped recruit some twenty thousand Bosnian Muslim volunteers into Hitler's Waffen SS.[24] Haj Amin al-Husseini, essentially the first leader of what has become known as the Palestinian people, was, quite literally, a Nazi.

True to form, the Muslim Brotherhood embraced the Mufti. Al-Banna even arranged for al-Husseini's political exile in Egypt after the Second

World War.[25] The Mufti returned to Jerusalem soon after and lobbied al-Banna to send Muslim Brotherhood volunteers to help battle the Jews. Al-Banna eagerly obliged and the Mufti organized the Ikhwan brigades that arrived to fight alongside invading Arab armies during Israel's War for Independence in 1948. Said Ramadan, Tariq's father and son-in-law of Hassan al-Banna, was chosen to lead the Brotherhood's efforts during the conflict. In the process, he became a military confidante of Jordan's King Abdullah.[26]

Israel prevailed. And as the tide of the war turned, improbably, in favor of the severely outgunned and outmanned Israeli forces, an embittered al-Banna vowed endless jihad against the reborn Jewish nation:

> If the Jewish state becomes a fact, and this is realized by the Arab peoples, they will drive the Jews who live in their midst into the sea.... Even if we are beaten now in Palestine, we will never submit. We will never accept the Jewish state.... But for politics, the Egyptian army alone, or volunteers of the Muslim Brotherhood, could have destroyed the Jews.[27]

Al-Banna's statements—and especially his actions—concerning Israel and the Jews laid the groundwork for today's murderous state of affairs, in which the Muslim Brotherhood and its various offshoots are the vanguard of global anti-Semitism and Hitler's true heirs.

━━━━━

The year 1948 was a pivotal year for the Muslim Brotherhood. Its fierce efforts to prevent the reestablishment of Israel ultimately failed. Even more disastrously, the Egyptian government outlawed the Ikhwan movement outright. The ban came after a wave of terror and violence perpetrated by Brotherhood members upon Egyptian government officials, Coptic Christians, and other opponents of the Brothers' sharia agenda for Egypt. As Iranian-born author Fereydoun Hoveyda describes in his book, *The Broken Crescent: The "Threat" of Militant Islamic Fundamentalism*, "Cinemas were bombed, hotels set on fire, unveiled women attacked, and homes raided. Prime ministers and other pro-Western high-ranking officials were assassinated."[28] The Brotherhood's victims included Egyptian Prime Minister Mahmud Fahmi Nokrashi, murdered by Ikhwan assassins. Al-Banna, in typical Brotherhood fashion, trained and equipped jihadists but took no responsibility for their actions. Hoveyda writes:

> Young aspiring terrorists from all over the world poured into Egypt in order to learn from al-Banna's men the art of eliminating the enemies of Islam. While training terrorists and directing murders, Sheikh Hassan denied involvement in the assassinations and attacks, using what Shiite clerics called *ketman* (holy dissimulation). Indeed, deceiving infidels was admitted by all Muslims, and Shiites even extended the dissimulation to other Muslims when the security of their "cause" was at stake.[29]

Nevertheless, the murder of Nokrashi proved a tipping point. The Brotherhood was banned and al-Banna himself was assassinated in 1949 by Egyptian government agents in Cairo. Hence, the godfather of modern-day jihad met what would be hailed as a "martyr's death" by his followers. Unfortunately for Egypt and the world, he left behind a fearsome terrorist organization that boasted at least one million members at the time of his death. And in those days, there was no denying that the Muslim Brotherhood was a terrorist organization. Just take a look at these *New York Times* headlines from the era:

- November 21, 1948, page 5: TERRORIST GROUP ARRESTED IN CAIRO, Police Action Against Members of Moslem Brotherhood Is Said to Solve Outrages
- December 9, 1948, page 12: EGYPT ENDS MOSLEM BROTHERHOOD; ORDERS ITS PROPERTIES CON-FISCATED, Proclamation of National Emergency State Accompanies Dissolution Decree—Bombings and Power Bid Laid to Organization
- December 16, 1948, page 17: ARMS UNCOVERED IN CAIRO, Cache of Moslem Brotherhood Seized by Police
- December 29, 1948, page 1: EGYPTIAN PREMIER IS SLAIN BY CAIRO STUDENT TERRORIST, The Assassin Is Member of Moslem Brotherhood—New Cabinet Formed
- January 14, 1949, page 8: 2 KILLED IN CAIRO BY FANATIC'S BOMB, Explosive Left for Prosecutor of Terrorists Is Carried to Street by Office Boy
- February 4, 1949, page 9: SUICIDE SQUADRON IN EGYPT REPORTED, Group of 200 Said to Have Been Formed Within Moslem Brotherhood
- February 13, 1949, page 5: MOSLEM BROTHERHOOD LEADER SLAIN AS HE ENTERS TAXI IN CAIRO STREET, Terrorist Leader Is Killed In Cairo[30]

The Muslim Brotherhood a "terrorist group"? Hassan al-Banna a "terrorist leader"? Muslim Brotherhood "fanatics" and "suicide squadrons"? Could this really be the same *New York Times* that doggedly served as the Brotherhood's most reliable media defender during the so-called Arab Spring, culminating in this gem by the paper's Cairo bureau chief, David K. Kirkpatrick, in December 2012?

[The Muslim Brothers] are not violent by nature, and they have over the last couple of decades evolved more and more into a moderate—conservative but religious, but moderate—regular old political force. I find that a lot of the liberal fears of the Brotherhood are somewhat outside. That said, you know, you don't know what their ultimate vision of what the good life looks like. But in the short term, I think they just want to win elections.[31]

Yes, a "regular old political force," a bit lively but perfectly reasonable, like the Whigs or the Tories. Your average Muslim Brother just wants "the good life," you see, and if that involves chopping hands, oppressing women, and subjugating Christians and Jews under sharia, who are we to judge? Kirkpatrick's assessment is even more galling considering that it came in the midst of a virtual coup d'etat by Mohammed Morsi and the Brotherhood, complete with reports of Ikhwan thugs raping women in Cairo and setting up torture chambers to brutalize political opponents. The good life, indeed. Contrary to the verbal bouquets thrown around by the *Times'* man in Cairo, the violent spasms and power grabs of the past few years have shown that the Muslim Brotherhood of today differs little from the openly jihadist outfit of yesteryear.

One major difference, however, is that the Brotherhood has learned the art of extreme caution, patiently gauging conditions on the ground and rarely, if ever, overplaying its hand and moving too soon. Yes, Mohammed Morsi's decree in November 2012 granting himself nearly absolute power, followed by his helping Egypt's Islamist-led parliament ram through a new sharia-based constitution, sparked massive protests and running street battles. But Morsi knew the Brotherhood had the numbers, the muscle, and the silent complicity of the Obama administration and would, as a result, win out in the end. He was also fresh off helping to broker a ceasefire between Israel and Hamas that saw him hailed as a pragmatist and statesman by President Obama and then-Secretary of State Hillary Clinton. With the region a tinderbox and Egypt's peace treaty with Israel hanging by a thread, Morsi realized the feckless Obama administration was invested in his success and wouldn't dare cut its billions of dollars of funding to his regime. Perhaps most important, the budding jihadist knew he had the Egyptian military's backing.

That wasn't the case in 1952, when, after supporting a military coup that overthrew the Egyptian monarchy, the Brotherhood expected a major role in the new government and pushed hard for Egypt to become an Islamic state governed by sharia law. The military junta, after early attempts to appease the Ikhwan, soon realized it was dealing with an implacable foe, as coup leader Gamal Abdel Nasser noted at the time:

> I have met several times with the Supreme Guide of the Brotherhood, who overwhelmed me with his demands. The thing he first asked for was for the government to ordain that women be veiled. Subsequently he made other demands, such as closing the cinemas and the theatres and other things as well that would make life gloomy and sinister. It was, of course, impossible to do such things.[32]

Who says history doesn't repeat itself? Nasser's remarks about the Brotherhood circa 1954 sound eerily like those of an analyst surveying the situation in Egypt today. Yet, while Morsi and the Brothers have been successful in their drive for absolute power, their predecessors had no such luck. The friction between the Ikhwan and Nasser's Free Officers reached a boiling point in October 1954, when a member of the Brotherhood's Secret Apparatus fired eight shots at Nasser while the latter was giving a speech in Alexandria. The assassination attempt failed and Nasser moved quickly to crush the Brotherhood, dissolving the organization and burning its headquarters to the ground. Thousands of its members—including chief propagandist Sayyid Qutb—were rounded up and arrested. Six were hanged.[33] The Brotherhood would be severely repressed in Egypt for most of the next five decades, its members frequently arrested, tortured, and executed. As a result, the movement went underground. Its leaders were patient, and worked insidiously to undermine the regime. And the slow-and-steady model, a phased strategy for weakening secular governments, soon became the norm for most Ikhwan satellites throughout the world.

One notable exception was the Brotherhood's Syrian branch, which spearheaded a violent insurrection in the late 1970s and early 1980s that ended in disaster for the Ikhwan in that country. As Islamism expert Hassan Mneimneh recounts:

> The confrontation escalated in March 1980 into uprisings in virtually all Syrian cities, with the open participation of numerous opposition groups. Though the [Hafez] Assad regime responded decisively over the next two years with spectacular acts of brutality and collective punishment, the Muslim Brotherhood remained an existential threat to the regime until February 1982, when it took over the city of Hama. This prompted Assad to dispatch his brother Rifat at the helm of "defense brigades" to squash the rebellion. Rifat accomplished his mission by steadily bombarding the city and killing an estimated 20,000 of its inhabitants.[34]

The Hama massacre signaled the neutralization of the Syrian Brotherhood—banned and largely ineffective until finding new life in Syria's recent civil war—and proved a cautionary lesson for the global Ikhwan on the virtue of patience, particularly in countries where military dictatorships unhesitant to employ brutal violence hold sway. Lesson learned: the fact that the Brotherhood is helping lead another insurrection today in Syria, some thirty years after its crushing defeat at the hands of Bashar al-Assad's father, Hafez, shows the remarkable resilience and staying power of the movement and its message. Like their Egyptian counterparts, the Syrian Brothers have been able to outlast some of the Arab world's most repressive strongmen. That's no coincidence. Hassan al-Banna's message of jihad and martyrdom, of anti-Semitic and anti-Western animus, struck a deep chord throughout the Muslim world and spawned generations of committed, fanatical Islamists bent on establishing a global caliphate.

Yet, for some, al-Banna didn't go far enough and slow-and-steady just wouldn't do. While still revering al-Banna as the godfather of modern jihad, these unholy warriors took their cues from a different Brotherhood icon, Sayyid Qutb—and changed the course of world history in the process.

CHAPTER FOUR

ACCESSORY TO AL-QAEDA

"**Y**ou are the first person I've given an interview to in a long time. The media, they tell lies about me."

Sheikh Abu Adam spoke in an almost mournful tone as he led my cameraman and me down a dimly lit hallway in his Munich flat. His burly bodyguards, both dressed in similar al-Qaeda–like garb, flanked us on either side, as they would throughout the next three hours. Our destination was a small back room of the apartment where a Middle Eastern–style spread of chicken, rice, and pita bread awaited us.

This was Germany but it could have easily passed for Gaza—a fitting atmosphere for the Sheikh, an Egyptian native of Palestinian origin whose real name is Hesham Sheshaa. At the time of our meeting, his three wives and ten of his twelve (some say he has more) children lived with him in the cramped flat. The sound of a baby wailing and small children screaming from the next room cascaded off the walls around us as we sat to eat, but the Sheikh—who bears an uncanny facial resemblance to Osama bin Laden—appeared unfazed. He stroked his long beard and adjusted his Islamic headdress before joining his bodyguards in devouring large helpings of chicken and rice.

"Before we do the interview, we must eat," he said between chomps. "There is much to discuss."

It was June 2012 and Germany's Salafist movement, of which Sheikh Abu Adam is a prominent voice, had increasingly come under the microscope of German intelligence as a major national security threat. Just two weeks before my interview with the Sheikh, one thousand German police fanned out across the country and raided the homes, schools, and mosques of Salafi Muslims suspected of terrorism-related activities.

Salafism is considered the most extreme interpretation of Islam—no small feat—and is the brand of choice for al-Qaeda and other Sunni Muslim terror groups. In dress, speech, and mannerisms, Salafists model themselves after Islam's prophet Mohammed and his earliest followers in the seventh century Arabian desert (the term *salaf* means "predecessors"). Long beards, flowing *dishdasha* robes, and pants worn above the ankle are some of their defining physical characteristics. They strictly adhere to every facet of Islamic sharia law and are openly, often violently, hostile to any society that does not follow suit, including Germany.

The Salafists, close cousins of the notorious Saudi Wahhabis, reject Germany's secular, democratic constitution and seek to make the Koran the ultimate authority over any manmade laws. If you think this sounds an awful lot like the Muslim Brotherhood, you're absolutely right. In fact, as recently as 2008, the "About Us" section of the Brotherhood's official website self-identified the MB as Salafi.[1] Indeed, the two movements share the exact same ideology and goals, and the Brotherhood's roots are indisputably in Salafism. But as we'll see shortly, there are some distinctions—mostly tactical—that have developed between the MB and hardcore Salafists like Egypt's Gamaa Islamiya in the years since the death of their mutual hero Sayyid Qutb in 1966. For instance, the Brotherhood's gradualist strategy and willingness to engage in electoral politics has been a sore point with Salafists—although that may very well be changing, if the thrust into Egyptian politics by Gamaa Islamiya and other Salafist groups in recent years is any indication.

As for Sheikh Abu Adam's home base of Germany, security officials there estimate that only about five thousand of the country's 4.3 million Muslims are Salafists. But these jihadists-in-waiting are Germany's fastest growing Muslim sect and are known for being verbally and physically confrontational toward non-Muslims.

A Palestinian Salafi imam named Ibrahim Abou Nagie created a firestorm during the first half of 2012 when he and his group Die Wahre Religion (The True Religion) led a drive to place a Koran in every German home. Abou Nagie's disciples set up stands in major German cities where they handed out thousands of free Korans, with non-Muslims the intended target. The goal, he said, was "to bring Allah's word to every household" in Germany.[2] Abou Nagie—who for years received welfare benefits from the German government—is just one of many high-profile Salafi preachers to draw law enforcement scrutiny for their role in radicalizing young German Muslims.

Several of these Salafi firebrands are based in and around the Rhineland cities of Cologne and Bonn in western Germany. I visited both cities and was struck by the number of Salafis I saw walking the streets, including a number of white Muslim converts. The ethnic mix was actually not surprising—there have long been reports of German jihad colonies in Pakistan's tribal regions, where German expats, including white converts, have devoted their lives to jihad and the al-Qaeda/Taliban cause.[3]

"We can see that a lot of jihadis with Salafist backgrounds are going to Afghanistan and to training camps, to Pakistan into training camps," German journalist Franz Feyder told me. "And what we can see as well is that a lot of jihadis are passing through the Horn of Africa. And they're going to fight in Somalia, going to fight in Yemen, going to fight in Kenya."

Feyder, an expert on Germany's Salafi scene, summarized German intelligence officials' view on the matter: "The Salafi movement in Germany is creating an environment for violence and radicalization. Not every Salafist is a terrorist, but every terrorist is a Salafist."[4]

The growing strength and confidence of the movement was on full display in May 2012, when hundreds of Salafists stormed a small anti-Islam rally in Bonn and attacked German police who were on the scene. Twenty-nine officers were injured as a result of the onslaught—including two seriously from knife wounds—and over a hundred Salafists were arrested.[5] A few months later, two Somali-born Salafists were jailed after attempting to bomb Bonn's central train station.[6] That incident wasn't Germany's first brush with Islamic terror, however. Dozens of German citizens have been arrested on terrorism-related charges since 9/11, including the gunman who murdered two U.S. airmen and injured two more in a jihadi attack at Frankfurt Airport in 2011 while yelling, "Allahu Akhbar."[7] The forerunner to these recent incidents was the infamous Hamburg Cell, consisting of a group of al-Qaeda operatives and sympathizers—including Mohammed Atta and two other 9/11 hijackers—that gathered in Hamburg in the late 1990s.

It is no doubt particularly disheartening for older Germans who suffered through Nazism and communism to see yet another anti-democratic, totalitarian ideology take root on German soil. Even more so because the German government—like virtually all of its counterparts in Western Europe—has exacerbated the problem over several decades with lax immigration laws, suicidal multicultural policies, and draconian political correctness. Simply put, the rise of German Islamism is an overwhelmingly self-inflicted wound. And it will surely come as no surprise to American readers to learn that the staunchly leftist German media has succeeded in branding anyone who voices concern over this troubling trend a "racist," "Islamophobe,"or worse, a "Nazi." When I interviewed courageous German anti-jihad activists, their most common complaint was about the bias and hostility of the left-wing German media.

But as Sheikh Abu Adam led us into his personal office in the basement of his apartment building, all was sweetness and light. He politely informed us that his bodyguards would be filming our interview to ensure that the Sheikh wasn't misquoted in my report. Then our conversation turned to his travels to Pakistan and other jihadi hotspots where he says he preaches against terrorism. He showed us video clips of himself in Pakistan's tribal regions, supposedly debating Taliban and al-Qaeda types and arguing against violent jihad. The Sheikh says his anti-terrorism work has drawn the ire of other Salafists and earned him death threats (hence the bodyguards).

"I try to convince them to leave jihad, to leave radicalism, to leave bomb attacks," he told me. "There are more and more radicals every day, also in Europe."

The Sheikh swears he isn't one of them. Needless to say, I wasn't buying it. For starters, all Salafists must support the idea of violent jihad. Remember, these are strict Koranic literalists who take every verse from Islam's holy book, including the infamous Verse of the Sword, which exhorts Muslims to "Slay the unbelievers wherever [Muslims] find them," quite literally. That doesn't mean all Salafists personally engage in violence or jihad. That isn't the case—although the movement's venomous anti-Western, sharia-fied ideology and lengthy track record of terrorism could certainly lead you to believe otherwise. It does mean, however, that all true Salafists, being the harshest of fundamentalists, must at least agree in principle with the numerous exhortations to violence against non-believers found throughout the Koran and Sunnah and regard these verses as open-ended and applicable to the modern day. Otherwise they wouldn't be Salafists.

That's why it came as no surprise when, during our interview, Sheikh Abu Adam showed me a recent letter he had received from the Bavarian government that identified him as—bingo—a radical Salafist and anti-Semite. I asked the Sheikh why German authorities would say such things about him and the Darul Quran mosque in Munich, where he is lead imam.

"I don't know!" he answered, seemingly dismayed. "All of my students, all—I don't have any exception—they are fighting against terrorism and they are very integrated in the society. All of them are very kind, loving people. They laugh. They communicate with all people."

A Bavarian television crew found something far less benign when it visited the Darul Quran mosque in 2011. It seems the Sheikh was presiding there over sharia courts operating outside of German law.[8] He told the German daily *Der Spiegel* that he encourages his followers to settle conflicts at the mosque, rather than going to German police, and that his judgments are "fairer than the [German] government's."[9] Considering that the average female Darul Quran attendee is clad in an all-encompassing *niqab* garment where only the eyes are visible, one can guess which way his judgments usually go when it comes to, say, marital disputes.

Coincidentally, that same *Der Spiegel* article described the Sheikh as someone who "teaches a reactionary kind of Islam...doesn't believe in separating religion from the state, and rejects moderate branches of his religion." But never fear, slippery Islamists: when right-wing meanies start asking tough questions, the *New York Times* has your back. The journalistic stalwarts at the *NYT*, manipulated repeatedly since 9/11 by Islamists great and small, ran a laudatory 2010 profile of the Sheikh titled "Munich Imam Tries to Dull Lure of Radical Islam."[10] As of this writing, the *Times* has yet to publish a follow-up conceding that it may have been wrong about the Sheikh, even with the sharia court controversy coming to light. To the liberal mind, when a guy like Abu Adam says he is a moderate who opposes violence he must be taken at his word, with no further background checks or research required. Doing anything more would be rank Islamophobia. After all, why would this kindly gentleman doling out chicken and rice to visiting journalists lie?

For a while, the German government also seemed to accept the *Times'* narrative of Abu Adam as tenderhearted peace activist. According to the Sheikh, his lectures on non-violence at various venues around Deutschland had the support of German officials, with whom he was apparently in regular contact. But the Sheikh's activities caught the attention of authorities for a different reason in late 2010, when he was arrested for brutally beating one of his three wives, reportedly breaking her nose and shoulder and inflicting several cuts and bruises.[11] He allegedly yelled misogynistic Koranic verses as he pummeled her and refused to allow German police to enter his apartment. The wife—who was reportedly beaten for telling the Sheikh she wanted to live a more Western lifestyle—ultimately declined to press charges, but not before the Sheikh spent almost three months in jail. He maintains that she acquired her injuries after taking a fall in their apartment.[12] He also has a bridge he'd like to sell you somewhere in Egypt.

As we wrapped up our interview, the Sheikh lamented the fact that German officials had turned against him—or in other words, wised up. Although the unabashed polygamist and his large brood receive generous welfare benefits from the government, he said he was unsure whether he would stay in Germany.

"I'm sacrificing myself and my family and my scholars because of you and then you write that I am radicalized?" he vented. "I'm fighting against the terrorists!"

Interestingly enough, one Islamic supremacist group the Sheikh does truly seem to oppose is the Muslim Brotherhood. At the time of our meeting, he had just returned from Egypt. As he and his bodyguards escorted us to our car, I asked his thoughts on that country's new Ikhwan overlords.

"The Muslim Brotherhood is not a religious group. They are a polit-ical group," he answered. "They are dangerous."

Dangerous indeed. But not for the reasons Sheikh Abu Adam had in mind.

━━━━━

As we'll see shortly, the Sheikh's negative view of the Ikhwan has absolutely nothing to do with the MB's declared endgame of a global caliphate ruled by sharia and everything to do with tactics. Indeed, if ideology were the determining factor, the Muslim Brotherhood and hardcore Salafists would be virtually indistinguishable. Both Islamist blocs seek a worldwide caliphate governed by Islamic sharia law. Both support violent jihad against the infidel and have engaged in it fre-quently. Both wish to see the state of Israel wiped off the map and both view the United States as a hated enemy. Let's also remember that the writings of seminal Brotherhood ideologue Sayyid Qutb—not to men-tion those of Hassan al-Banna—have inspired legions of Salafi-jihadists over the past several decades, including the founding leadership of al-Qaeda.

The Brotherhood admittedly has its roots in Salafism and the two factions desire the same endgame, so it comes as no surprise that they have collaborated frequently through the years. According to Islamism expert Gilles Kepel, the jihad against the Soviets in Afghanistan during the 1980s, in which Osama bin Laden and many of his future al-Qaeda soldiers played a major role, was one prime example:

> In Afghanistan all the different factions within the Islamist movement . . . found common ground under the banner of armed jihad. The ultimate success of the jihad in Afghanistan dealt serious blows not only to the communist world, but also helped to silence Ayatollah Khomeini's claim to hegemony in

the Muslim world after the Iranian Islamic revolution of 1979. By the end of the 1980s, therefore, the Brothers and other Islamist radicals who were in Afghanistan were convinced that the sky was the limit. The Brothers had invested heavily in Afghanistan—sending university students, doctors from their medical associations, money, weapons—and they cherished their part in the victory.[13]

As terrorism expert Lorenzo Vidino writes in his 2009 book, *The New Muslim Brotherhood in the West*, a group of top Brotherhood leaders returned to Afghanistan a few years after the Soviet withdrawal to bask in their victory—and promise an even greater one to come against the Great Satan:

> ... Swiss authorities found a videocassette with images of a 1993 trip to Afghanistan made by a group of senior Brotherhood leaders to congratulate Afghan Islamist leaders on their victory against the Soviet Union. The group was led by the future [Supreme Guide] of the Egyptian Brotherhood, Mustafa Mashour.... Mashour, a widely respected leader who had spent most of the 1980's in Germany, gave a speech that was not supposed to circulate beyond Brotherhood circles. He started by praising the Afghans for their victory and said that jihad must continue to liberate other occupied Muslim lands, from Palestine to India and Chechnya. *But Mashour did not stop there. "I will assure you," he said, "That as the Soviet Union has fallen, so will America and the West succumb, with the help of God."*[14] [emphasis added]

Mashour's last statement is a helpful reminder that the Obama administration is funding and arming—to the tune of billions of dollars annually—an organization that wishes to see America destroyed. Taxpayers, rejoice.

As the Afghanistan model shows, there's nothing quite like the prospect of jihad against the infidel and a global caliphate to convince Islamists to put aside petty differences. We're seeing that play out once again today in Egypt, where the Brothers and various Salafist parties control the bulk of the parliament and have struck up an alliance to advance their shared goal of an Islamic state.

"Remember that when Morsi claimed dictator's powers in November 2012, he called on the Islamists to help back the regime against the protestors," MB expert and investigative journalist Patrick Poole told me in a January 2013 interview. "If there is any difference [between the Brotherhood and Salafists] it is one of degree, not of kind. Think division of labor, much like the 'social' and 'military' wings of Hamas. The Salafis are the shock troops that the MB call in when they need help—and then when the Brotherhood comes under pressure from the West they supposedly 'crack down' and reign in the Salafists. But the MB couldn't survive without the Salafis."

In addition to their strategic differences on the timing of jihad and violence—which we'll explore in greater detail shortly—there have been three main areas where the Brothers and the Salafists have not always seen eye-to-eye over the past few decades. Mind you, as Poole said, these differences are narrowing every day thanks to the Islamist ascendance triggered by the so-called Arab Spring, which has brought the MB and Salafists even closer together:

1) Salafists tell the truth. In fact, the Janus-faced Sheikh Abu Adam and his double game are a rarity among the Salafist breed. They are generally very open and up front about their desire for a global caliphate comprised of sharia states that will confront Israel and the West. The Brotherhood, on the other hand, has mastered the Islamic pastime of

taqiyya—deception—working stealthily and incrementally to accomplish the very same aims as the Salafists. On the rare occasion that a Brotherhood official does slip up and share details about the movement's very immoderate goals, the Ikhwan, always protective of its "moderate" image in the West, quickly issues a denial, clarification, or retraction. It's a much more furtive brand of Salafism—and undeniably effective.

2) The Salafists strictly oppose any and all modern innovation (or *ijtihad*) in Islam and believe the answers to all of life's issues can be found in the faith's sacred texts, as interpreted by Muslim scholars during the roughly four-hundred-year period that began with Islam's founding in the seventh century and ended around the tenth century AD (when the so-called "Gates of Ijtihad" closed). Therefore, any new interpretations or independent judgments—known to most non-Muslims as, um, "freedom of thought"—are harshly condemned by Salafists.[15]

The Brotherhood, though, has a sly take here. Like their Salafist kindred spirits, the Brothers are Koranic fundamentalists whose interpretation of sharia includes subjugation of women, stoning, et al., and is medieval to the core. Yet Western Brothers I've interviewed have spoken favorably of reviving ijtihad for the present day and the Brotherhood's English-language website features several articles in support of the notion. On one hand, this is no surprise. Western Brothers in particular must cope with the technological advancements, permissiveness, and democratic nature of the societies in which they live. True, the freedom found in Europe and the United States is anathema to the Brothers' backward agenda. But as we'll see, it is frequently used to their advantage. The Brothers realize that what worked for Islamists in seventh century Medina doesn't work in ultra-secular, twenty-first-century Madrid or even modern-day Morocco, for that matter. Today's average Joe-hammed in the West faces challenges, cultural norms, and attitudes that his desert-dwelling predecessors did not, a fact that many diehard Salafists seem to disregard.

But not the Brotherhood. As our old friend Tariq Ramadan is fond of saying, Islamists must "Islamize modernity"—be realistic, recognize the unique conditions on the ground today and somehow make the quest for a caliphate ruled by sharia more palatable to modern sensibilities. And hey, when it comes to packaging evil, old ideas of Islamic conquest in a new, creative way, ijtihad could come in quite handy. Most important, it would allow the Brotherhood and its scholars to essentially set the tone for global Islam and become the ultimate authority on all things sharia-related (some would say the MB's spiritual guide, Sheikh Yusuf al-Qaradawi, already fills that role on his wildly popular weekly program on Al-Jazeera). This would greatly enhance the Ikhwan's despotic goal of speaking for all the world's Muslims and controlling how Islam is interpreted and practiced throughout the globe. In other words, Islam would be whatever the Brotherhood's braintrust tells you it is.

3) The Brotherhood's satellites in the Islamic world have embraced the political process, running in—and winning—elections; its operatives also actively lobby Western governments and have access to the halls of power in Washington, D.C., and Brussels. This makes sense: like other totalitarian movements, Islamism must first seize political power—and keep it for good—before it is able to realistically implement its utopian goals. In short, the Brotherhood views politics as a necessary evil used to attain absolute power.

Many Salafists, though, disdain politics as a manmade abomination, a domain reserved only for secularists and infidels, where Allah has no say. Al-Qaeda leader Ayman al-Zawahiri and a good number of Salafists consider the Brothers to be sellouts for participating in the political game and playing by the *kafirs'* rules. Al-Zawahiri even wrote a book, called *The Bitter Harvest*, that fiercely criticized the Ikhwan on that count.

For many Salafists, Qutb's strategy of jihad, insurrection, and over-throwing both secular or insufficiently Islamist Arab rulers and Western Crusader governments is the only acceptable way to obtain power—

forget taking it slow or working through the system. But that may be changing. In Egypt, even the notorious Gamaa Islamiya—the Blind Sheikh and Zawahiri's old organization—is now playing the political game. The toppling of secular Arab regimes throughout the region has left chaos and power vacuums aplenty—and the Salafists want to capitalize.

And they're moving quickly. In June 2012, a Gamaa Islamiya member named Hani Nour Eldin received a visa and participated in "high-level" meetings at the White House and State Department along with a group of his fellow Egyptian parliamentarians. Gamaa Islamiya, or the Egyptian Islamic Group, is a State Department–designated terrorist organization. Eldin himself was arrested in 1993 on terrorism charges after a shootout erupted between Gamaa Islamiya members and security officials at an Egyptian mosque. Yet he somehow secured a visa and was welcomed at 1600 Pennsylvania Avenue. Go figure.

At his meetings with senior Obama administration officials, Eldin reportedly asked that Gamaa Islamiya spiritual leader Omar Abdel-Rahman, the notorious "Blind Sheikh," be transferred to Egyptian custody as a "gift to the [Egyptian] revolution."[16] Rahman, beloved by al-Qaeda and Salafi/jihadis worldwide, is currently serving a life sentence in a North Carolina federal prison for his role in the 1993 World Trade Center bombing and a 1995 plot to bomb New York City landmarks.

It's tempting to think that Eldin's White House and State Department visits were just egregious, unintentional oversights—bureaucratic bungling of the worst kind, yes, but nothing more than an unfortunate mistake that was quickly corrected. The truth, however, is much worse. When members of Congress later pressed Department of Homeland Security chief Janet Napolitano about Eldin's D.C. adventure, she was coldly indignant, saying the Egyptian jihadist had been vetted by three different U.S. government agencies and that "no derogatory information was found." In other words, this was no blunder, no mistake. Eldin, a member of a violent terrorist group that has worked closely with al-Qaeda, was welcomed with open arms into the halls of power by the Obama administration. But that's not all. According to Napolitano, in the future, the Obama administration will "continue to have visitors to [America] that the State Department and others feel are useful to bring to the country, to have discussions moving forward, who say they're members of a political party that in the past has been so designated [as a terrorist organization]."[17]

Perhaps these visiting jihadi dignitaries can peruse the copy of Thomas Jefferson's Koran that President Obama likes to show off at annual White House Iftar dinners. According to Obama, the fact that our third president owned a Koran is "a reminder…that Islam—like so many faiths—is part of our national story."[18] What Obama neglects to mention is that Jefferson owned a Koran in order to learn the ideology behind the Muslim Barbary pirates who were plundering American and European ships along North Africa's Mediterranean coast. In 1805, after he became president, Jefferson sent U.S. Marines onto "the shores of Tripoli," where they routed the pirates in America's first-ever military confrontation with Islamists.[19] For some reason, Obama neglects to mention that important little fact. As for Jefferson, if only today's Western leaders possessed a shred of his intellectual curiosity and honesty about the Islamist enemy we face, Hani Nour Eldin and his ilk would be welcomed to America wearing handcuffs.

Islamists, very much including the Muslim Brotherhood, seek global domination and the subjugation of anyone opposed to their totalitarian aims. Of course, Muslim Brothers will never say that in English.

But if you let him, Anjem Choudary will happily wax poetic about the Islamists' true goals all day long, and with a British accent to boot. In my 2011 book, *The Terrorist Next Door*, I first introduced readers to Choudary, a forty-something Salafi firebrand who's been dubbed "Great Britain's Most Hated Man." Choudary and his followers—some of whom have been arrested on terrorism charges—regularly hold rallies in London calling for the downfall of the British state and the institution of sharia law in the UK. I interviewed him once again in an East London park in June 2012 to get his views on Islam in Britain and the so-called Arab Spring.[20] Choudary, never camera shy, had much to say:

> **Choudary:** Al-Qaeda believe in fighting the people who are occupying our land and eventually taking the authority and implementing the sharia. In that, they are absolutely correct. And we believe in the same thing. It's just that we live in the West.... Britain is Dar Al Harb [The Land of War]. Because they are, you know, anathema to God's law. They're not implementing it, they're violating its sanctity—and therefore, this is war against Allah and his messenger. But we are not allowed to actually fight them here at the current time—

> **Stakelbeck:** Not at the current time. Will there be a time?

> **Choudary:** Well, you know Erick, we are not like the Christians. If you hit me on the left cheek I'm not going to give you my right cheek. I'm going to defend myself. So at the moment we are propagating Islam peacefully. But if they attack us we have the right to defend ourselves.

> **Stakelbeck:** What if they don't attack? ... Then would there be a cause for offensive jihad?

> **Choudary:** If we have enough authority and we have enough power, then we are obliged as Muslims to take the authority away from those who have it and implement the sharia. Now, I hope that can come in a very peaceful way. I hope we can do that in a way where there is no bloodshed.

He "hopes," but he certainly isn't making any promises. With this exchange, Choudary articulated perfectly what the Muslim Brotherhood believes. Only, a Brotherhood spokesman wouldn't be caught dead uttering it on camera, least of all in a Western media hub like London. Therein lies a major difference between the Ikhwan and Salafists like Choudary. It came as no surprise, then, when Choudary, like his fellow Salafi, Sheikh Abu Adam, criticized the Brothers' tactics:

> **Stakelbeck:** One group that has really benefited from the Arab Spring is the Muslim Brotherhood. What are your thoughts on the Brotherhood?

> **Choudary:** The Ikhwan al-Muslimeen, over the last seventy to eighty years, have changed, they've split, you know, they have different factions. You have people like Sheikh Omar Abdel Rahman [the Blind Sheikh], and even from there, people like Sheikh Ayman al-Zawahiri, who believe in jihad, who believe in the pure form of the sharia. On the other hand you have people who believe in democracy...these are also within the realm of the Muslim Brotherhood.... Those who we have in charge in Egypt now are not calling for the pure form of sharia. What we find, in fact, is that they are trying to please the masses to get into power. And that is not Islam.

To Choudary, the Brotherhood's participation in the Egyptian political process was an affront that would invariably lead to a watered-down version of sharia. Yet the fact remained that the Brotherhood's stealth strategy had helped it wrest control of the Arab world's most populous and important country. Choudary bristled when I suggested the Muslim Brotherhood's blueprint for power was superior to the Salafists':

Choudary: Our purpose in life is to please [Allah]. So if people are going to do that by you know, just trying to achieve a temporary objective in this life and by any means necessary, even if it is not according to the traditions of the prophet [Mohammed], then they're not getting reward for that action. And in Egypt, for example, they must implement the sharia. The apostate regime of Hosni Mubarak before them needed to be removed—and we could have used force to remove them.

You can just picture an Obama administration official—like, say, self-professed foreign policy guru Joe Biden—listen to the preceding exchange and think to himself, "Hmmm. These Salafists sure are a violent, unpredictable bunch. And with their big beards and man-dresses, the optics are just all wrong for a Western audience. No way can we do business with them. They look like terrorists! Which, uh, I guess a lot of them are. Anyway, the Brotherhooders participate in politics, wear suits and trim their beards. They even speak English. And a lot of them have gone to school here. Oh, and most important, they are *not* blowing anyone up! At least not yet. Although I guess their Hamas brothers are over in Gaza. But they're just killing Israelis, so no harm to us. The right-wingers say they're bad but I say malarkey! I think we need to push these Muslim Brothers in a big way. They could be the answer we're looking for in the Muslim world. This could be a big bleepin' deal!"

Contrary to our elites' rosy view, the Muslim Brotherhood has been steeped in violence and radicalism since its beginnings, right down to its official logo, which features a Koran with two crossed swords and the Arabic inscription, "Make Ready" underneath. As if the swords weren't enough, "Make Ready" refers to Sura 8, verse 60 of the Koran, which states:

> Against them make ready your strength to the utmost of your power, including steeds of war, to strike terror into (the hearts of) the enemies, of God and your enemies, and others besides, whom ye may not know, but whom God doth know.[21]

Needless to say, you won't be seeing any Jesus Fish magnets next to the MB logo on car bumpers in Cairo.

From their incendiary emblem to their official motto—which, remember, reads in part: "Jihad is our way, dying in the way of Allah is our highest hope"—Hassan al-Banna and his Society of Muslim Brothers laid down the jihadi gauntlet from the very outset. Today, nearly a century after the Brotherhood's creation, both logo and motto, tellingly, remain unchanged.

That's one reason why it was so stunning—and infuriating—to hear the Obama administration's Director of National Intelligence, James Clapper, portray the Brotherhood as an Egyptian version of the Peace Corps in his now infamous February 2011 Congressional testimony about the MB. At the time, the so-called Arab Spring was in full swing, Egyptian President Hosni Mubarak was on the verge of being overthrown and the U.S. government and the American people were eager to glean more information about Mubarak's likely successor, the Brotherhood. Enter Clapper—America's top intelligence official—who sat before his microphone, glanced at his notes and proceeded to describe the Ikhwan as a "largely secular" organization that has "pursued social ends" and a "betterment of the political order." He also claimed that the Brotherhood "has eschewed violence and has decried Al Qaeda as a perversion of Islam" and has "no overarching agenda, particularly in pursuit of violence, at least internationally."[22] Mind you, he did so with a straight face.

Although administration officials immediately tried to walk back Clapper's preposterous comments and douse the firestorm they created, President Obama's continuing Brotherhood-friendly policies suggest the beleaguered DNI merely stated the views of his superiors in the White House.

Since Clapper is America's top intelligence official, you'd assume that he was aware of the very un-secular comments that had been emanating from Brotherhood leaders in the months and years prior to his testimony. That includes a notorious 2010 sermon by the Egyptian Muslim Brotherhood's current overall leader and Supreme Guide, Mohammed Badie, in which he predicted the imminent "demise" of the United States, called for the rise of a "jihadi generation," and encouraged Arabs and Muslims to resist "Zio-American arrogance and tyranny." Badie's rant was delivered just five months prior to Clapper's congressional testimony extolling the Brotherhood's altruism and moderation. So did Clapper know about it? That's an open question. Clearly, for America's top intelligence official to be unaware of a virtual call to arms against the United States—issued by the world's most influential Islamist organization—would be nothing less than dereliction of duty.

Similarly, you have to wonder if Clapper was aware that Badie's predecessor as MB Supreme Guide, Mahdi Akef, published a 2004 open letter in which he called for jihad against U.S. troops in Iraq and Afghanistan. "Islam considers the resistance to be Jihad for the sake of Allah and this is a commandment, a personal obligation incumbent on all of the residents of the occupied countries," Akef wrote. "[This commandment] takes precedence over all other [religious] duties. Even a woman is obligated to go to war, [even] without her husband's permission, and youth are permitted to go out and fight."[23] Akef repeated his calls to jihad against U.S. troops in a 2007 sermon, adding a broadside against the enemy "concealed in Jerusalem" for good measure.[24] Because no

Brotherhood sermon is truly complete without at least one viciously anti-Semitic statement.

By the way, does this sound like an organization that has "eschewed violence" and can be counted on to respect American interests in the Middle East and around the world?

Also in 2004, the Brotherhood's top spiritual leader, Yusuf al-Qaradawi, was one of ninety-three Islamic scholars—including several others from the Brotherhood—to sign a communiqué declaring that it was a "Shari'a duty" for all Muslims worldwide to aid in the "resistance" against Coalition forces in Iraq. The fatwa also forbids Muslims to help American or British troops there in any form.[25]

Does this sound like an organization that believes al-Qaeda—which has murdered an untold number of U.S. troops using the same "resistance" tactics the Brotherhood endorses—is "a perversion of Islam?"

The Brotherhood differs with al-Qaeda on means, but certainly not ends. Worldwide sharia law and the reestablishment of the caliphate are the order of the day for both organizations. Whereas the Brotherhood follows a patient strategy of gradualism to achieve those goals, al-Qaeda wants to set the world on fire and violently impose the sharia system on Muslim and non-Muslim alike *right now*. The MB's view is that al-Qaeda, while its heart is in the right place, is too rash, too impatient—lacking in tact as well as strategic vision and sophistication. In my interviews with MB-connected figures, I've sensed their occasional annoyance with hardcore Salafists like al-Qaeda who refuse to take part in the political process and favor an "all jihad, all the time" strategy. The Brothers are far too savvy to fall into that dead end. They learned the hard way in their early years in Egypt that jihad cannot be rushed and can only come when conditions are ripe. If only al-Qaeda were a bit more flexible and forward thinking, the Brothers would argue, AQ could have everything it desires without all the sticky mess of drone strikes against its mountain hideouts. Yes, the granddaddy of all modern Islamic terror groups still has more than a few things to teach the young upstarts.

If there were a jihadi superpower summit, the Ikhwan, wily as always, would say to their al-Qaeda brethren, "My dear brothers, we stand with you in your struggle. But patience must be the order of the day. Why rush into jihad now when we Muslims are overmatched militarily against the West? Any short-term gains you accomplish will be negated when your actions bring the infidels' wrath down upon all of our heads. Your martyrdom operations against the Americans and Europeans are blessed in the eyes of Allah. But they are not necessary at the moment and are counterproductive to the cause. Just think: we are accomplishing the very things you yearn for without firing a shot or sacrificing any of our mujahideen. Yes, it may take years, even decades. But *inshallah*, it will happen. Patience, brothers. Patience."

A version of the hypothetical scenario I just outlined actually occurred in April 2012 in Tunisia, when Rachid Ghannouchi, leader of that country's ruling Ennahda Party (the Tunisian branch of the Muslim Brotherhood) was captured on video meeting with a group of young Salafist leaders. According to Magharebia, a comprehensive website covering North Africa and sponsored by the United States Africa Command:

> ... Ghannouchi said, "The secularists are still controlling the media, economy and administration. Therefore, controlling them would require more time." He added that "the police and army's support for Islamists is not guaranteed, and controlling them would also require more time."
>
> "I tell our young salafists to be patient ... Why hurry? Take your time to consolidate what you have gained," Ghannouchi said before advising them to "create television channels, radio stations, schools and universities" to push their agenda.

The Ennahda leader said, "We've met with Hizb ut-Tahrir, and the salafists, including Sheikh Abou Iyadh and Sheikh al-Idrissi."

Abou Iyadh, also known as Seif Allah Ben Hassine, is currently wanted by Tunisian police in connection with the September 14th [2012] attack on the US embassy.

In the video, Ghannouchi said he was "not afraid" to include an article in the new constitution on Sharia law. He went on to mock secularists who accept Islam and fear Sharia. "They are like those who accepted content but rejected the name itself," he said.

He also told the salafists about achievements that were made for them after Ennahda came to office. "The government is now at the hands of Islamists, the mosques are ours now, and we've become the most important entity in the country," he said.

"The Islamists must fill the country with associations, establish Qur'anic schools everywhere, and invite religious preachers because people are still ignorant of Islam," Ghannouchi continued. In his first reaction to the leaking of the video, Ghannouchi said that his words were "taken out of context," adding that the secularism he denounced was "the radical and extreme secularism."[26]

Hassan al-Banna himself could not have said it better.

Ghannouchi, by the way, is a big deal in the MB universe; the Brothers I've interviewed speak about him in reverent terms. In public, he dutifully plays the role of "moderate" for secular Tunisians and his Western admirers, even condemning Salafists for their role in the September 2012 attack on the U.S. Embassy in Tunis. But with his private statements to the Salafists—statements he claimed were "misunderstood" after the video came to light—the mask slipped and his double game was exposed. In the video, Ghannouchi even brags of meeting with the leader of the same embassy attacks that he later condemned, showing, yet again, that while the tactics differ for the MB and AQ, their endgame is the same. As Middle East authority Daniel Pipes puts it, "Their differences are real. But they are also secondary, for all Islamists pull in the same direction, toward the full and severe application of Islamic law (the sharia), and they often cooperate toward this end, sometimes covertly."[27]

Indeed, the inherent superiority of the MB's slow burn strategy over al-Qaeda's uncompromising, "kill 'em all" methods has been on full display for all to see. In a span of under two years, the Brotherhood scored (mostly) bloodless electoral triumphs in Egypt, Tunisia, and Morocco. It could very well be looking at similar victories in Libya, Yemen, Syria, and Jordan in the not-so-distant future. And the Brotherhood's stock has risen in Western capitals to the point where an Egyptian MB delegation visited the Obama White House in April 2012 and Egypt's Ikhwan president, Mohammed Morsi, was hailed by the Obama administration as a peacemaking pragmatist for his role in brokering a ceasefire between Israel and Hamas later that year.

Conversely, since 9/11, al-Qaeda affiliates have seized tenuous control of broad swaths of northern Mali and Somalia—two chaotic, medieval backwaters—plus small chunks of southern Yemen, parts of Pakistan's prehistoric tribal regions, and a small portion of pre-Surge Iraq. All the while, AQ operatives have been relentlessly targeted by Western militaries and intelligence services, taking heavy manpower losses as a result. If you're a sharia-breathing Islamist, whose track record would you rather have? The results don't lie. Incrementalism works—in large part because, using tools of stealth and subterfuge, it seeks to slowly dominate a culture, which makes its political gains more powerful and lasting.

The Brotherhood's strategic documents, as we saw in Chapter Two, lay out the gradualist approach favored by Rachid Ghannouchi—one of the modern Brotherhood's most revered thinkers—in painstaking detail, offering the MB blueprint for victory over the West. The differences between the Muslim Brotherhood and al-Qaeda are merely tactical, not ideological.

For instance, following the May 2011 killing of Osama bin Laden by U.S. Navy SEALs, the Egyptian Brotherhood released a statement referring to the 9/11 mastermind in reverent tones as "sheikh" and condemning his "assassination." The statement also doubled down on the Brotherhood's support for "resistance" against U.S. forces in Iraq and Afghanistan.[28] Mind you, this is the same Muslim Brotherhood to which the Obama administration has committed billions of dollars in Egypt. Move over, Saudi Arabia and Pakistan: there's a new untrustworthy, hostile Islamist "ally" on the block!

Not long before bin Laden's death, Mohammed Mahdi Akef, who served as the Ikhwan's Supreme Guide until 2010, praised bin Laden as a "mujahid," or holy warrior, in an interview with an Arabic news service:

Interviewer: As we talk about resistance and jihad, do you consider Usama Bin Ladin a terrorist or an Islamic Mujahid?

Akef: Most certainly he is a Mujahid. I do not doubt his sincerity in resisting occupation for the sake of God Almighty.

Interviewer: Does this not contradict your previous description of Al-Qa'ida as US-made?

Akef: The name is US-made, but Al-Qa'ida as an ideology and organization came as a result of injustice and corruption.

Interviewer: Then, do you support the activities of Al-Qa'ida, and to what extent?

Akef: Yes, I support its activities against the occupier, but not against the people.[29]

The Brotherhood quickly issued a clarification on Akef's comments, distancing itself from al-Qaeda but reaffirming its support for so-called "resistance against occupation." Always shrewd operators, the Brothers realize the best way to fool naïve Westerners into believing that you are a peace-loving pragmatist is to distance yourself from the ultimate modern-day symbol of Islamic terrorism, al-Qaeda. By employing this strategy, the Brotherhood has successfully positioned itself to Western governments as the sane, reasonable Islamist alternative to those crazy cave dwellers who are blowing stuff up. Yet as Akef's comments and the ensuing clarification showed, the MB and AQ do indeed agree fervently when it comes to defensive jihad, or as they call it, resistance against illegal occupation. That means blowing folks up in Israel—an imperialist, occupying power in the Islamists' view—is just fine. Same with infidel U.S. troops in Iraq and Afghanistan, or anywhere else where they are desecrating Muslim soil and cruelly oppressing the ummah.

Defensive jihad is the tip of the iceberg. The U.S. government's Muslim outreach mavens may be shocked to learn that the "moderate" Ikhwan and extremist al-Qaeda actually agree on many things. Granted, some of their differences, like al-Qaeda's refusal to participate in politics, are significant. But there's a reason that several top al-Qaeda leaders belonged to the Muslim Brotherhood before AQ and it isn't because the Ikhwan is warm and fuzzy about freedom and democracy. As Pulitzer Prize–winning journalist Ian Johnson told me in a 2012 interview:

The Brotherhood is not al-Qaeda. They're not piloting the airplanes. But they're creating the ideological mindset that turns people into terrorists. It's true that not all Muslim Brotherhood [members] are terrorists, but all terrorists pretty much started by reading the works of the Muslim Brotherhood. It's the gateway drug, if you will, that leads to radicalism.

Johnson's book, *A Mosque in Munich*, gives a definitive historical account of the Brotherhood's infiltration of the West. His assessment of the group vis-à-vis al-Qaeda is echoed by Alain Chouet, former head of the security intelligence service of the French Directorate-General for External Security, who warned in 2004 that, "Al Qaeda is only a brief episode and an expedient instrument in the century-old existence of the Muslim Brotherhood. The true danger is in the expansion of the Brotherhood, an increase in its audience."[30]

The number of Muslim Brotherhood alumni who have gone on to become top al-Qaeda leaders should be more than enough to convince any sane policymaker about the Ikhwan's inherently radical, anti-Western nature. Virtually every major Sunni Muslim terrorist of the modern era started out with the MB before moving on to bigger and bloodier jihadi activities. And all were indelibly influenced by the violent, revolutionary theories of key Brotherhood ideologue Sayyid Qutb. The Foundation for the Defense of Democracies in Washington, D.C., compiled this jaw-dropping list:

Partial List of al Qaeda and MB members

Osama bin Laden—There is evidence that bin Laden was recruited by the MB while studying as a young man in Saudi Arabia. As early as his high school years Osama may have been recruited by the MB. At King Abdel-Aziz University, Osama attended Mohammed Qutb's lectures. Mohammed taught the same jihadist doctrine as his more infamous brother, Sayyid Qutb.

Ayman al Zawahiri—Zawahiri joined the MB at the age of 14 and quickly became [a] revered figure among his fellow

Brothers despite his young age. Zawahiri founded the Egyptian Islamic Jihad (EIJ), an organization that holds many of the same beliefs as the MB but simply refuses to renounce violence inside Egypt. Beginning in the 1980s, Zawahiri and the EIJ worked closely with Osama bin Laden. In the 1990s, the EIJ formally merged with bin Laden's organization.

Khalid Sheikh Mohammed—KSM is the mastermind of the September 11 attacks. Before becoming one of the most infamous al Qaeda terrorists alive, he was a member of the MB in Kuwait.

Mohammed Atta—Atta, an Egyptian, was the lead hijacker for the 9/11 operation. Before that, he was a member of the MB.

9/11 al Qaeda cells in Hamburg and Spain—The al Qaeda cells in Hamburg and Spain at the time of 9/11 were run by men who were formerly members of the Syrian Muslim Brotherhood (SMB). Mamoun Darkazanli and Mohammed Zammar, who ran the Hamburg cell for 9/11, were both members of the SMB. Imad Yarkas, who led al Qaeda's cell in Spain and was bin Laden's key point man in Europe, was also a former member of the SMB. Some of Yarkas' underlings were once members of the SMB as well.

Abdullah Azzam—Azzam was a key jihadist thinker, whose teachings helped launch the jihad against the Soviets in Afghanistan in the 1980s. Before he was assassinated in 1989, Azzam was a co-founder of both al Qaeda and Hamas. Azzam, who was one of Osama bin Laden's spiritual mentors, was a member of the Palestinian Muslim Brotherhood.

Sheikh Omar Abdel Rahman—Rahman, who is known as the "Blind Sheikh," was the spiritual leader of Gamaat Islamiyya. The organization's roots are in the MB and, like

Zawahiri's Egyptian Islamic Jihad, became its own jihadist group after the MB's leadership decided to avoid using violence inside Egypt. The Gamaat became a core part of the al Qaeda joint venture in the 1990s, and al Qaeda even plotted to spring Rahman from prison after he was convicted of his involvement in the 1993 World Trade Center bombing and a follow-on plot against NYC landmarks.

Sheikh Abdul Majeed al Zindani—Zindani founded the Yemeni branch of the MB. He has been designated [a terrorist] by the U.S. Treasury Department for his decades-long relationship with Osama bin Laden, finding that he served "as one of [bin Laden's] spiritual leaders" and recruited terrorists for al Qaeda's training camps.

Hassan al Turabi—Turabi was one of the most prominent MB members throughout the 1990s. He founded the MB's chapter in Sudan. From 1992 until 1996, Turabi hosted Osama bin Laden and al Qaeda in Sudan. He has been dubbed the "Pope of Terrorism" in the European press because of his many ties to international terrorism.

The report concluded:

As can be seen from this partial list, there is a continuum between the MB and al Qaeda—not a sharp break. MB members move seamlessly into al Qaeda and al Qaeda-affiliated organizations. The reasons for this easy transition should be obvious. The MB, like al Qaeda, believes that Muslims should value death more than life (al Banna's "art of death"). They both justify suicide bombings. They both hate the U.S. and Israel, depicting the world as enthralled in an imaginary conflict between "Zionist-Crusaders" and Muslims. And they

both believe that the Muslim world should be united under a
revitalized caliphate governed by Sharia law.[31]

If you should ever have the misfortune, as I often have, to come across a
European bureaucrat or D.C. think tanker who asks why you oppose
engagement with the Muslim Brotherhood, simply hand them the above
list. Really, what more needs to be said? The Brotherhood is the gateway,
period.

Take a look at some of the hardened jihadists who've led branches of
the Muslim Students Association, which was founded in 1963 by a group
of Muslim Brothers at the University of Illinois at Urbana-Champaign.
The MSA is the largest and most influential Muslim organization on
North American college campuses today, with nearly six hundred chapters spread throughout the United States and Canada.[32] Investigative
journalist and MB expert Patrick Poole told me in a 2011 interview that
the MSA is "the mother ship of all the Muslim Brotherhood front groups"
in America.[33]

"The Muslim Students Association has been a virtual terror factory,"
said Poole. "Time after time after time, we see these terrorists—and not
just fringe members, these are MSA leaders, MSA presidents, MSA
national presidents—who've been implicated, charged and convicted in
terrorist plots."

The dishonor roll includes al-Qaeda cleric Anwar al-Awlaki, who was
killed by a U.S. drone strike in Yemen in 2011 after helping devise several
terror plots against American interests, including the Fort Hood jihadi
rampage and the failed Christmas Day Underwear Bomber scheme.
Before moving on to become al-Qaeda's most influential English-speaking mouthpiece, al-Awlaki served as president of the MSA at Colorado
State University in the mid-1990s. Similarly, Omar Hammami, a leader
of the al-Shabaab terrorist group in Somalia, was once president of the
MSA chapter at the University of South Alabama. Then there is

Abdurahman Alamoudi, who served as national president of the MSA during the 1980s. Alamoudi is now serving a twenty-three-year prison sentence for his role as a senior al-Qaeda financier.[34]

This roll call of Muslim Students Association alums-turned-global terrorists should come as no surprise. The MSA is a Muslim Brotherhood–linked organization whose impressionable young members are steeped in the radical writings of MB luminaries like Hassan al-Banna, Sayyid Qutb, and Abu A'la Maududi. It is no coincidence that the NYPD has compiled a list of twelve former MSA members—including the three mentioned above—who have been arrested or convicted on terrorism charges in the U.S. or abroad.[35] The Department, which correctly identified the MSA as an "incubator" of Islamic radicalism in a 2007 report, reportedly monitors MSA members at various colleges on the East Coast—and with good reason. There is indisputably a direct correlation between Muslim Brotherhood ideology and terrorist violence.

When the more restless Muslim Brothers tire of the organization's patient, long-term approach, they simply leave and join violent Islamist groups with a jihad-now agenda. Many of these former MBers decry the Brothers' willingness to work within the political system and consider the Ikhwan corrupted, even as they hearken back to Brotherhood luminaries Qutb and al-Banna, who re-injected into modern Muslim consciousness the idea of jihad to establish a global caliphate. As a matter of fact, don't discount the very real possibility of rapprochement between the MB and the al-Qaeda wing of the Salafi movement.

For instance, on the day before his inauguration as Egyptian president in June 2012, the Muslim Brotherhood's Mohammed Morsi called for the United States to free the notorious "Blind Sheikh," Omar Abdel Rahman, from an American federal prison where he is serving a life sentence for his role in the 1993 World Trade Center bombing and a later plot to blow up New York City landmarks.[36] Morsi repeated his call for the U.S. to free the Sheikh into Egyptian custody a few months later, vowing to do "everything in [his] power" to "secure freedom" for the al-Qaeda favorite and Salafi icon.[37] Then, in a January 2013 interview with CNN's Wolf Blitzer, Morsi again said he wanted Rahman "to be free" and vowed to lobby President Obama on the terror kingpin's behalf. "There could be things like visitation, assistance, his children, his family, assisting him," Morsi told Blitzer. "He is an old sheikh and sick and blind. We need to respect that in this sheikh."[38]

Poor guy. Yes, he plotted to kill thousands of Americans and has been a close confidante of al-Qaeda. But he's old, frail, and blind, so all should be forgiven. Besides, he was just waging jihad against unbelievers as mandated in the Koran and Sunnah. Cut him some slack, people! Morsi and the MB's affection for the Sheikh is obvious—they clearly consider this unrepentant terrorist a hero of jihad and an exemplary Muslim. Interestingly enough, reports began to surface during the second half of 2012 charging that the Obama administration was, yes, considering transferring the Sheikh to Egypt, where he would ostensibly finish out his prison term under the benevolent eye of Morsi and the Muslim Brothers[39] (most likely in an extravagant villa on the Nile where he's fanned and fed grapes). The White House denied the reports but the rumblings I've heard from intelligence sources suggest that the administration has indeed considered transferring the sightless terror mastermind out of American custody. It sounds unfathomable. Yet no one should be shocked. Remember, we're talking about the Obama administration, led by a man who bowed deeply and reverently to the King of Saudi Arabia in plain view of other world leaders as cameras rolled. It's pretty tough to appeal to a guy's sense of shame after that kind of display.

As for Mohammed Morsi, as of this writing, he hasn't seen his wishes granted yet regarding the Blind Sheikh. But don't cry for ol' Mo-Mo. He's used his position as president to unilaterally release a number of convicted terrorists and jihadists from Egyptian prisons, including Mohammed Zawahiri, brother of the current top al-Qaeda kingpin. In fact, at least two thousand Islamists have been released from Egyptian custody since the fall of Hosni Mubarak in February 2011.[40] Some of them were involved in the storming of the U.S. Embassy in Cairo on the eleventh anniversary of the 9/11 attacks, a violent episode in which the black flag of al-Qaeda was raised above the building. The newly released Mohammed Zawahiri was there and helped lead the charge.

Between his campaign to free the Blind Sheikh and his release of numerous hardened jihadists, Morsi is clearly extending an olive branch to Egypt's Salafis, who, other than the Ikhwan, are now the country's most potent force. And why wouldn't he? The Muslim Brothers and the Salafi al-Nour Party not only dominate the Egyptian Parliament; the two sides, as we've seen throughout this chapter, share the same goals and ideology. If the Brothers can rein their more impulsive Salafi brethren in a bit, the latter can be used for street muscle at home and possibly even terror attacks abroad, assuming the Ikhwan decide to return to their violent ways and resume their long-running jihad against Israel. None other than Osama bin Laden seems to have been banking on that very possibility before he met his demise.

Documents seized in the raid of bin Laden's compound in Pakistan reveal that he was well aware of the MB's growing influence thanks to the so-called Arab Spring and was considering a sort of "if you can't beat 'em, join 'em" approach to the Brothers for the short term. He wrote:

> ...The movements calling for half solutions like the Brotherhood have witnessed a spread of the proper ideology among their membership in recent years, especially in the growing generations...it was mentioned in many of the media vehicles that there is a sizable direction within the Brotherhood that holds the Salafi doctrine, so the return of the Brotherhood and those like them to the true Islam is a matter of time, with the will of Allah.

So the Brotherhood was a "half solution" in bin Laden's eyes, but that's better than no solution at all. And besides, he argues, they'll come around to al-Qaeda's way of thinking soon enough. He went on to encourage Salafists to coexist peacefully with the Ikhwan for the time being:

> It would be nice to remind our brothers in the regions to be patient and deliberate, and warn them of entering into confrontations with the parties belonging to Islam, and it is probable that most of the areas will have governments established on the remnants of the previous governments, and most probable these governments will belong to the Islamic parties and groups, like the Brotherhood and the like, and our duty at this stage is to pay attention to the call among Muslims and win over supporters and spread the correct understanding, as the current conditions have brought on unprecedented opportunities and the coming of Islamic governments that follow the Salafi doctrine is a benefit to Islam. The more time that passes and the call increases, the more the supporters will be of the people, and the more widespread will be the correct understanding among the coming generations of Islamic groups.[41]

In essence, bin Laden seems to have been saying that while the Brothers are no longer true Salafis in his eyes, they do unquestionably have the power, and are enforcing at least some semblance of Islamic government that AQ and its allies can eventually co-opt. Makes sense. But the Brotherhood is far too cunning and disciplined to be outflanked in the manner bin Laden suggests. From the MB's inception, its members have prided themselves on always being one step ahead and on the cutting edge.

Yes, the MB and hardcore Salafists share the same ideology and have worked together frequently to achieve their mutual goals. That cooperation will only increase in the years to come, as the Salafists play a vital role as foot soldiers in the Brotherhood's multi-pronged offensive in the Muslim world and beyond. But make no mistake: the Brotherhood will be the unquestioned leader and trendsetter of this Sunni Islamist surge. America's next great enemy may be pure evil, but whether they're hoodwinking Western governments or outpacing rival Islamist movements, they're darn good at what they do.

CHAPTER FIVE

HATCHING HAMAS

I stood in the midst of a hundred Hamas supporters as they touched their foreheads to the ground in unison.

It was noontime on Friday—prayer time in Sheikh Jarrah, a predominantly Palestinian Muslim enclave in eastern Jerusalem, just outside the Old City.

Veneration of Allah was now in full swing and since I was clearly not Palestinian and clearly not praying, I found myself on the receiving end of some rather unpleasant stares.

As an openly Christian journalist who has spent years on camera and in print supporting Israel and condemning Hamas by name, I can't say it was the most comfortable situation I've ever been in. Ditto, I'm sure, for the two-man camera crew accompanying me—both of them Israeli.

By the time a stern-faced imam strode to the front of the crowd and began delivering a blistering sermon in Arabic, we felt a bit like guests at an elaborate feast where we were the main course.

In a decade-plus of covering the global Islamist movement, I had visited Friday prayers at dozens of mosques across the United States and Europe. This time, however, stood apart for two reasons. First, the setting was not a Muslim house of worship but the Jerusalem headquarters of the International Committee of the Red Cross (ICRC). And second, the throng of men in the street in front of the ICRC building had gathered for much more than prayers; they had come to pledge their full-throated support for three heroes of Hamas's jihad against the hated "Zionist entity," Israel.

Those same three Hamas parliamentarians now stood just a few feet away from me, holding court and greeting well-wishers under a makeshift tent they had set up on Red Cross property—with the apparent consent of ICRC officials.

By now, you're probably wondering how three representatives from one of the world's most notorious terrorist groups managed to set up shop on property owned by the world's most renowned humanitarian relief organization. The short answer is that the ICRC, like many international bodies, has taken a fashionably leftist tilt, especially when it comes to Israel and its Muslim opponents.

My visit was in early 2011, but the Hamas "sit in" at the Red Cross had actually begun months before, when Hamas parliament members Khaled Abu Arafa, Mohammed Totah, and Ahmed Attoun showed up at ICRC headquarters and announced that they would be holding a protest.

The Israeli government had recently revoked the men's residency cards because they were suspected of engaging in Hamas activity in Jerusalem and, when questioned, had refused to renounce their affiliation with the terror group. Membership in Hamas—an organization devoted to eliminating the Jewish State—is outlawed in Israel, for obvious reasons.

Their residency cards gone, Attoun, Abu-Arafa, and Totah were given until June 2010 to leave Israel. Instead, they turned up at the ICRC offices to draw international attention to their cause. A rather cagey move on their part, I have to admit. After all, theirs was the kind of narrative that sets hearts aflutter in EU circles and in the newsrooms of the BBC and *New York Times* (not to mention left-wing Israeli dailies like *Haaretz*)—entities that never miss a chance to portray Israel as heavy-handed and reactionary.

Sure enough, the "Hamas Three" found a willing host in the Red Cross. It was a safe bet. According to the respected Italian pro-Israel journalist, Guido Meotti:

> The Red Cross is waging a "soft war" against Israel and the Jews. In 2001 Rene Kosirnik, head of the International Red Cross's delegation to Israel, called the Israeli communities in Judea and Samaria a "war crime."
>
> The organization is serving as a mouthpiece for Palestinian propaganda against Israel on a variety of issues, including Israel's security barrier aimed at preventing suicide attacks—and the blood libel of the 2002 battle in the Jenin refugee camp that the Red Cross described as a "massacre" (independent investigators subsequently found that no massacre was committed, rather 11 Israeli soldiers died in house to house fighting with terrorists because the IDF refrained from having the area strafed—this to avoid civilian casualties despite having warned residents to leave).
>
> A case in point is how the Red Cross allocates budgets worldwide.

For all of North Africa, the Red Cross has one office in Tunis.

For "Israel/Occupied Territories/Autonomous Territories," the Red Cross has offices in Jenin, Tulkarm, Nablus, Kalkilya, Ramallah, Jericho, Bethlehem, Hebron, Gaza, Khan Yunis, Majdel Shams, Jerusalem, and Tel Aviv.

During the Second Intifada, Red Crescent ambulances commonly served as "Trojan horses" to transport terrorists and weaponry through the "West Bank" and Gaza....[1]

In other words, the ICRC building in eastern Jerusalem might as well have hung a flashing neon sign out front that said "Jihadists Welcome." Yet when one of my CBN colleagues interviewed ICRC spokeswoman Cecilia Goin, she was adamant that the Red Cross was not willfully providing the Hamas men a safe haven.

"This is a pure humanitarian activity that we are doing," said Goin. "Pure humanitarian help to them. We don't talk about politics—this is not the place of the [Red Cross]."

Of course, Goin then proceeded to make a blatantly political statement: "This is east Jerusalem, which is occupied territory," she intoned. "This is something that has to be clear. And Israel is the occupying power...[the Hamas trio] are protected people living in East Jerusalem. So the Israeli authorities must respect the Geneva conventions, which they signed."

Ladies and gentlemen, meet your new and improved non-partisan, non-political Red Cross!

According to Goin, under "international humanitarian law," Attoun, Abu-Arafa, and Totah were "protected people" living in "occupied territory." Her sympathy for their supposed plight is even more galling when you consider that for five and a half years, Hamas refused to allow the Red Cross access to visit kidnapped Israeli soldier Gilad Shalit in Gaza.

When the ICRC demanded proof from Hamas that Shalit was alive, a Hamas spokesman responded dismissively, saying, "The Red Cross should not get involved in Israeli security games aimed at reaching Shalit. It should take a stand that results in ending the suffering of Palestinian prisoners."[2]

That's the real Hamas—the Hamas that demands safe haven from the Red Cross, but will not give it access to an Israeli hostage; the ruthless, murderous Hamas that has slaughtered hundreds, if not thousands, of Israelis and, yes, Palestinians as well. But when I approached Attoun, Abu-Arafa, and Totah under their tent at the ICRC as Friday prayers ended, they were all smiles. After all, I was accompanied by a cameraman and holding a microphone. Which meant, in their view, that like the countless other BBC, Reuters, and AP stooges they had no doubt encountered over the years, I was a "friendly" who would be sympathetic and allow them to air their grievances against Israel for a large audience.

The throng of Hamas supporters pressing against us—including children who kissed the three terrorists' hands in deference—apparently agreed. Their earlier scowls turned to eager smiles once they realized that the tall, white infidel and his two friends were television journalists. When I told Mohammed Totah, the trio's de facto spokesman, that I worked for CBN News he didn't bat an eye. This was no surprise. I often joke that the various Islamists and jihadists I've interviewed must have assumed that CBN stood for "Chechen Broadcasting Network" when they agreed to speak with me.

The real answer, though, is that they simply can't resist the lure of a camera and the opportunity to share their views and hopefully sway a naïve Western audience to their side. Sure enough, during our ten minute interview, Totah was in full victim mode, calling on the "international community" to rally behind him and his two comrades and condemn Israel for its unjust treatment of the Palestinians.

His answers were all pretty boilerplate and boring—which was exactly the intention. Every Islamist worth his seventy-two virgins knows that you say one thing to a clueless Western audience to garner sympathy and another thing entirely to an Arabic-speaking audience to incite the masses.

This clever tactic was on full display when I asked Totah if Hamas could ever recognize Israel's right to exist. After all, Hamas's founding charter—which we'll examine shortly—clearly states that Israel must be "obliterated."

Totah thought about it for a second, then answered: "The Israelis came in 1948 to our historical Palestine. They occupied 78 percent of our land. And in 1967 they occupied the other 22 percent. This is not acceptable and the international community must say so."

Do the math and you'll recognize that Totah and his Hamas brethren believe that every last inch of Israel is, in actuality, a nation called "Palestine" that is currently occupied by people who have no right to be there.

Totah's own "right" to be on the grounds of the ICRC eventually came to an end. First, his partner-in-jihad, Attoun, was lured off the ICRC grounds and arrested by undercover Israeli police and then, after about a year and a half, Israeli police raided their tent and took Totah and Abu Arafa into custody. The Islamist circus at the Red Cross was finally closed.

You may be wondering why I'm spending so much time talking about Hamas—or the Islamic Resistance Movement—in a book about the Muslim Brotherhood. After all, while Hamas is identified by the U.S. government as a Specially Designated Terrorist Organization, rendering the group a diplomatic pariah, global Brotherhood leaders have been distinguished guests at the White House. And while Hamas sends suicide bombers and rockets against Israeli civilians on a regular basis, we're told that the Brotherhood has abandoned its blood-soaked past and renounced violence. Plus, the Brotherhood and its offshoots exist, in Egypt and elsewhere, as freely elected political parties that actually govern nation-states, whereas Hamas today "governs" only the cramped, seething cauldron of Gaza.

For now, at least, the view in Brussels, Foggy Bottom, and on the Beltway cocktail circuit is that the Muslim Brotherhood and Hamas are completely different animals with little common ground: one is supposedly respectable, reasonable, and open to dialogue while the other—although we are assured it has legitimate grievances and is acting only out of desperation wrought by "occupation" and Israel's blockade of Gaza—is going about things in an extreme and counterproductive way.

Never mind that as soon as they took power, the Egyptian Brothers violated the Camp David accords and re-militarized the Sinai Peninsula bordering Israel, shut down opposition media outlets, spewed anti-Jewish propaganda, and called for a return of an Islamic caliphate. In most Western political and media circles it is taken for granted that rigid extremists like Hamas are part of the problem and Islamist "moderates" like the Muslim Brotherhood are the solution.

But there is a massive hole in this theory. Namely, as Mosab Hassan Yousef, son of one of Hamas's founders, told me in a 2010 interview, "Hamas *is* the Muslim Brotherhood." Yousef, a longtime Hamas insider and heir apparent, eventually became repulsed by the movement's murderous brutality and deceit. He became an Israeli spy, converted to Christianity, and is now one of Hamas's fiercest critics. In our interview, he made abundantly clear that Hamas and the Brotherhood are inextricably linked—until death for the sake of Allah do they part.

But don't take my bigoted, Zionist, Islamophobic word for it, or even Yousef's. Rather, take a look at this excerpt from Hamas's founding charter—written by its leaders in April 1988, a few months after the group's creation:

The Relation between the Islamic Resistance Movement
and the Muslim Brotherhood

Article Two

The Islamic Resistance Movement is one of the wings of the Muslim Brotherhood in Palestine. The Muslim Brotherhood movement is a global organization and is the largest of the Islamic movements in modern times. It is distinguished by its profound understanding and its conceptual precision and by the fact that it encompasses the totality of Islamic concepts in all aspects of life, in thought and in creed, in politics and in economics, in education and in social affairs, in judicial matters and in matters of government, in preaching and in teaching, in art and in communications, in secret and in the open, and in all other areas of life.[3] [emphasis added]

Crystal clear and to the point. But in case you're still not convinced, here's another Hamas ode to the Brother-ship, from Article Seven of the Charter:

The Islamic Resistance Movement is one link in the chain of jihad in confronting the Zionist invasion. It is connected and linked to the [courageous] uprising of the martyr 'Izz Al-Din Al-Qassam and his brethren the jihad fighters of the Muslim Brotherhood in the year 1936. It is further related and connected to another link, [namely] the jihad of the Palestinians, the efforts and jihad of the Muslim Brotherhood in the 1948 war, and the jihad operations of the Muslim Brotherhood in 1968 and afterwards. Although these links are far apart, and although the continuity of jihad was interrupted by obstacles placed in the path of the jihad fighters by those who circle in

the orbit of Zionism, the Islamic Resistance Movement aspires
to realize the promise of Allah, no matter how long it takes.
The Prophet, Allah's prayer and peace be upon him, says:
"The hour of judgment shall not come until the Muslims fight
the Jews and kill them, so that the Jews hide behind trees and
stones, and each tree and stone will say: 'Oh Muslim, oh
servant of Allah, there is a Jew behind me, come and kill him,'
except for the Gharqad tree, for it is the tree of the Jews."
(Recorded in the Hadith collections of Bukhari and Muslim).[4]
[emphasis added]

Again, we see that Hamas's founders were explicitly clear from the outset
about who and what they were: namely, the Palestinian wing of the
Muslim Brotherhood. By including the infamous "Hadith of the Gharqad
Tree and the Jews" in their charter, they also left no doubts about what
they planned to accomplish: the establishment of a Palestinian Islamic
emirate in place of Israel, *Judenrein* and governed by sharia. Indeed, the
entire Hamas Charter is rife with calls to genocide against the Jews inter-
spersed with plenty of theological ammo in the form of anti-Semitic
Koranic verses and hadiths. There is also a healthy dose of conspiracy
theories (including a shout-out to *The Protocols of the Elders of Zion*,
an infamous anti-Semitic forgery), and Muslims worldwide are encouraged to join the Palestinians in their jihad against Israel. Because, according to the Charter:

Israel will exist and will continue to exist until Islam will
obliterate it, just as it obliterated others before it.[5]

That statement, not coincidentally, is the mirror image of another that is
included in the Charter, on its very first page. It is from none other than
the Muslim Brotherhood's founder, Hassan al-Banna:

"Israel will exist, and will continue to exist, until Islam abolishes it, as it abolished that which was before it."

The martyr, Imam Hasan al-Banna', Allah's mercy be upon him.[6]

We see, once again, that the Islamic Resistance Movement has inarguably followed the genocidal lead of its parent organization, the Ikhwan, from the very outset. Hence, twenty-five years of Hamas suicide bombings, rockets, missiles, and mayhem against the Jewish state have led, according to an estimate by the Council on Foreign Relations, to over five hundred deaths in more than 350 separate attacks since 1993 alone.[7] The dead include citizens from several countries including, among others, the UK, China, Romania, Ukraine, Sweden, and yes, America. As of early 2013, at least fifty-three U.S. citizens had been killed and eighty-three more wounded in Palestinian terror attacks over a twenty-year span.[8] Many of these casualties—which include American tourists, students, and expatriates living in Israel or areas under Palestinian control—have been inflicted by Hamas.

In his comprehensive book, *Hamas: Politics, Charity, and Terrorism in the Service of Jihad*, terrorism expert Matthew Levitt—a former high-ranking analyst at both the Department of the Treasury and the FBI—details the Palestinian Muslim Brotherhood's long reign of terror:

Since its founding in 1987, Hamas has committed countless acts of violence against both military and civilian targets, including suicide and other bombings and Qassam rocket, mortar fire and shooting attacks. In its early years Hamas conducted small-scale attacks like the 1989 abductions and murders of Israeli soldiers Avi Sasportas and Ilan Sa'adon. But the group is best known for its suicide bombing attacks. Between February 1989 and March 2000 Hamas carried out at least twenty-seven attacks, including twelve suicide bombings and three failed bombings. These attacks caused approximately 185 deaths and left over 1,200 people wounded.

With the onset of the second Intifada in September 2000, the pace of Hamas attacks increased dramatically. From September 29, 2000, through March 24, 2004, Hamas executed 52 suicide attacks, killing 288 people and wounding 1,646 more. In total, Hamas conducted 425 terrorist attacks during this period, killing 377 people, and wounding 2,076.

Hamas attacks increased throughout this period. In 2003 alone, Hamas was responsible for 218 acts of violence. That figure more than doubled in 2004, in which Hamas carried out 555 terrorist attacks. Also in 2004, Hamas mortar attacks increased by 500 percent and its Qassam rocket attacks increased by 40 percent compared to the previous year.[9]

Hamas's culture of death is driven by indoctrination that extends virtually from womb to tomb. From earliest childhood, Hamas teaches its adherents the Koran-mandated necessity of destroying Israel; the inferiority and inherent evil of the Jewish people in particular and non-Muslims generally; the glories of martyrdom and suicide attacks and the abundant rewards in the afterlife for those who sacrifice their lives for Allah. If you live in Gaza, these points are bombarded into your brain all day, every day on Hamas television (including in cartoons and children's programming), in schools, in mosques, in billboards, in murals and posters that adorn neighborhoods, and in parades honoring each new suicide bomber or "martyr." The ceaseless calls to genocide are inescapable. Hamas even holds summer camps in Gaza where boys under the age of fourteen engage in paramilitary training.[10] This is standard stuff in Hamas-stan. Remember, these are the folks who first brought you the pleasant images of camouflage-clad three-year-olds brandishing assault weapons and wearing mock suicide vests at Gaza rallies. Muslim Brothers worldwide help perpetuate the madness by providing tons of ideological, logistical, and financial support to their Hamas comrades.

Despite the continuing daily onslaught of pro-jihad brainwashing, the number of Hamas suicide bombers has decreased dramatically since 2006—thanks to Israel's construction of a security barrier in and around Palestinian areas of Judea and Samaria (known to the "international community" as the West Bank) from which many of the bombers originated. The constant barrage of Hamas rockets from Gaza into Israel, however, continued unabated until December 2008, when Israel initiated Operation Cast Lead. Some nine thousad rockets fired from Gaza had struck southern Israel over a seven-year period prior to Cast Lead.[11] This month-long Israeli military campaign succeeded in weakening Hamas and curtailing its ability to target Israel. But it did not stop the rocket attacks out of Gaza altogether. In fact, Hamas rockets continued to hammer Israeli towns and cities on a regular basis until November 2012, when Israel was forced to conduct another operation, called "Pillar of Defense," that severely weakened Hamas's launching capabilities and eliminated its top military commander in Gaza, Ahmed Jabari.

Just one week after Operation Pillar of Defense ended, I was given an on-the-ground tour of Israel's border with Gaza by the Israeli military and briefed on the multi-faceted and evolving threat posed by Hamas. I also spent a day talking to shell-shocked but resilient residents in the Israeli city of Sderot, just a mile from the Gaza border. Sderot has lost some 25 percent of its population over the past decade due to the constant rocket barrages.[12] Close to half of the city's children under the age of six suffer from Post-Traumatic Stress Disorder, as do more than a third of their parents.[13] Their precarious existence is overwhelmingly the Palestinian Muslim Brotherhood's handiwork. During a previous stay in Sderot, I paid a visit to police headquarters, where the shells of some of the thousands of rockets that have struck Sderot over the years are famously displayed as a reminder to the world of the tiny city's struggle for survival. President Obama visited there, too, in June 2008, just prior to his election. In between photo ops and empty promises to stand with Israel, he might have noticed that the largest rockets on display were labeled not in Arabic, but Farsi—the language of Iran. Indeed, the Iranian regime has long served as Hamas's largest supplier of funds—to the tune of hundreds of millions of dollars a year—as well as terror training and weaponry.[14]

For years, Hamas, along with Hezbollah, Syria, and Iran, formed the so-called Middle East "resistance bloc" devoted to Israel's destruction. The relationship between Hamas and Iran, however, became strained due to the Syrian Civil War, which saw Hamas vacate its Damascus headquarters and publicly side with the Muslim Brotherhood–dominated Syrian rebels against the regime. This defied the mullahs in Tehran, who were trying desperately to prop up their proxy, Syrian dictator Bashar al-Assad. Despite the friction and Hamas's logical decision to move more closely into the orbit of Egypt and the other rising Muslim Brotherhood governments in the region, Iran continues to provide money and weapons to the Gaza regime. For now, at least, eliminating the "Zionist entity" must take precedence over any petty, intra-jihadi disputes.

The Iranians are also the primary bankrollers and facilitators of the Gaza-based terror group, Palestinian Islamic Jihad. PIJ is yet another violent Muslim Brotherhood offshoot, founded by former Ikhwan members in the late 1970s with the goal of—you guessed it—wiping Israel off the map. To that end, PIJers have engaged in dozens of suicide and car bombings and launched an untold number of rockets against the Jewish State through the years. They've also been known to coordinate terrorist activities with Hamas. Tellingly, three months after 9/11, operatives from the two groups released a joint statement warning that "Americans are the enemies of the Palestinian people" and "are a target of future attacks."[15] That might help explain the 2003 roadside bombing of a U.S. diplomatic convoy in Gaza, which killed three American security guards.

It's still unclear which terror faction is responsible for that attack, but it's a safe bet that one or both of the Ikhwan's Palestinian offshoots had more than a casual involvement in its planning and execution.

———

Hamas may have been weakened by Operations Cast Lead and Pillar of Defense, but with the help of hundreds of millions of dollars provided annually in weapons and funding from jihadist sponsors like Iran, the group is steadily rearming in the belief that the final showdown with the hated Jews is not far off. It knows no other way. Hamas leaders have spent a quarter of a century working diligently to fulfill the genocidal aims of their charter, with the enthusiastic support of their Muslim Brothers around the world. Not a single word of Hamas's 1988 charter has been altered, even though Hamas now has responsibility for governing 1.7 million people in Gaza. In other words, forget the liberal pipe dream, heard most recently during the so-called Arab Spring, that Islamist parties will become moderate and pragmatic once in power. For Hamas to change would mean a complete repudiation of its founding motto (included in Article Eight of its Charter), which reads:

> Allah is its goal, the Prophet its model to be followed, the
> Koran its constitution, Jihad its way, and death for the sake
> of Allah its loftiest desire.[16]

Now, where have we heard that pleasant little jingle before? If I'm not mistaken, it is virtually identical to the founding motto of another notorious, Jew-hating Islamist group:

> Allah is our objective. The Prophet is our leader. Qur'an is our
> law. Jihad is our way. Dying in the way of Allah is our highest
> hope.

That, as you may recall, is the official creed of the Muslim Brotherhood—and despite supposedly rejecting violence today, the MB, like its Hamas offspring, has never altered its violent credo.

While Hamas certainly maintains a degree of independence, it has never severed its ties with the Brothers. It remains firmly in the MB camp and functions openly as one of the Ikhwan's many satellites worldwide, coordinating its activities with Egyptian Brotherhood leaders in Cairo—which means, in turn, that the Brotherhood has *never* abandoned violence. The organization has merely become shrewder about when and where to use it. What works for Hamas, MB's branch in the Palestinian territories, might not work for MB branches in Egypt or Morocco. The jihad option is always there, if needed, as has been the case in the Palestinian territories, or the Brotherhood can rely on propaganda and incitement.

Azzam al-Tamimi, former spokesman for the Jordanian branch of the Muslim Brotherhood and a longtime Hamas confidant, told me the following in an August 2012 interview I conducted with him via email:

> Hamas is a part of the global Brotherhood. The relationship with the MB in Egypt is excellent and is expected to reflect in forms of cooperation that will ease things for the Palestinians. In his recent meetings in Cairo with Hamas leaders, President Morsi told these leaders that Egypt would do what they want.[17]

I'm sure Israelis are comforted to hear that, not to mention American taxpayers, who continue to pour billions of dollars into Egypt and the Palestinian territories thanks to our government's mindless Middle East policies.

In his book, *Hamas: A History From Within*, al-Tamimi, who now directs an Islamic think tank in London, describes an infamous 1983 meeting of global Brotherhood members that resulted in the decision to create Hamas and steer it toward violent jihad. Al-Tamimi writes:

> It is now known that Palestinian Ikhwan members in the diaspora had also been pressing for military action. Their efforts were assisted by the unification of their organizations at the end of the 1970s, a project that reached its culmination in the historic conference convened secretly in Amman in 1983. Representatives of the Palestinian Ikhwan attended from within Palestine, both from the Gaza Strip and the West Bank, as well as from Jordan, Kuwait, Saudi Arabia, the other Gulf countries, Europe, and the United States. *The purpose of the meeting was to lay the cornerstone for what became known as the Islamic "global project for Palestine," a project proposed to the conference by the delegates from Kuwait. At this conference, a unanimous decision was taken to give financial and logistic support to the effort of the Ikhwan in Palestine to wage jihad.*[18] [emphasis added]

Al-Tamimi goes on to describe how the Kuwaiti branch of the Muslim Brotherhood provided their Palestinian brethren with $70,000 in start-up money "to be used for the purchase of weapons and ammunition and to send a number of individuals to Amman to receive military training." Thus, the seeds for Hamas were laid by the global Brotherhood in 1983. By the time the first Palestinian intifada against Israel erupted four years later, al-Tamimi writes, Hamas leader Sheikh Ahmed Yassin had the group's terror apparatus up and running in the form of two branches called al-Mujahidun al-Filastinyun (The Palestinian Mujahideen) and Majd (Glory). The former group was a military organization whose "main mission was to attack Israeli soldiers and Jewish settlers in the

Gaza Strip," while the latter was a security organization "whose princi-pal task was to apprehend, prosecute, and execute Palestinian collabora-tors working for Israel."[19] Both were eventually combined into Hamas's current military wing, the Izz al-Din al-Qassam Brigades. The rest, as they say, is jihadi history. In the words of al-Tamimi:

> The project could not have been more successful. Today Hamas is seen by a good proportion of the Palestinians as the true and legitimate representative of the Palestinians.[20]

Indeed. So what does that mean for the never-ending boondoggle known as the "Peace Process," a black hole that sucks every U.S. administration in and quickly spits it out? Al-Tamimi offered me some illuminating advice:

> Neither Hamas no[r] the MB will ever accept that Israel has the right to exist on land which they believe to be Arab and Islamic. Yet, a long-term truce arrangement allows for a de facto, not a de jure, recognition…yet, a Jewish state as in the Zionism project, will always be viewed as a colonial entity that will one day come to an end.[21]

I think he just said, in essence, that the global Muslim Brotherhood will never recognize Israel's right to exist and will actively work toward destroying the Jewish State. Nevertheless, somewhere in Foggy Bottom, a State Department bureaucrat is reading this right now and muttering to himself, "The Palestinians will come around soon. I just know it. Peace is achievable. If only Israel would give up more land, Hamas would stand down!" No, they won't. In fact, Hamas sees jihad as the only way to "liberate all of Palestine." According to the Hamas/MB insider, al-Tamimi:

> Jihad is an Islamic duty to defend rights and rise against
> oppression. The global MB sees Israel as the occupying power
> that oppresses the Palestinians who have every right to resist
> and struggle for freedom. The violence used in this case is
> considered legitimate. This is not any different from what other
> nations who happen to be victims of colonialism would do.[22]

With that, al-Tamimi articulated what is essentially the official Brotherhood policy on Hamas suicide bombings against Israel. In my interviews
around the world with Brotherhood-connected individuals, regardless of
country, they all give some variation of al-Tamimi's answer. It usually
goes something like this: "Hamas has a legitimate and internationally
recognized right to resist an illegal occupation, and due to the desperate
situation of the Palestinian people, has no other choice but to engage in
suicide bombings against the vastly superior and ruthless Israeli military
machine." Obviously, al-Tamimi and the others have done an excellent
job of coordinating their talking points on this subject; the discipline and
synergy in their messaging is quintessential Ikhwan.

The various arguments excusing Hamas suicide attacks were largely
crafted by Sheikh Yusuf al-Qaradawi, the Muslim Brotherhood's revered
and wildly influential Spiritual Guide. Al-Qaradawi, who reaches an
audience of tens of millions across the Middle East each week with his
highly rated Al-Jazeera program, *Sharia and Life*, is one of the most vocal
proponents of Palestinian suicide bombings. Once he gave them his blessing and theological justification, the global Brotherhood was all in. And
"bless" them al-Qaradawi has: frequently and enthusiastically. In countless interviews and sermons throughout the past three decades, he has
argued for the necessity of Palestinian "martyrdom operations" against
Israeli women and children and has assured his massive global audience
that such attacks are perfectly consistent with the teachings of the Koran
and hadiths. Al-Qaradawi, who is currently banned from entering the

United States, once prayed on Al-Jazeera for Allah to kill every Jew, "down to the very last one."[23] He summarized his position on Hamas suicide attacks in a 2010 interview on Egyptian television:

> According to Islamic law, in any country that is invaded and occupied by foreign infidels, all the local people should conduct resistance against the occupation, using all the means at their disposal. The jurisprudents said that a woman can set out on Jihad without her husband's permission, a child can set out on Jihad without his father's permission, and a slave can set out without his master's permission. All the people should set out on Jihad....
>
> [The Jews] are the most miserly of all people and the most protective of their lives, yet they devote their lives and their money [to their cause]. The Muslims worldwide must contribute to the regaining of Palestine. Palestine is not merely Islamic land. It is the land of the Al-Aqsa Mosque and of the holy places.
>
> [...] The martyrdom operations which I approve are the ones that target the occupiers. That is why I sanctioned martyrdom operations in Palestine. When I was asked, in London, how I could permit martyrdom operations in Palestine, I said that they are a necessity, because these people want to defend themselves, the things that are holy to them, and their land. I said to them: "You want them to stop the martyrdom operations? Then give them Apache helicopters, planes, tanks, and missiles, and then they will abandon martyrdom operations." *They do not have bombs, so they turn themselves into human bombs. This is a necessity.*

I permit this for the Palestinians, but not for those who attacked the Twin Towers in the US, because in that case, the

passengers of four civilian planes were killed, who were not
to blame. In what way were those passengers to blame? Many
of them were Arabs or Muslims, and were from various countries, and had nothing whatsoever to do with politics. Take
the people inside the towers—they were just employees in
companies, and some were even Muslims, who prayed on
Fridays. How were they to blame?

I only sanction martyrdom operations in defense of a
plundered and occupied land.[24] [emphasis added]

And that is the magical distinction that al-Qaradawi and other top Brotherhood ideologues always draw on to prove their inherent moderation.
In their view, suicide bombings are perfectly acceptable in Israel, Chech-
nya, Bosnia, Afghanistan, Iraq, Kashmir, and other Islamic lands where
Muslims are outgunned and "occupied" by infidel foreign powers. Al-
Qaeda's operations, on the other hand, are apparently a no-no in the eyes
of Allah because they are offensive actions. Ironically, Sayyid Qutb, one
of the Brotherhood's most revered ideologues, was the modern-day godfather of "offensive jihad" and a major influence on al-Qaeda's leadership. Let's also remember that the Brotherhood and al-Qaeda share the
exact same goals: sharia law for one and all and the establishment of a
global caliphate. Their differences are tactical, not ideological.

With that in mind, it's no coincidence that many of the same organizations and individuals who have been convicted of providing financial
support to al-Qaeda since 9/11 also helped bankroll Hamas. In addition,
when it comes to the United States, Palestinian Brotherhood leaders have
engaged in a series of incendiary statements and actions in recent years
that bear a striking resemblance to those of al-Qaeda. Some examples:

■ In 2004, leading Hamas operative Ismail Elbarasse was arrested
after authorities witnessed his wife videotaping Maryland's Chesapeake

Bay Bridge from their SUV as Elbarasse drove. The photos taken by Elbarasse's wife included close-ups of cables and other features "integral to the structural integrity of the bridge," according to court papers.[25] During a raid of Elbarasse's home that same year, federal agents uncovered documents revealing the Muslim Brotherhood's strategic plan to conquer North America. Elbarasse has since fled the United States.

■ Hamas's influential political chief, Khaled Meshaal, has stated that, "[Hamas's] battle is with two sides, one of them is the strongest power in the world, the United States, and the second is the strongest power in the region [Israel]."[26] Likewise, before being killed in a 2004 Israeli missile strike, Hamas leader Abdel Aziz al-Rantissi called on Iraqis to "strike and burn" U.S. forces and "teach them the lesson of the suicide actions."[27] Al-Rantissi also published a piece, titled "Why Shouldn't We Attack the United States?" on a Hamas website in which he wrote that striking America was not only "a moral and national duty" for Hamas, "but above all, a religious one."[28]

■ In 2006, *Time* magazine reported that Hamas was considering broadening its jihad to include U.S. targets. According to *Time*'s account:

> In furtive, underground meetings held in the West Bank and Gaza, a growing number of Hamas commanders say they are running out of patience with the U.S. and want to strike back. Insiders say the radicals are trying to exploit the exasperation within the movement at what they perceive as the Bush Administration's one-sided support of Israel and its attempts to press Palestinian President Mahmoud Abbas to dissolve the Hamas cabinet.
>
> "The U.S. has become very hostile to the Palestinians," one Hamas field commander told TIME. "We shouldn't stand by idly while the Americans are plotting against us."[29]

Seven years on, these potential plans seem to have been put on hold indefinitely, or at least until the time is right. Perhaps that time is sooner than we think.

■ In an August 2012 appearance on Hamas's Al-Aqsa TV, the Deputy Speaker of the Hamas parliament, Sheik Ahmed Bahr, bellowed, "Oh Allah, destroy the Jews and their supporters. Oh Allah, destroy the Americans and their supporters. Oh Allah, count them one by one, and kill them all, without leaving a single one." He also declared that jihad was a duty incumbent on every Muslim, and that women could engage in jihad without their husbands' permission in order to "annihilate those Jews."[30]

Perhaps the ultimate indicator of the Egyptian and Palestinian Brothers' continued shared affinity for violent jihad was their reaction to the death of Osama bin Laden in May 2011. The Brotherhood in Cairo condemned the killing of the terrorist mass murderer, and the Brothers' Palestinian branch, Hamas, mourned bin Laden's passing as well. Hamas Prime Minister Ismail Haniyeh said, "We condemn the assassination of a Muslim and Arab warrior and we pray to God that his soul rests in peace. We regard this as the continuation of the American oppression and shedding of blood of Muslims and Arabs."[31]

On 9/11, after learning the Twin Towers had been destroyed, Palestinian women and children were filmed dancing in the streets. A decade later, bin Laden was still a hero to Hamas.

———

Hamas's centrality to the Brotherhood's overall strategic plan makes perfect sense given the Brothers' unending obsession with reclaiming "Palestine" for the ummah. As we learned in Chapter Three, driving the hated Jews into the sea and once again raising the banner of Islam over "Al Aqsa" has been at the very core of the Ikhwan's existence from the beginning. A memo prepared by Hamas's political bureau in 2000 explained:

> Hamas is the intellectual and dynamic successor of Jama'at al-Ikhwan al-Muslimin (the Muslim Brotherhood) in Palestine, whose foundations were laid down in the 1930's and 1940's when Ikhwan branches were founded in Yaffa, Haifa, Jerusalem, and Gaza.... The role of the Ikhwan reached its zenith in Palestine during the participation of the brigades of the Ikhwan volunteers from Egypt, Syria, Jordan, and Iraq and the battles against the Zionist gangs on the eve of [Israel's founding].[32]

The Brotherhood's Palestinian branch continues that legacy today. It's not uncommon to see banners and posters displayed in Gaza featuring the images of Hamas leaders next to that of Hassan al-Banna, the Brotherhood's founder.[33] Hamas makes no secret about its affiliation with the Ikhwan, and vice versa.

In the wake of the so-called Arab Spring, the ties between Hamas and the various Brotherhood satellites across the Middle East and North Africa have only strengthened. In January 2012, Hamas Prime Minister Ismail Haniyeh embarked on a tour of the region that included five days in Tunisia hobnobbing with that country's newly elected Muslim Brotherhood government. When Haniyeh landed at Tunis-Carthage Airport, he was greeted by hundreds of hardcore Islamists chanting, "Kill the Jews—it's our religious duty."[34] The ruling Ennahda Party, which is Tunisia's Muslim Brotherhood, condemned the incident even though some of its members were among the chanters.[35] Ennahda had no objections, however, when Haniyeh appeared before a crowd of five thousand in a Tunis stadium a few days later and called on all Arab Spring revolutionaries to join Hamas in fighting Israel. Some in the crowd wiped their feet on the Star of David as chants of "Death to Israel," "The Tunisian revolution supports Palestine," and "The army of Mohammed is back," cascaded throughout the stadium.[36] Such scenes were rare in Tunisia—where some 1,500 Jews still live—before the revolution that swept Ennahda into power. Sadly, those beleaguered Tunisian Jews might have to get used to a frightening new normal. Because wherever the Muslim Brotherhood is in power, the ideology of its deadliest creation, Hamas, is sure to follow.

CHAPTER SIX

THE TURKISH MODEL: CALIPHATE ACCOMPLI

"Do people know that the world's most influential Islamist lives in the Pennsylvania mountains?"

"I doubt it," my cameraman whispered back to me. "But we'd better keep our voices down."

Wise advice. We were in the middle of a guided tour of the Golden Generation Worship and Retreat Center, which resembles a large ski lodge but is actually the global headquarters of the Fethullah Gülen movement, led by the charismatic Turkish cleric of the same name.

Our earnest young guide happily chatted us up as we toured the idyllic surroundings, which included a duck pond, picnic tables, and several modern living quarters, some still under construction, that would house Gülen devotees from around the world who came to visit. He explained that he, like others we saw walking the grounds of the site, had left a stable life in Turkey to follow Gülen to the twenty-five-acre spread in Pennsylvania's Pocono Mountains, about a two hour drive northwest of Philadelphia.

"I'd love to interview the 'Master Teacher,'" I told him, referring to Gülen by the English version of the name ("Hocaefendi" in Turkish) his followers had given him. "Is he available?"

"Oh no," our guide answered. "He is here but is unable to meet with you. He is not feeling well. I'm sorry."

I was disappointed, but not surprised, given that the reclusive Gülen rarely grants interviews. Plus, I had left numerous messages at the Retreat Center prior to our trip up from Washington, D.C., and had received no response. The powers-that-be likely thought I would just go away and stop bothering them. Perhaps that's why the group of Turkish men manning the front entrance seemed so surprised when I showed up to the mountain compound with two videographers in tow.

Yet from the outset, we received the kind of polite treatment that has become a hallmark of Gülenists in the United States in their interactions with those outside the movement. The young men we encountered at Gülen headquarters were casually dressed with no flowing, Salafi-style beards or outward signs of Islamist tendencies. As he led us around the state-of-the-art facilities, our guide talked proudly about his academic career in the States and how the Gülenists frequently engaged in interfaith dialogue with local Christians.

If you think it all sounds a bit too perfect, you're getting warm. I was drawn to the Poconos not by visions of leafy walking paths and free Turkish delight, but to try to get a handle on Fethullah Gülen's true intentions. Michael Rubin, a respected scholar of the Middle East, has compared Gülen to Iran's Ayatollah Khomeini, warning that if "Hocaefendi" were to return to Turkey, as has been rumored from time to time, he'd likely be greeted by the same type of fanatical masses that hailed the arrival of Iran's notorious tyrant. "Istanbul...may very well look like

Tehran 1979," wrote Rubin. "As Khomeini consciously drew parallels between himself and Twelver Shiism's Hidden Imam, Gülen will remain quiet as his supporters paint his return as evidence that the caliphate formally dissolved by Atatürk in 1924 has been restored."[1]

Frank Gaffney, a former assistant Secretary of Defense under the Reagan administration, has said he believes Gülen "envisions himself being the next Caliph," and is running "a Muslim Brotherhood kind of operation, stealth jihad" from the Poconos. "I would venture there isn't one member of Congress today who has ever heard of [Gülen's] name," Gaffney added. "Let alone understands what he is up to."[2] And Gülen is up to quite a lot. The imam oversees a multi-billion-dollar global empire that includes a network of schools, media outlets, think tanks, businesses, and charities. According to the *Wall Street Journal*:

> [Gülen's] Followers have established hundreds of schools in more than 100 countries and run an insurance company and an Islamic bank, Asya, that its 2008 annual report said had $5.2 billion in assets. They own Turkey's largest daily newspaper, Zaman; the magazine Aktion; a wire service; publishing companies; a radio station and the television network STV.... Helen Rose Ebaugh, a University of Houston sociologist and author of "The Gülen Movement"...says followers donate up to one-third of their income to independent Gülen-linked foundations.[3]

Gülen's followers number between three and eight million worldwide and are spread over six continents. But his home country of Turkey remains the main power base for his *cemaat*, or Islamic civil society movement. It's estimated that Gülenists make up some 80 percent of Turkey's federal police force,[4] and they control a significant chunk of the nation's judiciary and overall bureaucracy. Much like the Muslim Brotherhood, many of Gülen's followers are well-educated professionals: businessmen, journalists, teachers, and intellectuals. Next to the ruling Justice and Development Party (or AKP) and the military, the Gülenists are Turkey's third major power broker.

When AKP—led by Islamist firebrand Recep Tayyip Erdogan, Turkey's current prime minister—ascended to power in 2002, it empowered the Gülenists even more, working hand-in-hand with them to Islamize Turkey and weaken the secular state that Mustafa Kemal Ataturk built after disbanding the Turkish-led Ottoman caliphate in 1924. As we'll see, the AKP has roots in the Muslim Brotherhood, and although there are no formal links (and Erdogan is a fiercely independent actor), the party is, in many ways, an MB satellite organization. The AKP's strategy has included decimating and demoralizing Turkey's so-called "Deep State," described by Istanbul-based writer Claire Berlinksi as, "a secret coalition of high-level figures in the military, the intelligence services, the judiciary, and organized crime," which had helped maintain Turkey's secular regime after Ataturk's death in 1938.[5]

The dual rise of Erdogan and Gülen has helped turn the Deep State on its head, with the Turkish military—which had long been the fierce guardian of Ataturk's secular legacy—finding itself increasingly targeted under AKP rule. Several leading current and retired military officials, along with other critics of Erdogan's regime, including journalists, now sit in Turkish jails, thanks to trumped-up charges—pushed by Gülenists who dominate Turkey's national police and judiciary—of plotting a coup against Erdogan's government.[6]

So who exactly is Fetullah Gülen, and how did he wind up in the United States? Born in 1941 in a small village in eastern Turkey, Gülen became a state-licensed imam at the age of seventeen after studying under Sufi clerics.[7] He was an ardent follower of the teachings of Said Nursi, a hugely influential Turkish Islamist who spent eleven years in prison for condemning Ataturk's secular vision. Nursi died in 1960, but Gülen furthered the controversial preacher's ideas and began calling for an Islamic revival in Turkey (much like the Muslim Brotherhood has done in Egypt and elsewhere).[8]

Over the years, the *Wall Street Journal* reports, Gülen, "built a national organization of Islamic study and boarding halls, gaining support of many wealthy Muslims but at times running afoul of the law."[9] In 1971, Gülen was arrested after a military coup in Turkey.[10] He was convicted the following year by the Izmir State Security Court, according to Turkish media, of "attempting to destroy the state system and to establish a state system based on religion."[11] Translation: he wanted to turn Turkey into an Islamic state governed by sharia. Gülen eventually received a pardon and never served time in prison, although some of his followers were jailed during Turkey's secular, pre-Erdogan era for allegedly attempting to infiltrate the Turkish military.

Despite this dubious track record, Gülen's supporters hail him as an Islamic reformer and brilliant visionary. He's been publicly lauded by both former President Bill Clinton and former Secretary of State James Baker, and President Obama visited a Gülen charter school in Washington, D.C.[12] Gülen met with Pope John Paul II at the Vatican in 1998.[13] His movement (he calls it Hizmet), which stresses education, interfaith dialogue, and the merger of Islam and science, has seen Gülen become an almost messianic figure to his followers, as Dr. Ariel Cohen, a Middle East analyst with the Heritage Foundation in Washington, D.C., explained to me in a 2011 interview.

"It's not just a religious movement; it's the 'Fetullah Gülen movement.' They call themselves that," said Cohen. "So it is, you can say, a cult. It is a highly personalized movement."

He added, "This is clearly the world according to the Koran, the world according to Islam, the world according to Fetullah Gülen. But what he's talking about is not the caliphate, is not the sharia state. He calls it the New World Islamic Order."

As with all stealth Islamists, something sinister lurks beneath Gülen's "moderate" surface. French-Turkish scholar Bayram Balci has written that the Gülen movement, "serve(s) to accomplish three intellectual goals: the Islamization of the Turkish nationalist ideology; the Turkification of Islam; and the Islamization of modernity."[14] The push to "Islamize modernity" is also quite popular among a certain powerful Islamist group whose initials are "M.B."

Much like the Brotherhood, Gülen and his followers employ the termite-like approach of eating away at societies gradually from within in order to establish Islamic states. Gülen laid out this approach clearly in a private sermon to his followers that was secretly videotaped and leaked to a leading Turkish television network in 1999. His remarks sparked an uproar when they hit the air:

> You must move in the arteries of the system without anyone noticing your existence until you reach all the power centers.... Until the conditions are ripe, they [Gülen's followers] must continue like this. If they do something prematurely, the world will crush our heads, and Muslims will suffer everywhere, like in the tragedies in Algeria, like in 1982 [in] Syria, ... like in the yearly disasters and tragedies in Egypt.... The time is not yet right. You must wait for the time when you are complete and conditions are ripe, until we can shoulder the entire world and carry it.... You must wait until such time as you have gotten all the state power, until you have brought to your side all the power of the constitutional institutions in Turkey.... Now, I have expressed my feelings and thoughts to you all—in confidence ... trusting your loyalty and secrecy. I know that when you leave here, [just] as you discard your empty juice boxes, you must discard the thoughts and the feelings that I expressed here.[15]

One can imagine a young Hassan al-Banna delivering a nearly identical speech in a Cairo back room during the 1930s.

Gülen's supporters insist the tape was doctored to twist his words, although they have never presented any evidence to back up their claim. He was charged in absentia by a Turkish court in 2000 of seeking to overthrow Turkey's secular government and establish an Islamic state (a feat, ironically enough, that Erdogan would begin accomplishing through legal means just two years later).

Gülen was eventually acquitted in 2008. By that time, he had been entrenched in the Poconos for several years, having arrived in the United States in 1999, supposedly to seek medical treatment (the German daily *Der Spiegel* claims Gülen had to flee Turkey after the video of his infamous secret sermon emerged).[16] Whatever the case, successive U.S. administrations have allowed Gülen to build his lucrative Islamist empire in the solitude of rural Pennsylvania. A federal judge granted him a green card in 2008, after two former CIA officers and a former U.S. Ambassador to Turkey personally vouched for him.[17]

But Gülen's influence in the United States reaches far beyond the bureaucratic elite. His movement is reportedly the country's largest operator of charter schools, with an estimated 135 such institutions spread out across twenty-five states.[18] When Gülen tells his followers to "build schools instead of mosques," he means it.[19] Although Gülen and school administrators deny that the schools have any connection to the movement, Berlinski notes, "federal forms required of nonprofits show that virtually all the schools have opened or operate with the aid of Gülen-inspired groups—local nonprofits that promote Turkish culture."

The schools, which stress math and science, have innocuous sounding names, like "Truebright Science Academy" and "Beehive Science and Technology Academy," that give no hint of any link to a famous Islamist imam. That hasn't prevented them from drawing U.S. law enforcement and government scrutiny, as Berlinski, a U.S. native now living in Istanbul, described in an in-depth 2012 piece for *City Journal*:

> The FBI and the Departments of Labor and Education have been investigating the hiring practices of some of these schools...particularly the replacement of certified American teachers with uncertified Turkish ones who get higher salaries than the Americans did, using visas that are supposed to be reserved for highly skilled workers who fill needs unmet by the American workforce...some of these new arrivals have come to teach English, which often they speak poorly, or English as a second language, which often they need themselves. They have also been hired as gym teachers, accountants, janitors, caterers, painters, construction workers, human-resources managers, public-relations specialists, and—of all things—lawyers.
>
> Two of the schools, located in Texas, have been accused of sending school funds—which are supplied by the government, of course, since these are charter schools—to other Gülen-inspired organizations.... Federal authorities are also investigating several of the movement's schools for forcing employees to send part of their paychecks to Turkey.... There is no evidence that Islamic proselytizing takes place at the American Gülen schools and much evidence that students and parents like them. Most seem to be decent educational establishments, by American standards; graduates perform reasonably well, and some perform outstandingly.
>
> So what are the schools for? Among other things, they seem to be moneymakers for the [Gülen movement]. They're loaded with private, state, and federal funding, and they have proved amazingly effective at soliciting private donations. The

schools are also H-1B visa factories and perhaps the main avenue for building the Gülen community in the United States.[20]

One Gülen school in North Philadelphia reportedly receives some $3 million annually in taxpayer money.[21] That means American taxpayers have officially come full circle: funding Islamist movements abroad—in Muslim Brotherhood–led Egypt and elsewhere—and now also at home.

Maddeningly, classified documents released by WikiLeaks in 2011 show that U.S. officials know exactly what Gülen is up to. "Gulen supporters account for an increasing proportion of [the] ... nonimmigrant visa applicant pool," a U.S. consular official in Istanbul observed. "Consular officials have noticed that most of these applicants share a common characteristic: They are generally evasive about their purpose of travel to the United States."

Another section of the leaked cable may explain the reason for that evasiveness. U.S. officials, it states, "have multiple reliable reports that the Gulenists use their school network (including dozens of schools in the U.S.) to cherry-pick students they think are susceptible to being molded as proselytizers and we have steadily heard reports about how the schools indoctrinate boarding students."[22]

A senior American official who spoke anonymously to the *New York Times* in 2012 summarized the situation: "We are troubled by the secretive nature of the Gulen movement, all the smoke and mirrors.... It is clear they want influence and power. We are concerned there is a hidden agenda to challenge secular Turkey and guide the country in a more Islamic direction."[23]

If American officials are indeed concerned about Gülen, the reality on the ground inside the United States—where Gülenists continue to establish charter schools nationwide and exert local influence—reflects something vastly different.

The notoriously multiculturalist Dutch government, on the other hand, cut public funding to the Gülenists in 2008 after conducting an investigation that found the movement discouraged members from integrating into Dutch society. Perhaps the Dutchmen perused one of Gülen's books, called *Cag ve Nesil* (*This Era and the Young Generation*), in which the so-called Master Teacher wrote, "Westerners will exhibit no human behavior," and lambasted fellow Turks who wish to align more closely with Europe as, "freeloaders," "parasites," and "leukemia."[24]

Gülen, who has reportedly only left his Poconos compound a handful of times since arriving over a decade ago, also found time to release a 2011 video message calling on the Turkish military to attack Kurdish separatists. The peace-loving advocate of interfaith harmony railed, "Locate them, surround them, break up their units, let fire rain down upon their houses, drown out their lamentations with even more wails, cut off their roots and put an end to their cause."[25]

Some nasty stuff there from ol' Hocaefendi. All was perfectly tranquil, however, as my camera crew and I departed the Golden Generation Worship and Retreat Center following our guided tour. No diatribes about slowly conquering Turkey from within or raining fire down upon the Kurds. Just friendly handshakes and admonitions from fervent Gülen supporters—some of whom have been known to weep tears of reverence when discussing their beloved imam—to drop by again sometime. Sharia with a smile: coming soon to a school district near you.

———

In a rare 2005 interview, Fethullah Gülen shared his thoughts on the possibility of a revived Islamic super-state:

> Today, those who believe that there is no need for a Caliphate say this because of the establishment of nation states and the development of ideas of independence. For these reasons,

some people believe that the Khilafah has lost its effectiveness. There are some people who believe in the dynamics of Khilafah since it is a means of unity among Muslims and facilitates cooperation between Muslim nations through exchanging their skills and opportunities. The possibility of rallying the masses can easily coalesce around the religious term, Caliphate/Khilafah.

Having said this, I would say that the revival of the Caliphate would be very difficult and making Muslims accept such a revived Khilafah would be impossible. The perception of the modern world regarding the revival of Khilafah must be considered.[26]

Gülen's supporters often cite the above statement as supposed proof that he is not interested in seeing the caliphate reestablished. A few points to consider on that end. 1) As we've seen, Muslim Brothers in the West similarly downplay the possibility of a new caliphate and profess to have no desire for it. At the same time, they cheerlead for Brotherhood Islamists in the Middle East for whom the renewed caliphate is a core goal. 2) Notice Gülen's careful, intentionally middle-of-the-road wording: "some people believe the caliphate has lost its effectiveness," but, on the other hand, he notes, "some believe in the dynamics of the Khilafa." 3) Yet Gülen never tells us what *he* believes about the caliphate. He suggests it would be difficult to accomplish, that it would be impossible to make Muslims today accept it and that it may lead to a negative world perception. But he never says that he personally opposes the caliphate, nor does he state definitively whether he thinks it is a good or bad thing. 4) Let's also remember that those remarks, Gülen's last recorded ones on the caliphate, were made in 2005—six full years before the outbreak of the so-called Arab Spring and the meteoric rise of caliphate-obsessed Islamists throughout the Middle East and North Africa.

Indeed, what was almost unthinkable as recently as December 2010—the rebirth of a unified Islamic super-state stretching from the Atlantic coastline in the west to the Himalayas in the east—is now perilously close to becoming reality. If, as some suggest, Gülen does harbor designs on being a potential caliph—the religious/political ruler who would lead this pan-Islamic union—he has plenty of competition. As we'll see shortly, from Iran to Egypt to Saudi Arabia to Turkey and beyond, the forces seeking the long-awaited return of the caliphate feel that the wind is at their backs and the time is at hand.

As for Turkey, it led the Ottoman Caliphate from 1571 until Ataturk formally disbanded it in 1924 in an act that all Islamists—including the current Turkish government—consider a catastrophe. At the height of the Ottoman period, the Turks controlled most of the Middle East, North Africa, and the Caucasus, and conquered a large slice of Southeastern Europe, including Romania, Bulgaria, Albania, Greece, the former Yugoslavia, and parts of modern-day Hungary. Turkish-led Ottoman armies even laid siege to Vienna on two separate occasions before being beaten back. Under the stewardship of Erdogan and AKP, Turkey today is actively seeking to regain those glory days as leader of the worldwide Muslim ummah and head of the caliphate, while slowly but surely erasing Ataturk's secular legacy. But before Erdogan can accomplish that, he could face a showdown with Gülen for the title of Turkey's Islamist Top Dog.

Although Erdogan invited Gülen to return to his native land during a June 2012 speech (some Turkey-watchers think the politically shrewd Erdogan was simply calling Gülen's bluff), there have been signs of cracks in the strategic partnership between AKP and the Gülenists in recent years.[27] Erdogan is threatened by the growing power and influence of the Gülen movement inside Turkey—particularly its domination of the police force and judiciary—and the Gülenists are growing increasingly bold in flexing their muscle and influence. Gülen declined Erdogan's invitation to return to Turkey, but if he were to change his mind in the near future, things would get very interesting.[28] For now, though, the sometimes uneasy AKP/Gülenist alliance is working swimmingly, as the two factions continue to push Turkey toward becoming an Islamic state governed by sharia—with even grander regional ambitions in mind.

Those ambitions are spearheaded by Erdogan, who, while serving as mayor of Istanbul in 1994, declared, "Thank God almighty, I am a servant of sharia."[29] In his decade-plus as Turkey's prime minister, he has kept that unnerving pledge—and then some. In classic, gradualist Muslim Brotherhood fashion, Erdogan has managed to neutralize and cow the Turkish military and "Deep State" to an astonishing degree. There are obvious parallels here with Egypt, except that, upon his election in June 2012, Egyptian President Mohammed Morsi—in very un-Brotherhood-like fashion—essentially scrapped gradualism and went for the jugular right out of the gate. His moves to rapidly Islamicize Egyptian society and consolidate absolute power for the MB and its hardcore Salafist allies have angered a chunk of the Egyptian populace and led to violent civil unrest.

The crafty Erdogan, on the other hand, has suffered no such pitfalls. Beardless, with a neatly trimmed moustache, and clad in well-tailored suits, Erdogan—like Morsi and other Brotherhood leaders—looks perfectly at home at forums alongside Western leaders. He is a disciple of Necmettin Erbakan, the father of modern Turkish Islamism, who served as Turkey's prime minister for a year until being ousted by the military in a 1997 coup over fears (well founded) that he sought to smash Turkey's secular legacy.

Erbakan was influential in the development of two political parties, the National Salvation Party (NSP) and Refah (Welfare) with strong ties to the Muslim Brotherhood over the course of his political career. Beginning with his time as a youth leader for Erbakan's NSP in the early 1970s, Erdogan was weaned on the Brotherhood's ideology and its tactics—

the latter of which explains his patient, savvy push for sharia in Turkey today.[30] Simply put, he learned from the masters.

He also learned from personal experience. Erdogan and other outspoken Turkish Islamists in the Welfare Party camp were arrested after the 1997 coup. Erdogan served four months in jail for inciting religious hatred after he publicly recited a poem boasting, "The mosques are our barracks, the domes our helmets, the minarets our bayonets and the faithful our soldiers...."[31] That declaration may explain why Erdogan's government is today engaged in a mosque-building frenzy throughout Germany and Austria, both home to large Turkish expat populations.

It wouldn't be until a decade after his release from prison that Erdogan once again began making bold public statements revealing his true colors. He learned, just as Egypt's Muslim Brothers did during the Nasser era, that moving to push an Islamist agenda before the timing is right (or "ripe" as Fethullah Gülen might say) can be disastrous. So the AKP—which was founded on the ashes of Erbakan's banned Welfare Party—went incrementalist.

And it has worked brilliantly. Under Erdogan's watch, Turkey has commenced a slow, steady march to sharia, sharply reoriented its foreign policy away from NATO and the West and toward the Islamic Middle East, and turned viciously against Israel, a former ally. Yet Erdogan retains solid popularity among the Turkish public (he's been reelected twice since 2002). This has dire implications for Turkey's immediate future, warns Middle East authority Daniel Pipes:

> Having outmaneuvred the "deep state," especially the military officer corps, in mid-2011, the AKP adopted an increasingly authoritarian cast, to the point that many Turks fear dictatorship more than Islamisation.
>
> They watch as an Erdogan "intoxicated with power" imprisons opponents on the basis of conspiracy theories and

wiretaps, stages show trials, threatens to suppress a costume television soap opera, seeks to impose his personal tastes on the country, fosters antisemitism, suppresses political criticism, justifies forceful measures against students protesting him, manipulates media companies, leans on the judiciary, and blasts the concept of the separation of powers. Columnist Burak Bekdil ridicules him as "Turkey's elected chief social engineer." More darkly, others see him becoming Turkey's answer to Vladimir Putin, an arrogant semi-democrat who remains in power for decades.

Freed of the military's oversight only in mid-2011, I see Erdogan possibly winning enough dictatorial power for him (or a successor) to achieve his dream and fully implement the sharia.[32]

On top of his despotic power moves at home (which include imprisoning journalists critical of his AKP at an alarming rate), Erdogan has become an absolute thorn in the side of the West on the international scene as well. He has become a key ally of the Iranian regime, supporting the mullahs' nuclear weapons program and opposing international sanctions against it. He has also aligned himself with Iran's main proxy, Hezbollah, meeting with delegations from the terrorist paramilitary organization in Beirut and defending it against charges of involvement in the 2005 assassination of Lebanese Prime Minster Rafic Hariri.[33, 34] Erdogan even reportedly allowed Iran to transfer weapons to Hezbollah in 2006 during the Second Lebanon War against Israel.[35]

But the AKP honcho has struck up a particularly close relationship with another Iranian proxy (and the Muslim Brotherhood's Palestinian branch), Hamas—not surprising, given that Erdogan is an MB acolyte who shares Hamas's naked animosity for Israel. In 2006, Erdogan became the first world leader to host Hamas official Ismail Haniyeh after the terror group won elections in Gaza. He later backed Hamas against Israel during 2008's Operation Cast Lead, calling Israeli airstrikes (which came in response to eight years of ceaseless rocket bombardment of Israeli cities and towns by Hamas terrorists in Gaza), "a serious crime against humanity."

A short time later, Erdogan precipitated a heated exchange with Israeli President Shimon Peres at the World Economic Forum in Davos, Switzerland, barking at the then-eighty-five-year-old head of state, "President Peres, you are old, and your voice is loud out of a guilty conscience. When it comes to killing, you know very well how to kill. I know well how you hit and kill children on beaches."[36] Erdogan then stormed off the stage in a dramatic flourish that made him the darling of Islamists worldwide. That reputation was only enhanced in May 2010, when a Turkish government–supported flotilla of six ships (manned by a leftist/Islamist coalition of anti-Israel fanatics) attempted to break Israel's lawful, UN-recognized blockade of Hamas-controlled Gaza.

One of the ships, the *Mavi Marmara*, contained some very interesting cargo. Dozens of hardcore jihadists from the Turkish "charitable" organization, the Humanitarian Relief Foundation (IHH), were on board, spoiling for a fight with the hated Jews. The IHH has been described by former federal terrorism prosecutor Andrew C. McCarthy as, "a jihadist organization camouflaged as a global do-gooder.... Founded in the early Nineties by Osman Atalay, a Turkish Islamist who fought in the jihad in Bosnia, the outfit has longstanding ties to Muslim Brotherhood satellites throughout the world."[37] IHH, according to McCarthy, "often coordinates closely" with Erdogan's office and helps build his base of support among Turkish Islamists.

It's unclear whether Israel was aware of the heavy terrorist presence aboard the *Mavi Marmara*. After the ship refused orders to turn back and continued advancing on Gaza, a team of Israeli naval commandos boarded it—armed only with paintguns and sidearms with live ammo (for use only in self defense). They were immediately set upon by heavily armed passengers waiting on deck and viciously attacked. Some of the Israelis were stabbed, and others were bludgeoned with pipes. At least one was thrown overboard. Locked in a struggle for their lives, the Israeli commandos fought back, killing nine of their Turkish attackers (including one Turkish-American U.S. citizen). But the saga of the Gaza flotilla—an enterprise supported by Erdogan's government[38]—was only beginning.

Erdogan reacted to the deaths of the nine jihadists aboard the *Mavi Marmara* with predictable fury, calling Israel a "terrorist state," demanding an apology and recalling the Turkish ambassador to Israel—all calculated moves that would only enhance his rock star standing in the eyes of the Arab world. He later expelled Israel's ambassador to Turkey, downgrading the former allies' diplomatic relations to the lowest possible level, and blocked Israeli participation in a 2012 NATO summit.[39] Erdogan went even further at a UN forum in Vienna in February 2013, calling Zionism "a crime against humanity," and comparing the movement for a Jewish state in Israel to "fascism" and, oddly enough, "anti-Semitism."[40]

Israeli leaders were furious over the remarks, but Islamist hearts fluttered with delight once again as Erdogan continued to stake his claim as pseudo-caliph and mouthpiece for the Muslim ummah. Despite the vicious stream of anti-Zionist insults emanating from Ankara, President Obama continued to pressure Israeli Prime Minister Benjamin Netanyahu to apologize to Erdogan for the *Mavi Marmara* incident. In March 2013, after meeting with Obama in Israel, Netanyahu called Erdogan, with Obama also on the line, and apologized. Erdogan's reaction was to decline reestablishing full diplomatic relations with Israel and announce that he would promptly be traveling to Gaza to meet with Hamas.[41] Check and mate. A few lessons for Bibi here which, in his gut, he surely already knew before even picking up the phone: 1) Islamists only mend fences with each other. Infidel apologies only embolden them. 2) Turkey is gone as an Israeli ally. And it's not coming back anytime soon. 3) Never trust President Obama to have Israel's best interests at heart. Always rely on him to side with Islamists.

On the positive side, the Obama White House rightly condemned Erdogan's slander of Zionism as "offensive and wrong."[42] It was a brief and fleeting dollop of sanity in what has been an enthusiastically pro-Erdogan policy on the part of the Obama administration. The Obama administration views Turkey as a model of "Islamic democracy" and cultivates ties with the AKP. In the process, Erdogan has struck up a cozy relationship with Barack Obama. The two have been chums ever since Obama visited Turkey during his first overseas trip as president in 2009. They've become so close that Obama talks to Erdogan more than to any world leader other than British Prime Minister David Cameron.[43] At the 2011 G-20 meetings in France, Obama greeted his European counterparts with handshakes but, tellingly, gave Erdogan a warm hug.[44]

Obama's public embrace of Erdogan sent a clear message to Israel and the world that the U.S. government, under Obama, would not only tolerate, but celebrate, a proudly Islamist anti-Semite. To further hammer home that point, during a joint press conference with Erdogan in March 2012, Obama called the budding modern-day Sultan, "an outstanding partner and an outstanding friend" with whom he was, "in frequent agreement upon a wide range of issues." Obama added, "I also appreciate the advice [Erdogan] gives me, because he has two daughters that are a little older than mine—they've turned out very well, so I'm always interested in his perspective on raising girls."[45] One of Erdogan's daughters, Sumeyye, is apparently a real chip off the old block: a headscarf-wearing Islamist politician who belongs to her father's AKP party.[46]

Think about that for a second. The president of the United States—leader of the Free World—taking parenting advice from and publicly embracing a man who once said, "Democracy is like a train that takes you to your destination and then you get off."[47] Next stop, Grand Sharia

Station. President Obama's man in Ankara has also defended the murderous Sudanese dictator, Omar al-Bashir—whose Islamist regime has slaughtered hundreds of thousands of Christians and Muslims alike in south Sudan and Darfur—by arguing, "A Muslim couldn't do such things. A Muslim could not commit genocide."[48] Non-Muslims who've borne the brunt of 1,400 years of Islamic jihadist campaigns may beg to differ with Erdogan's assessment.

As for those large Turkish expat communities abroad, Erdogan laid down the gauntlet during a 2008 speech in Cologne, Germany, telling an audience of twenty thousand cheering Turkish immigrants that, "assimilation is a crime against humanity."[49] He repeated that message in a 2011 address to ten thousand German Turks in Dusseldorf, reminding them that while they are part of Germany, they also belong to what he called, "our great Turkey." Much like his Ottoman forebears, Erdogan would clearly like to extend his domain beyond the Middle East and into Europe—which explains his disturbingly successful attempts to exercise influence over Turkish immigrant communities in places like Germany and Austria.

Erdogan's government is even making inroads in the United States through major outreach to Native American tribes. It sounds like a bizarre pairing on the surface, but the AKP is going to great lengths to forge business and cultural ties with this long-suffering group. And it's working. In 2011, a bill was introduced in the House by Republican Congressman Tom Cole (who has Native American ancestry) that would grant Turkish-owned companies preferential treatment when it comes to Native American tribal area projects. Marc J. Fink of the Middle East Forum noted the proposed bill—which ultimately failed—with concern:

> The bill was the culmination of a curious multi-year effort by Turkey to ingratiate itself with Native American tribes: tribal students now study in Turkey with full scholarships; Turkish

high officials regularly appear at Native American economic summits; and dozens of tribal leaders have gone to Turkey on lavish all-expense paid trips.... Is it really in America's national security interests to have thousands of Turkish contractors and their families flooding into America's heartland and settling in semi-autonomous zones out of the reach of American authorities? Especially if their intent is to form intimate business and social ties with a long-aggrieved minority group?[50]

Of course not—and that's exactly the point. It's all part of Erdogan's strategy to reestablish Turkey as a global player and regional giant while at the same time spreading Islamist ideology far and wide. And Muslims across the Middle East and North Africa—many of them starved for a new caliphate led by a bold leader who will take on Israel and the West—are taking notice. Erdogan was greeted by adoring crowds during a strategic, September 2011 solidarity tour of Tunisia, Libya, and Egypt—three "Arab Spring" countries where his Islamist allies were newly ascendant. He received a hero's welcome from thousands of cheering Egyptians as he arrived at Cairo airport in a public spectacle that the Muslim Brotherhood helped organize.[51]

Erdogan used his Egypt stop to once again lambast Israel (always the surest way to win an impressionable Islamist's heart) and called on Egypt's new Brotherhood overlords to cultivate a secular Islamic democracy similar to what his AKP has supposedly established in Turkey. Muslim Brotherhood leaders ended up perturbed by Erdogan's advice on governance and more than a bit unnerved by the confident swagger of their non-Arab guest. "We welcome Turkey and we welcome Erdogan as a prominent leader," Essam el-Erian, deputy leader of the Brotherhood's ruling Freedom and Justice Party, huffed. "But we do not think that he or his country alone should be leading the region or drawing up its future."[52]

Likewise, Syrian dictator Bashar al-Assad—who, as of this writing, was still clinging to power amid that country's bloody civil war—may be a murderous tyrant, but in his assessment of Erdogan, at least, he is on target. "Erdogan thinks that if the Muslim Brotherhood takes over in the region and especially in Syria, he can guarantee his political future...." al-Assad told an interviewer in 2012, referring to Erdogan's open support for Syria's Brotherhood-heavy rebel factions. "He personally thinks that he is the new sultan of the Ottoman [Empire] and he can control the region as it was during the Ottoman Empire under a new umbrella. In his heart he thinks he is a caliph."[53]

Jordan's King Abdullah has expressed a similar view of Erdogan. A 2013 profile of the Jordanian monarch in *The Atlantic* magazine reported that he is "wary" of Erdogan and views Turkey, along with Egypt, as part of a new "Muslim Brotherhood crescent." According to the piece, Abdullah correctly "sees Erdogan as a more restrained and more savvy version of Mohammed Morsi."[54]

El-Erian, al-Assad, and Abdullah are no dummies. Although each comes from a vastly different ideological viewpoint, they all realize that Erdogan is a force to be reckoned with: a hugely popular figure in the Muslim world who, as head of a NATO member nation, also has the ear of Western leaders. Not to mention Turkey boasts a strong military, growing economy, and a long and fairly recent history of leading the caliphate. Fronted by an ambitious, politically astute despot who is fawned over by the U.S. president and idolized by legions of restless young Muslims worldwide, Turkey is an emerging juggernaut. At the time of this writing, Istanbul was a finalist to host the 2020 Summer Olympics—a bid that, if successful, would make Turkey the first Muslim nation to hold the Games. Erdogan has also announced plans to build a mega-mosque in Istanbul that will boast the tallest minarets in the world. Since he took power in 2002, Turkey has added an astounding 17,000 new mosques and counting.[55] Right about now, Ataturk is turning in his grave.

Erdogan, seeing the potential for another Arab fascist domino to fall en route to a revived caliphate, has been at the forefront of funding and supporting Sunni Islamist rebels against the Assad regime in neighboring Syria. In short, he seems to be everywhere these days, and his AKP's "Turkish model" of patient, gradual Islamization, combined with its so-called "Zero Problems with Neighbors" foreign policy, is all the rage among younger Muslim Brothers whom I've interviewed. They cite it, repeatedly and with admiration, as a model for Islamic governance. Ironically enough, so do the same clueless Western officials that Erdogan would like to subjugate.

——

"When we look at the region, we will find that Saudi Arabia, Iran, Egypt, and Turkey are the most important countries. For this reason, there has to be some sort of cooperation among these nations."[56]

When he made these remarks during his 2011 visit to Cairo, Recep Tayyip Erdogan showed that he was well aware of Turkey's main competition for Middle East supremacy. What was more relevant, however, is what Erdogan didn't say: that he would indeed like "cooperation" among these major Muslim powers, but under the aegis of Turkey. Turkey has many things working in its favor in this regard—including Erdogan smartly positioning himself as a major player at the Organisation of Islamic Cooperation (OIC), the Muslim world body that, as we saw in Chapter Two, already provides a framework for the caliphate.

The problem for Erdogan is that the Islamist regimes in Riyadh, Tehran, and Cairo also aspire to lead a renewed caliphate. Additionally, Turks are not Arabs, and Arab Islamists are fiercely supremacist and loathe ceding authority to non-Arabs like Erdogan. Iran faces the same ethnic-based problem, as would Pakistan.

As for Saudi Arabia, its vast oil wealth combined with its status as the birthplace of Islam and Mohammed ensure that it will always at least be part of the conversation. The Saudi Royals—custodians of the Two Holy Mosques in Mecca and Medina—have long viewed themselves as the standard bearers for Muslims around the world and have used billions of their petro-dollars to build radical mosques and madrassahs on six continents. The Saudis have money, oil, and the sentimental value of being the birthplace of not only the very first caliphate, but of Islam itself, all working in their favor. But their chances of emerging at the head of a pan-Islamic union are slim to none.

Although the Saudi regime was largely untouched by the so-called Arab Spring, unemployment and discontent remain rampant among its heavily Islamist citizenry. It's no stretch to say that the Saudi Royals, along with Jordan's King Abdullah, could very well be the next dominoes to fall in the region. Islamists worldwide consider the Saudis as corrupted, decadent pawns of the West who are unworthy of presiding over Islam's holiest sites. At the end of the day, the Saudi regime just does not possess the prerequisite Islamist street cred or military might to be taken seriously as a caliphate leader. By the time you read these words, the House of Saud could be history. That's how rapidly—and unpredictably—things are moving in the Middle East these days.

Then there is Egypt—currently ruled by an organization that has long been the most vocal advocate of a revived caliphate. Remember, the death of the Ottoman Caliphate in 1924 spurred Hassan al-Banna to create the Muslim Brotherhood. His dream, like that of Sayyid Qutb and every Ikhwani that has come after them, was to restore the caliphate and unite the Muslim ummah. It is the main reason for the Brotherhood's very existence. Now that the MB has taken control of Egypt—the Arab world's most populous and influential country—you'd think its leadership of the caliphate would be inevitable. The Brothers also have billions in Western aid and military hardware at their disposal and lead the world's most influential Islamist movement.

Yet the situation inside Egypt at the moment appears far too precarious for Mohammed Morsi and the Brotherhood to be able to lead the Islamic world, though that is exactly what the Egyptian Muslim Brotherhood is planning to do. That requires quelling the continued civil unrest that has plagued its short reign, and ensuring that the Egyptian military doesn't launch a coup. At the same time, Egypt is wracked by rampant poverty and food shortages for which the Brotherhood has yet to provide an answer. These serious domestic troubles would seemingly make it difficult for the Brotherhood to fix its sights outside of Egypt in the foreseeable future. Still, the Brothers are saber-rattling against Israel, forging closer ties with Iran, and encouraging their satellites to rise up everywhere from Syria to Jordan to the UAE.

Mohammed Morsi is not one to stand pat. He has essentially abandoned the longtime Brotherhood strategy of gradualism and is moving at warp speed to push through everything the Brothers have been waiting to accomplish for the past eighty-five years. If Iran, as I suspect, is due to have its military capabilities and prestige weakened by an Israeli first strike against its nuclear weapons facilities, the Brothers have little standing in their path to Islamic domination other than Turkey—which is led by a Brotherhood acolyte and ally in the form of Erdogan. Either way, the Brothers win. And as we've seen with Erdogan, a healthy dose of Israel-baiting—the type of which Egypt's Brothers regularly engage in with glee—will take the Muslim Brotherhood a long way in its quest to win Muslim hearts and minds.

No other Islamist movement or regime can match the MB's reach, which extends to at least eighty countries, or its influence as a powerful, seminal source of modern Islamism. If the Brotherhood's satellites and allies continue to gain power across the Middle East and North Africa, there is an excellent chance that the seat of the revived caliphate will be in Cairo, with the Brotherhood's Supreme Guide as a de facto caliph and the famed Al-Azhar University serving as an ideas-and-propaganda factory.

Iran's mullahs, however, have other ideas.

———————

I can just hear the deep thinkers that comprise the Obama administration's foreign policy team on this one: "Stakelbeck, you really are a right-wing fearmonger, aren't you? News flash: Iranians are Shia. And practically every other country that would belong to this Callystrate—or whatever it is you're raving about—is Sunni. Everyone knows that Sunni and Shia can never work together—they hate each other! Always have and always will. Take your cockamamie analysis someplace else. Besides, we've got Iran under control. Trust us."

Ah, the Left's favorite canard about the Middle East: Sunni and Shia Islamists hate each other even more than they hate Christians and Jews; so much, in fact, that they would never work together under any circumstances. Don't get me wrong: there is no love lost between Sunni and Shia. The two factions share a longstanding enmity and are at each other's throats today in Syria, Iraq, Pakistan, and elsewhere. But there is one holy cause that unites both Sunni and Shia and is able to achieve a truce—however temporary—in their Islamic family feud. And that is working toward the destruction of Israel and the West. In other words, as Iran expert Ken Timmerman has phrased it, "when it comes to killing Christians and Jews, Sunni and Shia get along just fine."

The Iranian regime is the main driver of this Sunni/Shia jihadi cooperation. A few examples:

- In December 2011, A U.S. district court in New York City ruled—to the complete obliviousness of the mainstream media—that the Iranian government and Hezbollah, both

Shiite, materially and directly supported Sunni al-Qaeda in carrying out the 9/11 attacks. A federal magistrate judge later ruled that Iran, along with al-Qaeda and the Taliban, should pay $6 billion in damages to the relatives of 9/11 victims.[57] Given that Iran's regime is busy spending most of its funds right now on building nuclear weapons and is devoted to America's destruction, that payout will likely take a while.

- Shortly after the 9/11 attacks, Shiite Iran began providing safe harbor to senior al-Qaeda leaders and bin Laden family members—something that continues to this day.[58]
- Shiite Iran is the main supplier of both weapons and money to Sunni Hamas. Iran's Shia proxy, Hezbollah, also has close ties to Hamas.
- Shiite Iran provides arms to the Sunni Taliban that are used to kill American troops in Afghanistan.
- Shia Hezbollah and Sunni al-Qaeda have a longstanding relationship that dates back to the mid-1990s, when al-Qaeda operatives visited Hezbollah training camps.[59]

The above list is just the tip of the iceberg. Yes, the interests of Shia and Sunni jihadists diverge violently in Syria, where Iran and Hezbollah are locked in a death match against al-Qaeda–linked groups and the Muslim Brotherhood over the fate of the Assad regime, an Iranian proxy. The two sides also clash in Iraq, where Iran is attempting to make its predominantly Shia neighbor an Iranian client state—and largely succeeding—over the fierce opposition of al-Qaeda in Iraq and other Sunni jihadists.

The theological—and in the examples just mentioned, strategic—differences between Sunni and Shia Islamists are well documented. Yet, in the larger scheme of things, both Sunni and Shia consider wiping Israel off the map and subjugating the hated, infidel West, led by the United States, as the more pressing jihad and overriding priority. The enemy of my enemy is my friend in this regard, and intra-Islam squabbling must always be put on the shelf when the opportunity arises to work together toward the demise of the Great Satan, America, and the Little Satan, Israel.

The Iranian regime sees the so-called Arab Spring as an opportunity to do just that. In the mullahs' view, the rapid rise of Islamists across the Middle East and North Africa is not an Arab Spring but an "Islamic Awakening": a divine signal from Allah that the return of the Muslim messiah is nigh. This messiah figure—known in Iranian Shia eschatology as the "Mahdi" or "Twelfth Imam"—will unite the Muslim world across sectarian lines and lead it to a final, bloody victory over all non-Muslims. In essence, the Mahdi is the ultimate and final caliph, and the Iranian regime believes it has been divinely designated to help usher in his return.

To the average, inside-the-Beltway talking head or Foggy Bottom careerist, this all sounds absolutely nuts—and indeed, it is. What the chattering classes can't grasp, however—much to the detriment of America's national security—is that it doesn't matter what they think about it. The only thing that matters here is that the Iranian regime is dominated by die-hard "Twelvers" who truly believe the Mahdi is at the doorstep and are shaping policy around his imminent reemergence. If U.S. officials refuse to even consider the fact that the Iranian regime (and its nascent nuclear weapons program) is ultimately driven not by geo-political considerations but by an apocalyptic, end-times ideology, then they have no one but themselves to blame when the other shoe drops.

If Iran's mullahs have their way, that "shoe" will come in the form of a renewed caliphate poised to stomp on the throats of Israel and the West. They made that point abundantly clear in a propaganda video produced shortly after the outbreak of the so-called Arab Spring. In March 2011, Reza Kahlili—a former CIA double agent who for years worked undercover inside Iran's elite Revolutionary Guards—provided me with an exclusive copy of the film, which he had obtained from his sources within the regime. Called *The Coming Is Upon Us: Israel Shall Be Destroyed*, it was approved at the highest levels of the Iranian government and produced in collaboration with the office of then-Iranian president, Mahmoud Ahmadinejad.

The documentary described ongoing upheavals in the Middle East as a prelude to the impending arrival of the Mahdi, who will unite the Muslim world—with Iran at the head of the pack—for a decisive showdown with Israel and America. According to Kahlili, "the purpose of the project was to inform Muslims across the globe of the immediate coming of the last Islamic messiah. The Iranian leaders, now more than ever, feel that all the stars are aligned for such an event" thanks to the ascension of Islamist governments brought on by the so-called Arab Spring. Kahlili told me that the Iranians planned to distribute the video throughout the Arab world in order to spark further uprisings and help pave the way for a new caliphate.[60] Only in the Iranian version, it would actually be more of an "Imamate," with an Iranian Ayatollah—and eventually, the Mahdi—at the helm of the Islamic coalition.

My report on *The Coming Is Upon Us* received heavy coverage from Fox News, talk radio, and the Drudge Report, and reportedly caused some rancor inside the Iranian regime, which had never intended for the film to leak out to Western media.[61] And yet the regime has not been shy in recent years about its devotion to the Mahdi or its desire to unite the Muslim world. Each September, as he stepped to the podium before the UN General Assembly and scores of world leaders, former Iranian president Mahmoud Ahmadinejad opened his addresses with a public prayer to the Mahdi. Likewise, Supreme Leader Ali Khamenei frequently encourages the Iranian public to prepare for the Mahdi's arrival. He used a July 2012 speech, for instance, to exhort Iranians to, "prepare for the coming...of the 12th Imam" and "be ready to fight." He added, "There will come a time when all the oppressive powers of the world will be destroyed and humanity will be enlightened in the era of Imam Mahdi."[62]

Under the stewardship of the Mahdi, Iran's leaders believe, the revived caliphate will rule the world and obliterate those "oppressive powers"—namely, the United States and Israel. That's why the current unrest across the region has them so galvanized. In September 2011, Khamenei hosted a two-day conference in Tehran on "Islamic Awakening" that was attended by several hundred guests from Arab countries. Attendees—Sunni and Shia alike—discussed ways that Islamists can utilize the so-called Arab Spring to gain power and work together toward common goals.[63] Khamenei drove this point home further in a later speech, imploring the Muslim world to, "make the most of this opportunity for the formation of an international Islamic power-bloc."[64] In other words, a twenty-first-century caliphate.

The nations that would belong to this renewed caliphate are practically all majority Sunni. Yet Iran is overwhelmingly Shia. Judging by its repeated calls for Islamic unity across sectarian lines, and its continued support for Sunni terror groups, the Iranian regime is not bothered by this fact. But how would Sunnis—who comprise 85 to 90 percent of the world's 1.5 billion Muslims—feel about being led by a nation from the minority Shiite sect, to which only some 10 to 13 percent of all Muslims adhere? On top of that fact, the majority of Iranians are ethnic Persians who share a long history of animosity and distrust with their Arab neighbors.

The trump card here is an Iranian bomb—provided Israel allows Iran to acquire one. That is a highly unlikely proposition in my view, but not impossible, given the Obama administration's relentless pressure on Israel to refrain from a preemptive strike against Iran's nuclear facilities. The acquisition of nuclear weapons and the long-range missiles capable of delivering them to the shores of the United States—two milestones Iran is working feverishly toward as of this writing—would make Iran the undisputed strong horse in the Middle East. All of a sudden, Iran would be able to flex its muscles and influence like never before and legitimately claim the mantle of leader of the Muslim World.

Yes, Sunni Pakistan already has some hundred-plus nuclear warheads in its arsenal. But the current Pakistani regime has not yet shown any aspirations to either lead or join a reformed caliphate. Of course, if hardcore jihadists were to seize power in Pakistan—a nightmare scenario not outside the realm of possibility—that could change in a hurry. Or perhaps Pakistan and Iran would simply combine their resources, form a united nuclear Islamic front, and dominate the world. The two nations have had generally frosty relations since the 1979 Iranian revolution, but, again, with things moving so rapidly in the wrong direction throughout the region, no scenario can be deemed impossible.

Many, if not most, Sunnis would violently resist the idea of an Iranian-led caliphate. In the case of Turkey and Egypt, each has its own designs on global Islamic supremacy and would seek equal footing with the Iranians in any strategic partnership. The Saudi Royals—Iran's hated enemy—would seemingly never accept an Iranian-led caliphate, although the looming possibility of a nuclear Iran marching into Shia-dominated eastern Saudi Arabia and claiming its oil fields could be more than enough to make the House of Saud reconsider.

The harsh reality, for Sunnis, is that a nuclear-armed, jihadist Iran would provide the best chance to crush Israel and the West and unify the Islamic world. That's why I believe Sunni Islamists would reluctantly fall in line—at least for a short time—behind the hated Persian Shia for the greater good, in their view, of destroying America and Israel. In the meantime, of course, those same Sunni nations would work post haste to acquire their own nuclear weapons in order to supplant Iran. For Iran, everything is contingent on obtaining the bomb. Without it, Iran at the head of a revived caliphate is simply not happening.

Shia and Sunni animosity does guarantee one thing. Once the envisioned caliphate wipes out all the Christians, Jews, Buddhists, Hindus, and other worthless kuffar, Sunni and Shia will resume their endless war against each other.

"Over 100 years' time we are closing a number of parentheses; the 1911 Tripoli war in 2011, the 1912 Bulgarian-Balkan migration in 2012, in 2017 it will be 100 years since Jerusalem's division from the Ottoman Empire in 1917, and in 2018 it will be a century since our separation from the Middle East."

It was March 2013 and Turkey's Foreign Minister, Ahmet Davutoglu, speaking before an audience of fellow AKP members, was seemingly mourning the fall of the Turkish-led Ottoman Caliphate while, at the same time, promising to resurrect it:

Without going to war with anyone, without declaring enemies and without disrespecting anyone's borders, we will be connecting Sarajevo to Damascus and Erzurum to Batum once again. This is the source of our strength. They may now appear to be separate countries; however, 110 years ago Yemen and Skopje were both part of the same country. The same can be said for Erzurum and Benghazi. However, when we make references to this, we are labeled as "neo-Ottomans." Those who have united Europe are not referred to as neo-Romans, yet those who unify the Middle Eastern geography become neo-Ottomans. It is an honor to be tied to the history of the Ottomans, the Seljuks, the Artuqids, and the Ayyubids. However, we have never set our sights on another nation's land.[65]

The nations vanquished in bloody campaigns by Ottoman Turks in centuries past would likely have a far different recollection of the old empire than Davutoglu. While he can deride the "neo-Ottoman" label all he wants, his remarks were nothing less than an open call for the reestablishment of the Ottoman Caliphate. His assertion that this can be accomplished bloodlessly is likely a nod to the Organisation of Islamic Cooperation (OIC), where fifty-seven Muslim nations and the Palestinians already work together in unison—and where Turkey has taken a leading role.

"It is our obligation to reestablish regional order in this geography and we will be embarking on achieving this day and night," Davutoglu continued. "We have to give our history its justice."

Davutoglu, in a symbolic act, later met with the living descendants of the last Ottoman Sultans at a reception in London.[66] The AKP's intentions should be clear and unambiguous to anyone who is paying attention, including even the Obama administration.

The caliphate is coming: an Islamic super-state united economically, politically, and militarily, speaking with one, powerful voice at the UN and controlling a sizable chunk of the world's oil wealth. Its sights will be set squarely upon first, Israel, then, the West. The only questions left to answer are, in what form will it come, which nations will be included, and who will be at the helm?

CHAPTER SEVEN

AMERIKHWAN: TERRORISTS IN SUITS

Al-Quds Market was the type of traditional Middle Eastern grocery found throughout the West Bank and Gaza, but with an added touch: the store's entire exterior was painted in the red, black, green, and white colors of the Palestinian flag. From the outside, needless to say, it looked like a no-go zone for a non-Muslim supporter of Israel.

That instinct was confirmed once I walked through the front door and glanced above the meat counter, where a large Palestinian flag featuring the Dome of the Rock—one similar to those flown at rallies for Hamas—greeted me.

Such a brazen display was to be expected in the terror hotbeds of Jenin or Gaza City. But I was in Hilliard, Ohio, thousands of miles from the seething cauldron of the Palestinian territories and a world away from the unbridled radicalism of the Muslim Middle East. Or so I thought.

I had come to Hilliard, a sleepy suburb of Columbus nestled in the American heartland, at the invitation of my friend, counterterrorism consultant and Hilliard native Patrick Poole. He had recently returned to his hometown after ten years away and was shocked by what he found.

"After a decade away, to come back and see all the changes Hilliard had gone through and then to find out that we had essentially become a center of jihad, one of the hottest centers of jihad in the country, was just mind blowing," he told me as I interviewed him at the local VFW Post.

At the center of this budding network, Poole explained, was an Egyptian native and leading global Muslim Brotherhood operative named Salah Sultan. When I arrived in October 2007, Sultan—hailed by local media and Islamic organizations as a pillar of the Columbus-area Muslim community—had already left his upscale single home in Hilliard behind and returned to the Middle East. His request for U.S. citizenship was soon rejected and he was denied reentry into the country, thanks, in part, to his undisguised support of Hamas during various trips abroad.

In 2006, for instance, Sultan appeared at a rally for the terror group in Turkey. One year later, he participated alongside top Hamas leader Khaled Meshaal in an event in Qatar honoring Muslim Brotherhood spiritual leader, Yusuf al-Qaradawi. Sultan is a longtime protégé and confidante of al-Qaradawi and has appeared with him at numerous events over the past several years.[1] This is the same Yusuf al-Qaradawi, of course, who has advocated for suicide bombings against Israeli women and children and U.S. troops alike.

Sultan's chumminess with al-Qaradawi didn't seem to faze the Muslim community back in Hilliard. If anything, it likely only enhanced his stature. During his time in town, Sultan was the religious director at the local Islamic school, Sunrise Academy, and was also the resident scholar of the newly built Noor Islamic Cultural Center—a sprawling mega-mosque with Brotherhood connections located in the heart of quiet little Hilliard. Heck, he may have even been a regular at Al-Quds Market.

Basically, Sultan had become entrenched in the Hilliard Muslim community and even beyond, thanks to his role in local interfaith events. So when Poole returned to town and blew the lid off his popular new neighbor's terror connections in a series of online exposés, the local mainstream media pounced. The *Columbus Dispatch*, in particular, seemed determined to discredit Poole's meticulously researched pieces as the ravings of a Muslim-hating bigot. One *Dispatch* piece accused him of making "hostile assertions"—simply for stating the verifiable facts about Salah Sultan's support for global terror.[2] Hilliard's Muslim community dutifully piled on, defending their brother Sultan as a peaceful scholar and castigating Poole as a fear-mongering Islamophobe.

Thankfully, Poole has since been vindicated many times over for his revelations about Sultan. And it didn't take very long. Shortly after the *Columbus Dispatch* published its piece portraying Poole as a right-wing extremist, Sultan appeared on Egyptian television and said of 9/11: "The entire thing was of a large scale and was planned within the U.S., in order to enable the U.S. to control and terrorize the entire world."[3]

Of course, the *Columbus Dispatch* conveniently chose not to report that maniacal little outburst. But Sultan was just getting warmed up. After leaving the United States, he ended up in Bahrain, where he hosted a television show that was eventually shut down by the Bahraini government for its radical message. A 2007 *Los Angeles Times* article warned about the rise of "extremist" groups, particularly the Muslim Brotherhood, within Bahrain and identified Sultan by name as a "controversial Sunni figure" that was making trouble in the country.[4]

Unfortunately, being removed from the airwaves in Bahrain didn't slow down Sultan's budding career as a multi-media mujahideen:

- In an interview with the official Muslim Brotherhood website following the 2008 U.S. presidential election, Sultan claimed that Jews assassinated President Kennedy and advocated that America become an Islamic theocracy.[5]
- In a December 2008 appearance on Egypt's Al-Nas TV, Sultan warned of the imminent destruction of the United States and promoted not only a notorious Islamic hadith calling for the extermination of the Jews by Muslims, but also the infamous *Protocols of the Elders of Zion*.[6]
- During a March 2010 interview on Hamas's Al-Aqsa TV, Sultan invoked the blood libel claiming that Jews kidnap and murder non-Jews and use the blood to make Passover matzos.[7]
- In yet another event broadcast on Hamas's Al-Aqsa TV, Sultan led a crowd in shouts of "Allahu Akbar," cheering forest fires in northern Israel that claimed the lives of dozens of Israelis in December 2010.[8]
- In an article published on the official Muslim Brotherhood website shortly after the death of Osama bin Laden, Sultan lauded the al-Qaeda butcher as a warrior who had "raised the banner of jihad for the sake of Allah" and had served a noble cause while at the same time questioning whether the arch-terrorist was really behind 9/11. He added that U.S. "terrorism" was greater than bin Laden's.[9]
- In 2011, Sultan appeared on Al-Jazeera openly calling for the murder of any Israeli citizen who enters Egypt— "tourist or not."[10]

And there you have it: the esteemed Islamic scholar, Salah Sultan—pride and joy of the Columbus, Ohio-area Muslim community and darling of the local Columbus media—in all his malevolent, America-hating,

Jew-baiting glory. Around the time of my visit to Hilliard, Sultan agreed over email to conduct a phone interview with me, but later canceled. Clearly, he had much more important Brotherhood business to which he had to attend.

He's now come full circle and is working for the government of Mohammed Morsi as Egypt's Secretary General of the Supreme Council of Islamic Affairs. It was a logical next step: Sultan was often seen by Morsi's side while actively endorsing the latter's campaign for president of Egypt in 2012. He also led a Muslim Brotherhood rally and gave a fiery speech in Cairo's Tahrir Square during a live June 21, 2012, broadcast on Al-Jazeera, a few days before Morsi's election victory.[11]

No word on whether Hilliard's very own Al-Quds Market catered the event.

═══════════

Salah Sultan—clad in sports coats, button-down shirts, and slacks, beard neatly trimmed—is about as far as you can get from the typical American stereotype of an Islamic jihadist. With his business casual attire, middle-aged paunch, and receding hairline, Sultan looks like he should be selling insurance in Des Moines, not marching alongside Hamas in Gaza. Therein lies the genius of the Muslim Brotherhood. The Brothers know full well that the typical, naïve Western view—including at the governmental level—is of bearded, turbaned Islamic terrorists hiding in caves, wearing suicide belts, and hijacking airplanes, or brandishing AK-47s as they mindlessly burn American flags in some Third World hellhole. Because, as Obama administration official Paul Stockton reminded us, "We are at war with al Qaeda, its affiliates, and adherents."[12] Period. End of story. The Muslim Brotherhood? Why, they're the *good* guys; they're the *moderates*; they're the people we can deal with. That's the message the Obama administration has hammered home to the American people for five years through both its words and its policies.

Much to the Obama administration's benefit—and the Brotherhood's—far too many Americans are so blissfully distracted by the latest
technical gadgetry, obsessed with social media updates, and riveted to the
Kardashians' every move that they just can't seem to find time to pay a
bit of attention to what's going on "over there." After all, the government
will protect us, and President Obama is a righteous dude who really seems
to care. He even got bin Laden, which means all that terrorism stuff is
yesterday's news, anyway. Now pass the nachos.

A disturbingly large chunk of Americans are becoming like facsimiles
of the zombies that they're busy shooting on their Xboxes and watching
on their flat screens. Unquestioning, unknowing, and concerned only
with their own well-being; trusting that the government will provide by
raiding the bank accounts of the "one percent" and redistributing the
money to everybody else; blindly believing in equality and forsaking any
judgment that might be fill-in-the-blank-phobic. The result? Barack
Obama is reelected. Oh, and Salah Sultan, a famously anti-Semitic
Islamist operative, becomes the toast of Columbus, Ohio, in the heart of
Middle America.

The Muslim Brotherhood has sized up the American public and its
leadership and found it wanting. The Brotherhood realizes full well that
for all the time Americans spend plopped in front of computers each day,
there seems to be a troubling inability to type in a Muslim-sounding name
and click "search," should the need arise. Current protocol in U.S. governmental and educational institutions apparently requires that when a
follower of the "Religion of Peace" wants a job, all due diligence must
be thrown out the window. Likewise, poor, vulnerable American Muslims
must be protected to the hilt, regardless of the facts, if accused of radicalism by bigoted conservatives.

This helps explain the various inroads made by a guy like Salah Sultan, who was defended to the bitter end by the *Columbus Dispatch*
newspaper despite a virulent track record that was readily accessible on

the internet for all to see. We've neutered ourselves as a society and suc-
cumbed completely to a suicidal brand of political correctness imposed
by the leftist gatekeepers of the media, government, and academia. We've
also just about dumbed ourselves down past the point of no return. And
the Brothers know it.

Sure, as long as that pesky Second Amendment is around and the
American military machine is still chugging (on the cheap and itself
degraded by administration-directed political correctness), we can defend
ourselves at home and abroad and kill a lot of terrorists who outwardly
seek to do us harm. And oh, those glorious drones!

But factor in an economy that is flatlining, and a people who are
divided, and the United States, circa 2013, is clearly ripe for a massive
enemy influence operation. The Ikhwan—always ahead of the curve—
saw this day coming. In fact, they've helped hasten it over the past several
decades by sending waves of well-groomed, eloquent operatives to the
United States and Europe who now hide in plain sight, fully intent on
hijacking Western civilization by building mosques, spreading their propaganda, and radicalizing fellow Muslims. Should they encounter resistance from their infidel hosts, the stealth Islamists' first line of defense is
to play the victim and plead for religious tolerance; once that approach
is exhausted, they rush to their allies in the mainstream media to demonize their enemies as bigots and Islamophobes; and after that wears thin,
they turn to their suicide-belted friends "from the old country" to wreak
just the right amount of havoc to cower the weaker elements of a society
into submission. Denial and deception—taqiya—are their weapons of
choice, not guns and bombs, though they keep terrorism in reserve. The
Brotherhood has turned this "double game" approach into a veritable
art form.

So, if these "terrorists in suits" have blended in among us, even
obtaining positions of influence in the halls of power, how are we to spot
them? Terrorism expert Lorenzo Vidino has written extensively about

the activities of the Muslim Brotherhood in the West, and has identified seven common traits to these individuals and organizations:

1) History. The leaders of these organizations typically are directly tied to the various Muslim Brotherhood movements in their countries of origin. As Vidino puts it, "They may have changed their tactics in order to adapt to the circumstances, their thinking on many issues might have evolved, but rarely do organizations started by Brotherhood members lose the basic ideological imprint of their founders."

2) Adoption of the Brotherhood's methodology. The creed and religious slogans generally mirror those established by Hassan al-Banna, educational efforts are imbued with Brotherhood ideology, and members are organized in accordance with the system laid out by al-Banna.

3) Muslim Brotherhood literature is prominent at events/bookstores. Familiar authors are heavily represented, including al-Banna, Sayyid Qutb, Maulana Maududi, and more modern authors like Yusuf al-Qaradawi and Tariq Ramadan (al-Banna's grandson).

4) Frequent interaction with other Brotherhood organizations. This can range from shared events to press conferences and extend to the personal level as well, such as intermarriage between families of prominent leaders.

5) Financial ties. According to Vidino, "the Brothers' financial interaction with the Arab Gulf elites has provided a bonanza." While the Saudis have backed off funding the Brotherhood since the 1991 Gulf War, and especially since the onset of the so-called Arab Spring, other Gulf States, particularly Qatar, have picked up the slack in bankrolling Ikhwan institutions in the West.

6) Informal allegiance to Yusuf al-Qaradawi. Although he has been banned from entering the United States since 1999 for his support of Hamas, al-Qaradawi—the Brotherhood's Qatar-based spiritual leader— is still looked to by many U.S. Islamic organizations as their chief Islamic jurist. Despite the travel ban, he even holds top positions in some of these

organizations, including a role as chairman of the Muslim American Society's Islamic American University. As Vidino puts it, "The Western Brothers play a crucial role in the global network led by al Qaradawi. It is evident that most of their networks and organizations refer to him rather than the [Supreme Guide] of the Egyptian branch. Though al Qaradawi may not be the pope of Sunni Islam, he unquestionably is the pope of the New Brothers and their Western branches." Based on my conversations with individuals in the West who Vidino identifies as "New Brothers," I can confirm that they revere al-Qaradawi and regard his pronouncements as the modern pinnacle of Islamic thought.

7) Membership in Brotherhood superstructures. While official umbrella organizations (like the Brussels-based Federation of Islamic Organisations in Europe) are more common in Europe, the Islamic Society of North America (ISNA) serves that role in the United States.[13]

These seven common traits are shared by, among others, the largest American Muslim organization, ISNA, and the loudest, the Council on American-Islamic Relations (CAIR). One additional trait I would add to the list is that Western Brothers uniformly support Hamas and do not recognize Israel's right to exist. A favorite tactic of these groups is to respond to Arab terror attacks against Israelis with statements condemning "terrorism in all its forms." These statements conveniently avoid naming or condemning any specific group, whether Hamas, Hezbollah, or Palestinian Islamic Jihad, and simply decry "terrorism." They are purposefully vague, and by including the phrase, "in all its forms," the Western Brothers cannily include supposed Israeli terror against Palestinians on the list.

Remember, the Brotherhood considers Palestinian suicide bombings against Israelis not as terrorism, but as legitimate resistance against illegal occupation. Still, the Western Brothers know that to keep up their moderate façade and remain in the good graces of Western media and governments, they need to feign some sort of public opposition when a Jewish child is blown to bits by a Hamas suicide bomber or rocket barrage. Invariably, their insincere, carefully parsed condemnations of "terrorism in all its forms" are more than enough to satisfy their many non-Muslim, Western supporters.

Although the covert nature of the Western Brotherhood organizations hearkens back to the founding principles of the Ikhwan in Egypt, the chief reason they continue in secrecy today is because of their mission to overturn governments, impose sharia law, and revive the global caliphate. At no time have these Western Brothers ever stopped supporting Islamic terrorist movements around the world, and when they've been caught doing so (for instance, via so-called Islamic "charitable organizations" that have been shut down by the U.S. government), they've quickly adapted their methods to continue providing that support.

Indeed, the Brotherhood has found the West useful territory for exporting global jihad. The United States, in particular, offers untold freedoms for an enterprising Islamist to exploit, all enshrined under the Constitution. America's general affluence also provides ample funding sources and a large pool of high quality, college-educated recruits for the Brotherhood to mine via the Muslim Students Association (MSA) and other MB fronts. As the saga of Salah Sultan shows, this phenomenon is not limited to large coastal cities with significant Muslim populations, like New York City or Los Angeles. In my 2011 book, *The Terrorist Next Door*, I described how Brotherhood-linked organizations are establishing networks throughout the Bible Belt and Midwest—intentionally burrowing into the very fabric of America's Judeo-Christian society with the intention of undermining it from within.

Clearly, we're not in Kansas anymore when it comes to the Brotherhood in America. Or maybe we are. In 2007, Major Thomas Dailey of the Kansas City Police Department's Counterterrorism Division offered stunning—and virtually unnoticed—testimony before Congress about Brotherhood infiltration in his heartland city:

In Kansas City, we face a silent, careful enemy. Disguised as legitimate Islamic organizations and charities we find the threads leading to Violent Islamist Extremism. Hidden within these groups are facilitators, communications, pathways for radicalization and funding sources for terrorism.... The possibility now exists that members of terrorist organizations and those posing as family members now reside in our community.... Areas of concern in Kansas City include an environment created for the support of terrorism through fundraising.[14]

While Dailey's testimony undoubtedly shocked our Ikhwan-illiterate Congress, it came as no surprise to anyone who's been following the Brotherhood's movements inside the United States. Indeed, Kansas City has long been a hub for MB activity, and some of the earliest conferences in the United States featuring known terrorist leaders and operatives were held there. According to the *Kansas City Star*:

Islamic extremists from around the globe flocked to Kansas City's Bartle Hall to bond in prayer, song and dance, and ominous appeals for bloodshed. They came by the hundreds to promote jihad, or holy struggle, at two conventions during a pivotal time for radical Islam—December 1989 and again the next winter. At the first meeting a masked terrorist from the Palestinian group Hamas spoke in Arabic for an hour. He pledged "oceans of blood" would oust Israelis from his homeland.[15]

The article confirmed that Muslim Brotherhood leaders were present at the 1990 Kansas City event. One Brother was captured on tape telling the audience that the borders of Jordan should be opened, "to Muslim youth so they may confront the Jews and the Americans at once."

Wait, did he say confront *Americans*? But I thought the Muslim Brothers were our friends? That's no way for friends to treat each other!

No, Dorothy, despite the Obama administration's protestations to the contrary, the Brotherhood is most certainly not America's friend—far from it. Nevertheless, the Brothers have been here chipping away at our foundations for quite a while, with successive administrations, Democrat and Republican alike, apparently unconcerned. The organization first laid roots in the United States in 1963 at the University of Illinois at Urbana-Champaign with the formation of the Muslim Students Association (MSA) by Brotherhood members. The MSA has a long history of turning out terrorists from its ranks. It served as the American launching pad for the Ikhwan, which was comprised mostly of university students for the first two decades of its existence on U.S. soil.

A U.S. Brotherhood leader named Zeid al-Noman outlined the MB's past and future trajectories during a speech that federal authorities believe he delivered in—where else—Kansas City during the early 1980s. In the speech, he repeatedly emphasized the importance of establishing "fronts" to further the MB's agenda (a goal that would come to fruition with the formation of ISNA, CAIR, and many others) and revealed that the American Brotherhood, though loosely connected in some respects, has a formal organizational structure and Shura Council that guide its overall direction. Al-Noman, in fact, was introduced as Masul ("official") of the Executive Office of the U.S. Muslim Brotherhood.[16]

Al-Noman said that one of the Brothers' major goals in America was to move from being a "students Movement" to a "Movement of the residents." The problem with being largely student-based, al-Noman explained, was that students were often transient, and "all the Ikhwans in one city might leave it or…the fundamental people the Movement relies on in this [particular] city might collectively leave," he said. "And, thus, leaving a sort of a vacuum behind them; a vacuum in work and also a vacuum in planning."

The Brotherhood needed a permanent and mature presence in America in order to really begin making headway. That's why al-Noman was encouraged that many of the students had begun to establish Islamic centers in their respective cities—a tactic that the Brotherhood developed in ensuing years:

> ... the presence of an Islamic center means the presence of residents, means the existence of contacts between students and the residents, means recruitment of the residents and winning them to the ranks of the Dawa'a, means forming permanent foundations in these cities.[17]

One of the places that the Brotherhood laid a "permanent foundation" was Plainfield, Indiana—once again, smack dab in the middle of the American heartland. Plainfield is the national headquarters of the Islamic Society of North America (ISNA), which became the MB's most important American organization shortly after it was created in 1982—fulfilling al-Noman's vision of the U.S. Brotherhood moving past being a mostly student-centric enterprise.

It was a vision the Brotherhood actually laid out a few years before al-Noman's speech, during a 1977 MB conference in Lugano, Switzerland. During that gathering, a task force comprised of senior Muslim Brotherhood leaders was created to move the Brothers beyond American college campuses and into the American mainstream. The eventual result of this task force would be the formation of ISNA, which is now the largest Islamic umbrella group in the United States and the preferred outreach partner for the U.S. government (despite ISNA's being named as an unindicted co-conspirator in the Holy Land Foundation terror financing trial).

Zeid al-Noman's address not only gave a fascinating glimpse inside the Brotherhood's formative years in the United States, but also shed light on an aspect of the Ikhwan's U.S. operations that the group's media and government allies would surely rather ignore. During the question-and-answer session that followed al-Noman's remarks, some audience members—all of them undoubtedly peace-loving moderates—seemed to have a strange preoccupation with violence:

> **Unidentified Male:** By "Securing the Group", do you mean military securing? And, if it is that, would you explain to us a little bit the means to achieve it.

> **Zeid Al-Noman:** No. Military work is listed under "Special work." "Special work" means military work. "Securing the Group" is the Groups' security, the Groups' security against outside dangers. For instance, to monitor the suspicious movements...which exist on the American front such as Zionist, Masonry...etc. Monitoring the suspicious movements or the sides, the government bodies such as the *CIA, FBI*...etc, so that we find out if they are monitoring us, are we not monitored, how can we get rid of them. That's what is meant by "Securing the Group."[18]

Two quick thoughts here: first, wouldn't it be nice if the Department of Homeland Security, rather than drawing up memos warning about Tea Partiers and pro-life activists, devoted resources to investigating the Muslim Brotherhood's "military work" on American soil? Second, if the U.S.-based Brothers aren't doing anything illegal and have the country's best interests at heart, as they assure us time and again, why are they so concerned about "ridding" themselves of monitoring by the CIA and FBI?

Al-Noman gave an indication why as the Q and A session rolled on, declaring, "while here in America, there is weapons training in many of the Ikhwans' camps...." The camps, he said, often included shooting ranges. He elaborated further that the Brothers had established a camp in Missouri, but avoided Oklahoma because of "harassments" by (rightly) suspicious local authorities. According to al-Noman, these MB camps were so important that if the wife of a Muslim Brotherhood member had just given birth, she would implore her husband to go to the camp rather than stay home and help tend to the newborn baby.[19]

What is clear from al-Noman's comments is that, as far back as the early 1980s, the Muslim Brotherhood—an organization which declares jihad its way and martyrdom its highest hope—was engaging in weapons training inside the United States. This should have been front-page news from coast to coast—but it wasn't. In fact, although al-Noman's speech was introduced as evidence by federal prosecutors in the Holy Land Foundation terrorism financing trial of 2008 (which saw five Amerikhwan convicted for funding Hamas), I'll wager this chapter is the first time many readers have ever heard about it. The U.S. government, on the other hand, has had al-Noman's speech in its possession for nearly a decade. And as we saw in Chapter Two, al-Noman's revelations aren't even the biggest ones to emerge from the Holy Land Foundation trial regarding the Brotherhood's nefarious intentions toward the United States. Sadly, instead of using these smoking guns to smash the Brotherhood's U.S. network, we have aimed the guns at our own heads by actively courting America's Next Great Enemy.

———

The Ikhwan's operations in the United States are not just some passing diversion—indeed, they have been directed at the highest levels of the international Muslim Brotherhood, dating at least as far back as 1977. That was the year of the aforementioned Lugano conference—held at the luxurious villa of Muslim Brotherhood "foreign minister" Youssef Nada—and featuring thirty top Islamist leaders from all over the world, including the Brotherhood's hugely influential spiritual guide, Yusuf al-Qaradawi. A senior Brotherhood official later told American authorities that he believed the conference provided a "blueprint" for the worldwide activities of the Muslim Brotherhood for most of the 1980s.[20]

One of the organizations founded by the MB following the Lugano conference was the International Institute of Islamic Thought (IIIT). Pulitzer Prize–winning *Wall Street Journal* reporter Ian Johnson has noted the importance of IIIT to the Brotherhood's mission in the United States:

> Despite IIIT's name, its function was not theological. Its goal was to provide the theoretical underpinnings for the spread of Islamism in the West. It would hold conferences and allow leaders of the Brotherhood and similar groups to meet and exchange ideas. It would also publish papers and books, helping to nurture the global rise of Islamist philosophy.[21]

IIIT would be incorporated in Philadelphia in 1980 and later relocated to Herndon, Virginia, near Washington, D.C., where it is still based today. It has long been the focus of federal law enforcement investigators who have examined its ties to terrorist financing, culminating in a 2002 raid in which, according to the search warrant, authorities were looking for "any and all information referencing in any way PIJ (Palestinian Islamic Jihad), Hamas, Al-Qaida...Usama Bin Laden, and any other individual or entity designated as a terrorist by the President of the United States, the United States Department of Treasury, or the Secretary of State."[22] All this, allegedly emanating from an organization based just a few miles from the White House.

One other target of the Herndon raids was IIIT employee Tarik Hamdi, who had coordinated media interviews for bin Laden and even transported a satellite phone battery to the al-Qaeda leader in 1998.[23]

But don't worry: liberals tell us talk of a Muslim Brotherhood plan to undermine America is just right wing, racist paranoia. If only it were so.

In Chapter Two, we saw that suspected Brotherhood operatives have infiltrated the Obama administration. What follows are three additional case studies that show just how deeply, and shrewdly, the Muslim Brotherhood has entrenched itself into American society. Their *stated* goal is nothing less than the destruction of Western civilization. And the worst part about it is that your government knows and apparently could not care less.

THE MASTERMIND

At first glance, it sounds like the quintessential immigrant success story. After a hardscrabble upbringing in Gaza, Mousa Abu Marzook arrived in the United States in 1981 to study at Colorado State University, where he received a Master's Degree in industrial sciences. In 1985, he moved his family to Ruston, Louisiana, to begin work on a doctoral engineering program at Louisiana Tech University.[24] Up until that point, Marzook's academic journey was the kind that countless ambitious immigrants have navigated in the United States. But then came a slight twist.

By October 1992, Marzook was leading a delegation from the terrorist group Hamas on an official visit to Tehran for meetings with the Iranian regime.[25] Mousa Abu Marzook, fresh off a decade spent at two well-respected American institutions of higher learning, was now head of Hamas's political bureau and a major player on the global jihadist scene. Like I said, just a *slight* twist.

Surprised at how this promising doctoral student's career turned out? Don't be. Time and again, Islamic terrorists have worked the U.S. educational system to their advantage. Look no further than the jihadist-ridden alumni of the Muslim Students Association (MSA), or 9/11 plotter Khalid Sheikh Mohammed's stint at North Carolina A&T, or convicted al-Qaeda terrorist Aafia Siddiqui's time at MIT. The list goes on. Clearly, Marzook had some illustrious—and murderous—company in his American educational pursuits.

It was during his time in Louisiana that Marzook not only assumed leadership of Hamas, but also oversaw the establishment of the Hamas support network in the United States. He did so by enlisting the backing of a number of operatives to assist in recruiting, terrorist training, and money laundering, and also by establishing a series of organizations to help keep Hamas running.

After Israel arrested most of Hamas's top leadership in the early 1990s, Marzook moved immediately to reorganize the terrorist group's infrastructure and keep it alive. His response was to move much of the organization's decision-making outside of Gaza and the West Bank and divide leadership responsibilities into three areas: the Political Committee, the Propaganda Committee, and the Jihad Committee. The Political Bureau would be headed by Marzook himself from Falls Church, Virginia, just outside Washington, D.C.; the responsibilities for propaganda would be handled by another U.S.-based Marzook associate, Ahmed Yousef; and the terrorist arm would be supervised by Mohammed Sawahla in London.[26] Marzook would also oversee the establishment of Hamas offices in Amman and Damascus.

In December 1992, another crisis confronted Marzook when Israel deported more than four hundred Hamas and Palestinian Islamic Jihad terrorists, including most of the Hamas terror command, to Lebanon amid howls of outrage from the UN Security Council, which—with the support of the United States—adopted a resolution that "strongly" condemned the deportation of "hundreds of Palestinian civilians."[27] Israel eventually allowed the terrorists to return thanks to withering international condemnation. Political commentator Daniel Greenfield has written that with its despicable pressure campaign against Israel, "the world saved Hamas."[28] Some observers believe that without the evil genius of Mousa Abu Marzook and his prolific fundraising on U.S. soil (which saw him raise millions for Hamas), the Hamas terror factory would have been snuffed out for good even earlier.[29]

Marzook was living in Jordan at the time of the deportations and responded by dispatching another trusted U.S.-based associate, Muhammad Salah, to coordinate cash distributions to the families of the deported, finance the purchase of weapons and explosives for retaliatory strikes against Israel, and scout potential targets for attacks. When it came to terror and mayhem, Marzook was clearly adept at thinking on his feet. Evidently, a quality American education can help take an enterprising jihadist a long way.

Marzook and his family lived in the Washington, D.C., area during part of this period of his leadership of Hamas. It is undoubtedly a period that American officials would rather forget, seeing as it happened right under their noses. Marzook did his best to help them in that regard. After being expelled from Jordan in 1995, he tried to reenter the United States and, upon being apprehended by authorities at JFK Airport in New York, denied any involvement with Hamas or terrorism. Regardless, the Clinton administration listed him as a Specially Designated Global Terrorist in August 1995. He would remain imprisoned until 1997, as U.S. officials debated what to do with him.

The Israelis wanted Marzook extradited to face charges of murder and terrorism but later dropped their request amid concerns over possible retaliatory terror attacks.[30] The U.S. ultimately deported Marzook back to Jordan. From there, he bounced to Damascus for several years before finding his perfect match: the new, Muslim Brotherhood–led Egypt, where he has resided since 2012 as Hamas's overall second-in-command.[31]

The strange case of Mousa Abu Marzook is notable for many reasons, the most obvious being that a committed jihadist was able to run one of the world's deadliest terrorist groups from within the friendly confines of the United States—including, for a time, from a suburb of the nation's capital. Another important detail: following Marzook's arrest in 1995 at JFK Airport, he became a *cause célèbre* for American Muslim organizations in the Brotherhood orbit. The Amerikhwan loudly declared Marzook's innocence, claiming that he was a victim of false evidence concocted by the Israeli government.

Yet in court filings submitted by federal prosecutors during his two-year detention, the U.S. government proved that Marzook had lived a double life in America, comfortably ensconced in the 'burbs while at the same time directing and approving Hamas terror attacks abroad. Although the U.S. Ikhwanis were ultimately unable to save Marzook from deportation, future pressure campaigns would be far more successful thanks to a Hamas-tied group whose genesis began in 1993: the Council on American-Islamic Relations, also known as CAIR.

THE '93 MEETING: KILLADELPHIA

In October 1993, I was a seventeen-year-old kid in Northeast Philadelphia gearing up for my final season of high school basketball. While I was preparing to launch jump shots, a group of Muslim Brotherhood operatives were gathered across town preparing to launch America's most notorious Islamist group.

The creation of the Council on American-Islamic Relations (CAIR) was just one alleged by-product of a three-day summit held in October 1993 at the Marriott Courtyard Hotel near the Philadelphia airport. The gathering featured several leaders of U.S.-based Muslim Brotherhood organizations as well as others from the Brotherhood's "Palestine Committee"—an Ikhwan apparatus formed, according to internal MB documents, to "serve the Palestinian cause on the U.S. front."[32] And serve it they have—in the form of repeated denunciations of Israel and open support for Hamas.

The Philadelphia meeting was a strategy-and-planning session called to formulate the Palestine Committee's response to the recently signed Oslo Accords, which set out an (ultimately doomed) strategy for peace between Israel and terror master Yasser Arafat's Palestinian Liberation Organization (PLO). The proposed peace plan was a direct threat to Hamas's agenda, which was then—and remains today—the complete destruction of Israel.

The Brotherhood's efforts to support Hamas were re-doubled at the Philly confab, and also led to a major organizational expansion for the MB movement in the United States. Unbeknownst to the participants, the FBI had obtained a warrant from the top-secret Foreign Intelligence Surveillance Court to wiretap the meeting. The transcripts from these wiretaps would later play a prominent role in the Holy Land Foundation terrorism financing trial and also shed light on the thinking behind the American MB's future direction.

Participants in the summit were concerned that the image of the U.S. Brotherhood groups was taking a beating because of their open opposition to the Oslo process. "Let's not hoist a large Islamic flag and let's not be barbaric-talking," cautioned Holy Land Foundation for Relief and Development CEO Shukri Abu Baker. "We will remain a front so that if the thing happens, we will benefit from the new happenings instead of having all of our organizations classified and exposed."[33]

What they needed was a presence in Washington, D.C., that presented a polished, professional, and managed message concealing their ultimate mission of supporting Hamas and its jihad against Israel. The new organization tasked with this job would need to work closely with the media and have the ear of lawmakers on Capitol Hill. Within a year of the Philly meeting, the Council on American-Islamic Relations was born.

According to 2008 testimony by FBI Special Agent Lara Burns at the Holy Land Foundation (HLF) trial, CAIR was formed as a direct result of the Philadelphia meeting and came under the umbrella of the Palestine Committee.[34] Its creation was a watershed moment for the Islamist movement in the United States.

The group—named, like fellow Brotherhood front ISNA, as an unindicted co-conspirator in the HLF terror financing trial—has seen past officials convicted on terrorism charges and was linked to Hamas by a federal judge. You'd think such a resume would make CAIR persona non grata in mainstream circles and possibly lead to its being shut down by the U.S. government—given that Hamas is listed by the State Department as a terrorist group.

But never underestimate the willful ignorance of America's elites. CAIR leaders continue to pop up frequently on network news shows and provide quotes to leading daily newspapers. No disclaimer or asterisk next to their names explaining their organization's ties to Hamas and rather problematic designation as an unindicted co-conspirator in the largest terror financing trial in U.S. history. Instead, hosts and scribes alike present CAIR to their audiences as the equivalent of a Care package, sent to educate ignorant America about the "real Islam" and how right-wing Christians and Jews are distorting it.

Still more dangerous than CAIR's manipulation of the media, however, is its continued access to local, state, and federal governments, where it attempts to affect the dialogue on Islamism, sharia, and the Palestinian jihad against Israel—and with great success, in many cases. CAIR officials continue to have the ear of the Obama administration, just as they had access to the Bush and Clinton administrations before it.

The birth of CAIR is one reason why, in a comprehensive assessment of HLF's role in support of terrorism, the FBI deemed the 1993 Philly summit a "significant" event which "represented a meeting in the United States among senior leaders of Hamas, [the Holy Land Foundation] and the [Islamic Association of Palestine]."[35] Needless to say, if I had known my future career path at the time, I might have skipped basketball practice and swung by the Marriott for a look-see.

It's doubtful, however, that I would have made it very far past the front door. Participants took extensive security measures in case they were being watched. As the FBI assessment noted, at the beginning of the meeting, those assembled were cautioned by Abu Baker to use code when referring to Hamas:

> During the meeting the participants went to great length and spent much effort hiding their association with the Islamic Resistance Movement, a.k.a. HAMAS. Instead, they referred to Hamas as "SAMAH," which is HAMAS spelled backwards. Most of the time, the participants referred to HAMAS as "the Movement."[36]

The transcripts reveal that Abu Baker specifically directed the attendees, "Please don't mention the name Samah in an explicit manner. We agree on saying it as 'sister Samah.'"[37] This discipline was apparently hard to maintain. One participant slipped during the conversation, saying, "Hamas...the Samah Movement. I mean Samah." His gaffe elicited nervous laughter from the rest of the group.[38] See, Hamas is just like you and me, a bunch of cutups—quite literally, when it comes to Jews.

The focus of much of the discussion in Philadelphia was the problems that the proposed Oslo peace plan between Israel and the PLO would present for Hamas and its support network in the United States. One participant complained, "There is no occupation now.... This will be classified as terrorism according to America.... How are you going to perform Jihad?" Yet some still wanted to continue openly to support the jihad: "In the coming stage, the most important thing we can provide in this stage is to support the Jihad in Palestine...it is the only way if we want to bring the goals of the [peace] accord to fail."[39]

The HLF's Shukri Abu Baker complained that when discussing the Palestinian issue with Americans, "I can't say...that I'm Hamas.... For American organizations, if you're against peace, you're a terrorist."[40] What the MB needed was not only an expansion of activities and efforts inside America, but a strategy of increased deception as well. After all, they were Islamically justified in doing so, as an exchange between Baker and another attendee, CAIR co-founder Omar Ahmad, showed:

> **Abu Baker:** I swear by your God that war is deception. War is deception.... Deceive, camouflage. Pretend that you're leaving while you're walking that way.... Deceive your enemy.

> **Ahmad:** This is like one who plays basketball; he makes a player believe that he is doing this while he does something else.... I agree with you. Like they say, politics is a completion of war.

> **Abu Baker:** Yes, politics—like war—is deception.[41]

Concerning the basketball reference, I believe that's called a "head fake." As for the notion that war is deception, why, that came straight from Mohammed himself, as recorded in a famous Islamic hadith (Bukhari, 52:269). In short, what the taqiyya masters gathered in Philadelphia needed were some new organizational tools and a rebranding of their efforts. Their war of deception would be waged in the media and in the political arena. Omar Ahmad laid out the plan:

> In order to strengthen the Islamic activism for Palestine in North America we must do two things: widening the Muslims' circle of influence and reducing the Jews' circle of influence.... Based on this study, I concluded three things and they

were almost discussed: having organizations which include media and research departments, another for politics and public relations, and another for money and law.[42]

To widen their circle of influence, the Amerikhwan would institute a plan to "infiltrat[e] the American media outlets, universities and research centers."[43] Nihad Awad, who is currently CAIR's National Executive Director, suggested a program of "training and qualifying individuals in the branches and the communities on media activism through holding special courses on media." Enlisting the media to assist in hopes of "broadcasting the Islamic point of view" was a key goal. Another Hamas-linked entity, the United Association for Studies and Research, recruited academics from respected universities in the Washington, D.C., area—including Georgetown and American Universities— to aid the cause. The endgame of this infiltration-and-co-opting strategy with universities and the media would result in the U.S. Brotherhood improving its "influence with Congress."

In his authoritative book on Hamas, terrorism expert Matthew Levitt summarizes the outcomes of the Philadelphia summit:

> The participants decided on five central goals: (1) "Support the holy struggle, Jihad"; (2) Publicly distance their movement from Hamas "to avoid media criticism and negative public perception"; (3) effect "Mass mobilization"; (4) "Actively solicit contributions and fundraising" for Hamas; and (5) "Influence the public opinion and the news media in the United States."[44]

Mission accomplished. Not only would the organizations represented in Philadelphia have more coordination and greater focus, their areas of operation would increase dramatically. As discussed during the Philly meeting, the Holy Land Foundation was in the process of opening a new branch office in Jerusalem that would more directly serve Hamas. This increased activity would not go unnoticed by authorities in Israel and the United States.

A few weeks after the 9/11 attacks, things began to unravel for the Holy Land Foundation, eventually culminating in the successful prosecution of top HLF executives—convicted of using their "charitable" organization to raise millions in funds for Hamas. As we've seen, evidence introduced in the HLFers' ensuing trial provided irrefutable proof that the Muslim Brotherhood is interested in subverting American foreign policy and America itself.

THE SURGEON

"Can you tell us about your organization's ties to the Muslim Brotherhood?"

The assembled left-wing press corps turned their heads around and gasped.

A tall, outspoken Islamophobe was in their midst, and he was asking questions—tough questions.

It was about time.

I had stood near the back of the room for thirty minutes, listening to Esam Omeish spin the several dozen media members who had gathered for his press conference. It was a masterful performance. Handsome, affable, and passionate, Omeish sounded utterly convincing as he denied charges of anti-Semitism and extremism while mournfully announcing his resignation from the Virginia Commission on Immigration. The gathering of reporters, clearly smitten, responded with googly eyes and a series of softball questions that supported Omeish's victim narrative.

Then I asked about the Muslim Brotherhood.

You could have heard a pin drop. Omeish, flanked by a cadre of Muslim, Christian, and leftist friends who had come to attest to his sterling character, looked a bit surprised. So did my media "colleagues," who, at the time, didn't know the Muslim Brotherhood from the Ya-Ya Sisterhood. Part of the reason was that it was September 2007, a few years before the Brotherhood would become a household name thanks to the so-called Arab Spring. The other part is that the mainstream media could care less about Esam Omeish's background. All they knew was that he was a persecuted minority being unfairly smeared by vicious right-wing bigots. After all, he told them so.

Omeish—taking advantage of his audience's sympathies as well as its ignorance—maintained that while there were some past links, his group no longer had any tie to the Brotherhood. He repeated this line when I approached him after the press conference: an event from which he was able to escape with his reputation damaged, but still intact.

It shouldn't have been. Omeish had resigned from the Virginia Commission on Immigration after multiple videos surfaced online of him seemingly praising Islamic terrorism. In one, he lauded his Palestinian "brothers and sisters" for "giving up their lives for the sake of Allah and for the sake of Al-Aqsa (Jerusalem)," adding that they were "spear[heading] the effort to free the land of Palestine—all of Palestine—for the Muslims."[45] In another video, captured at a public rally held across the street from the White House in 2000, Omeish said of the Palestinians, "You have known that the jihad way is the way to liberate your land."[46]

These and other videos showing Omeish making inflammatory remarks about Israel had been uncovered by the Investigative Project on Terrorism and led directly to him stepping down from the immigration commission. Predictably, Omeish claimed that his comments were "taken out of context" and that he was a victim of a "smear campaign" driven by "anti-Muslim intolerance."[47]

He had been appointed to the commission just a month earlier by then-Virginia governor (now Democrat Senator) Tim Kaine, who wanted to have a diverse group that included a Muslim representative.[48] When it came to selecting the Libyan-born Omeish, Kaine and his staff apparently didn't do their homework. On paper, Omeish's credentials as a top surgeon at a Washington-area hospital and a graduate of Georgetown University School of Medicine seemed to make him the perfect choice. His extracurricular activities were the problem. In addition to delivering anti-Israel harangues in public, Omeish was on the board of directors of the terror-tied Dar Al-Hijrah Islamic Center in northern Virginia and also served, at the time of his appointment by Kaine, as president of the Muslim American Society (MAS).

MAS, which declares on its website that it has "expanded its reach into thousands of communities across the United States," was founded by members of the Muslim Brotherhood in 1993 and now boasts more than fifty chapters nationwide. By the early 1990s, much of the MB network in the U.S. had been established. One critical component that was still missing, however, was on-the-ground ideological training of MB members. The Brotherhood addressed that need by creating MAS.

A detailed investigative profile of the operations of the Muslim Brotherhood in America published in 2004 by the *Chicago Tribune* identifies the critical role MAS provides to the Ikhwan's overall strategy in the United States.[49] One of the incorporators of the group was the then-leader of the Muslim Brotherhood in the U.S., a Panama City, Florida, doctor named Ahmed El-Kadi. The other two incorporators—Jamal Badawi and Omar Soubani—were listed as members of the Brotherhood's Board of Directors in documents seized by U.S. authorities.[50] Outside direction was also provided by Mohammad Mahdi Akef, who would later serve as the Supreme Guide of the Muslim Brotherhood in Egypt.

MAS leaders had decided early on that they would not publicly identify themselves as the Muslim Brotherhood. As the *Chicago Tribune* explained:

Documents obtained by the Tribune and translated from Arabic show that the U.S. Brotherhood has been careful to obscure its beliefs from outsiders. One document tells leaders to be cautious when screening potential recruits. If the recruit asks whether the leader is a Brotherhood member, the leader should respond, "You may deduce the answer to that with your own intelligence."

Evidently, MAS's deception extends not just to non-Muslims, but even to fellow Muslims who are potential recruits. The internal documents obtained by the *Tribune* provide a fascinating glimpse of how one obtains membership in the Brotherhood:

Not anyone could join the Brotherhood. The group had a carefully detailed strategy on how to find and evaluate potential members, according to a Brotherhood instructional booklet for recruiters.

Leaders would scout mosques, Islamic classes and Muslim organizations for those with orthodox religious beliefs consistent with Brotherhood views, the booklet says. The leaders then would invite them to join a small prayer group, or usra, Arabic for "family." The prayer groups were a defining feature of the Brotherhood and one created by al-Banna in Egypt.

But leaders initially would not reveal the purpose of the prayer groups, and recruits were asked not to tell anyone about the meetings. If recruits asked about a particular meeting to which they were not invited, they should respond, "Make it a habit not to meddle in that which does not concern you."

Leaders were told that during prayer meetings they should focus on fundamentals, including "the primary goal of the Brotherhood: setting up the rule of God upon the Earth."

After assessing the recruits' "commitment, loyalty and obedience" to Brotherhood ideals, the leaders would invite suitable candidates to join. New members, according to the booklet, would be told that they now were part of the world-wide Brotherhood and that membership "is not a personal honor but a charge to sacrifice all that one has for the sake of raising the banner of Islam."

Did Esam Omeish and others who have been involved with the Muslim American Society go through a similar process? We may never know the answer. But federal prosecutors have stated that "MAS was founded as the overt arm of the Muslim Brotherhood in America," even specifically citing the *Chicago Tribune* investigative report as support.[51] Additionally, the internal educational curriculum of MAS is composed almost entirely of the works of hardcore Muslim Brotherhood ideologues, namely Hassan al-Banna, Yusuf al-Qaradawi, and the godfather of modern jihadist ideology, Sayyid Qutb.

Omeish himself confirmed the influence of the Brotherhood upon MAS in a 2004 letter to the editor of the *Washington Post* (written when Omeish was still MAS president):

We, MAS, are a religious, educational, activist, and civic organization espousing the comprehensive understanding of Islam as explained by the prophet of Islam, Muhammad (peace be upon him), and as outlined and applied more recently by modern Islamic movements, of which the Muslim Brotherhood is pre-eminent.

The moderate school of thought prevalent in the Muslim Brotherhood represents a significant trend in Islamic activism in the United States and the West, and we in MAS accordingly have been influenced by that moderate Islamic school of thought....

The influence of Muslim Brotherhood ideas has been instrumental in defining our understanding of Islam within the American and Western context in order to espouse the values of human dialogue, tolerance and moderation....[52]

Despite his immigration commission debacle, Omeish soon had another high-profile opportunity to showcase the supposed "moderate school of thought" within the Muslim Brotherhood, when he ran for the Virginia House of Delegates as a Democrat candidate in 2009. Although his bid was unsuccessful, Omeish did receive 15.7 percent of the vote, finishing third overall.[53] Not bad for a guy who had been captured on tape praising "the jihad way." Incidentally, the third highest contributor to Omeish's campaign was the Virginia-based International Institute of Islamic Thought—another organization launched by the Muslim Brotherhood.[54]

It's a good bet that we haven't heard the last of Esam Omeish on the public stage. In September 2012, he attended a reception for Egyptian president Mohammed Morsi during the Brotherhood stalwart's first visit to the United Nations. Omeish later wrote on his Facebook profile, "His Excellency provided great insights and we share important perspectives." Perhaps Omeish will share some of those perspectives during future meetings at the White House. An exposé by the Investigative Project on Terrorism found that Omeish visited 1600 Pennsylvania Avenue three times during President Obama's first term, meeting with officials from the

White House Office of Public Engagement.[55] No word on what was discussed.

One thing, however, is certain. With an administration in power that fully supports the Muslim Brotherhood agenda, the Amerikhwan is ready to expand its territory like never before.

Let the mosqueing of America commence.

✖ CHAPTER EIGHT ✖

MOSQUES, ENCLAVES, VICTORY

I t was hard to believe that the gaping hole staring up at me would be filled by a large mosque in the near future.

It was even harder to believe the location of the project—which, when completed, would boast a price tag of well over $1 million.

The 2800 block of Voorhies Avenue in Sheepshead Bay, Brooklyn, is not a bustling commercial center or a major thoroughfare; it is a quiet, residential street lined with tidy row houses. Like most blocks in this working class neighborhood nestled along the Atlantic coastline, it boasts a multi-ethnic mix of residents: Irish, Russian, Jewish, Italian—but, at the time of my visit in June 2011, not one Muslim family. In fact, according to neighbors, the nearest area with a significant Muslim presence was blocks away.

Nevertheless, someone was determined to build a large, three-story mosque smack dab in the middle of this cramped residential block where parking was at a premium. To the neighbors' utter dismay, that "someone" was the Muslim American Society, or MAS, an organization that federal prosecutors have described as the Muslim Brotherhood's U.S. arm.[1]

"We have Holocaust survivors who live in these buildings around here," local resident Victor Benari told me. "And people, of course, are in shock."

Benari, a short, thoughtful man with glasses, settled in Sheepshead Bay after moving from Israel in 1999. Now he and the large local Jewish population—including some who survived Auschwitz—faced the prospect of living alongside followers of an organization that had worked with the Nazis to liquidate Jews.

As we stood together on the rooftop of a nearby apartment building and surveyed the large crater below—where a construction crane stood at the ready—Benari shook his head at the bitter irony of it all.

"People invested money to buy these houses and live in a nice, quiet neighborhood," he said. "The mosque will be able to hold hundreds of people—at least. What happens when they come here to pray? Will they walk here? I doubt it. They will probably drive…what about the parking? And the noise? And what about the call to prayer five times a day? Do people want to hear that over loudspeakers?"

No, they don't. But to Islamic supremacists conducting a not-so-subtle settlement jihad, an infidel's concerns are but a mere trifle. That was certainly the case a few miles from Sheepshead Bay, at Ground Zero, where Muslim Brotherhood–tied Islamists forged ahead with plans to build a mega-mosque at the scene of the worst Islamic terror attack in U.S. history—despite the opposition of some 70 percent of the American people.[2]

At the time of this writing, the so-called Park51 project—a planned $100 million, fifteen-story "Islamic community center" which would have inhabited a building damaged by landing gear from one of the planes that struck the Twin Towers—has fizzled, with the building housing little more than a glorified Muslim prayer room frequented by a few dozen Friday worshippers.[3]

The good people of Sheepshead Bay, however, have had no such luck. Despite heated protests by local residents against the MAS mosque throughout 2010 and 2011 that drew national media coverage—most of it, predictably, depicting the protestors as knuckle-dragging nativists— construction on the facility, as I write this, is nearly complete.

Benari joined with other neighbors to form a group called the Bay People that was dedicated to stopping the mosque, and for a while they had some success. Their complaints over building and zoning violations coupled with quality-of-life concerns resulted in some construction stop- pages, not to mention thousands of dollars in fines for the property's owners.

But in the end, despite a valiant effort, the Bay People's pleas fell on deaf ears. Other than support from a few local officials, they could not muster any sort of significant backing from New York City's mostly left- ist lawmakers. And appealing to pandering New York City Mayor Michael Bloomberg—the Ground Zero mosque project's most vociferous and shameless public supporter—was never a realistic option.

"We welcome Muslim families to build a house and to be a good neighbor," Victor Benari explained as we walked along the Brooklyn waterfront. "But we will not welcome this facility in the wrong place and backed up with the wrong organization behind it."

That brings us to the heart of the matter. Benari and the Bay People were careful to frame their opposition to the mosque around quality-of- life and zoning issues rather than the Islamist nature of the Muslim American Society. But I quickly found during our meeting that the Bay People knew full well who—and what—their new neighbors would represent.

"There are clips of Mahdi Bray, a [former] leader of MAS, speaking at an event in D.C., supporting Hamas and Hezbollah, 100 percent," said one Sheepshead Bay local, referring to an infamous anti-Israel event Bray appeared at in 2000 across the street from the White House.

"They're tied to the Muslim Brotherhood," added another neighbor. "How do you deal with people who embrace enemies of the United States? I don't think that anybody can."

Unless, of course, you work for the Obama administration.

As for MAS's Muslim Brotherhood ties, they were extensively documented in a groundbreaking 2004 *Chicago Tribune* article that would have won a Pulitzer Prize in a world where real investigative journalism was the norm. The *Tribune* piece contains several direct quotes from senior Brotherhood leaders, past and present, that leave no doubt that MAS was founded as a Brotherhood front group:

> In recent years, the U.S. Brotherhood operated under the name Muslim American Society, according to documents and interviews. One of the nation's major Islamic groups, it was incorporated in Illinois in 1993 after a contentious debate among Brotherhood members.
>
> Some wanted the Brotherhood to remain underground, while others thought a more public face would make the group more influential. Members from across the country drove to regional meeting sites to discuss the issue....
>
> When the leaders voted, it was decided that Brotherhood members would call themselves the Muslim American Society, or MAS, according to documents and interviews.
>
> They agreed not to refer to themselves as the Brotherhood but to be more publicly active. They eventually created a Web site and for the first time invited the public to some conferences, which also were used to raise money....

[Former U.S. Muslim Brotherhood head Ahmed] Elkadi and Mohammed Mahdi Akef, a Brotherhood leader in Egypt and [until 2009] the international head, had pushed for more openness. In fact, Akef says he helped found MAS by lobbying for the change during trips to the U.S....

Shaker Elsayed, a top MAS official, says the organization was founded by Brotherhood members but has evolved to include Muslims from various backgrounds and ideologies.

"Ikhwan [Brotherhood] members founded MAS, but MAS went way beyond that point of conception," he says.

Now, he says, his group has no connection with the Brotherhood and disagrees with the international organization on many issues.

But he says that MAS, like the Brotherhood, believes in the teachings of Brotherhood founder Hassan al-Banna, which are "the closest reflection of how Islam should be in this life."

"I understand that some of our members may say, 'Yes, we are Ikhwan,'" Elsayed says. But, he says, MAS is not administered from Egypt. He adds, "We are not your typical Ikhwan."[4]

To review, according to its top officials, MAS was founded by Brotherhood members and adheres to the pro-jihad, anti-Semitic teachings of MB founder Hassan al-Banna. In addition, MAS has been known to distribute the violent writings of Brotherhood icon Sayyid Qutb at its events.[5] But not to worry, Sheepshead Bay: these aren't "your typical Ikhwan." And hey, MAS even disagrees with the international Brotherhood on "many issues"—although I have yet to hear one.

The reality is that the Sheepshead Bay mosque was a quintessential, Ikhwan-style operation from its conception. The double lot on Voorhies Avenue was purchased in 2008 by a Yemeni immigrant named Ahmed

Allowey for a whopping $800,000.[6] Allowey then sold the property to the Muslim American Society, which promptly had the two homes demolished and began construction on the mosque before neighbors on Voorhies Avenue even knew what was happening.

When I spoke to members of the Bay People, all of them expressed frustration that they were left completely in the dark about the mosque project by Allowey and MAS, not to mention by local officials. Incredibly, the Bay People said they only found out about the planned mosque after someone asked a worker at the Voorhies Avenue site what exactly was being built. And, well, there goes the neighborhood.

Now, I'm sure Ahmed Allowey, who also owns a laundromat and lives in a modest home in Sheepshead Bay not far from the mosque, is a fledgling tycoon. But $800,000 is a lot of money—particularly for a Yemeni immigrant who only arrived in the United Sates in 1997. It also seems an awful steep price to pay for two modest homes in working-class Brooklyn.

I would have loved to have asked Allowey about his finances and his relationship with the Muslim American Society, but he did not respond to my phone calls or answer his front door when I came a-knockin'. I also had no luck when I dropped by a Muslim American Society mosque in Brooklyn to inquire about the project on Voorhies Avenue. A young girl in a hijab politely referred me to a MAS official, who never returned my calls. A very transparent bunch, these Ikhwan disciples.

MAS, for its part, seems to have unlimited funding at its disposal. In addition to the Sheepshead Bay mosque, MAS also opened a massive mosque in Boston in 2008 that cost over $15 million (with more than half of those funds reportedly coming from Saudi sources)[7] and the group has more projects in the works. Given MAS's unsavory Ikhwan ties and the numerous reports over the past decade of foreign funding of American mosques—including estimates that some 80 percent of these structures have Saudi influence behind them[8, 9, 10]—it's fair to ask where MAS and other mosque developers in the U.S. are getting their money. Indeed, as we'll see in this chapter, the Brotherhood and the Saudi regime, despite some differences, have worked together closely over the past several decades to establish mosques throughout the West.

Is the mosque in Sheepshead Bay one of them? We may never know, as MAS is under no obligation to reveal its funding sources. But before leaving Brooklyn, I had an intriguing conversation with a resident of Voorhies Avenue who lived very close to the site of the future mosque but wished to remain anonymous for safety reasons. He told me that in 2010, shortly before ground was broken on the facility, two Arab Muslim men approached him about selling his home.

The neighbor told me one of the men was young, well dressed, spoke fluent English, and claimed to be a real estate agent. The other was clad in Islamic garb and spoke no English. Needless to say, the neighbor assumed the second man was from out of town. He told me the pair offered him up to $600,000 to buy his home, well above the market price. He declined their offer. In the process, he likely prevented the mosque on Voorhies Avenue from taking on even larger dimensions. If true—and after talking to others in Sheepshead Bay, I have no reason to believe it isn't—the neighbor's story represents an admirable show of defiance against a rising Islamist tide in Brooklyn and beyond.

———

Why Sheepshead Bay? Why would a Muslim Brotherhood–linked organization want to erect an expensive, three-story mosque in the middle of a quiet, tree-lined residential street where not one Muslim family lived? Notice that I use the past tense there. Because once the double parking and overflow traffic hit narrow Voorhies Avenue, and the call to prayer echoes through the neighborhood five times a day, and overflow Friday prayers perhaps spill outside, with worshippers prostrate in the middle of the street (this happens regularly at Madina Masjid, another three-story mosque located across the river in Manhattan's East Village),[11] it's a safe bet that Sal, Angelo, Moshe, and other unfortunate local infidels will be posting "For Sale" signs on their modest front lawns, post-haste. It's an even safer bet that Muslims will move in and replace them.

I've seen this pattern repeated time and time again over the course of my eleven years spent covering the Islamist movement in the West. An Islamist organization—usually linked to the Muslim Brotherhood and flush with cash from Saudi Arabia and/or the Gulf states—spends big bucks to buy up several acres of property in a town where hardly any Muslims reside. Plans are announced to build an "Islamic Cultural Center" where all faiths are welcome and diversity will be celebrated in a new, multiculti mini-utopia. But blindsided local residents, after doing some research, quickly learn of the nefarious connections of the mosque's leadership and see a potential hub for terrorist plotting in their midst—one with financial backing from overseas radicals to boot.

Yet, when these same neighbors demand to know where the money is coming from to pay for the planned mega-mosque, smooth-talking Muslim spokesmen involved with the project just smile and calmly reassure all comers that the funds have been "locally raised." The local city council, petrified of being called racist, ultimately approves the so-called Islamic center against the will of the people. On cue, the mainstream media and Islamic groups then team up to condemn critics of the mosque as "bigots" and "Islamophobes." Neighbors are left feeling demonized, abandoned, angry, and alone. And the mosque is built—even though its leadership has been exposed as having ties to the extremist Muslim Brotherhood, a hatred for Israel, and a fondness for sharia law.

I highlighted several examples of this trend in my book, *The Terrorist Next Door*. In a chapter called "Mega-Mosque Nation," I described the plight of Murfreesboro, Tennessee, a rural town in the buckle of the Bible Belt where locals protested—fiercely but again, in vain—against a fifteen-acre, multi-million-dollar mega-mosque planned by radical Islamists.[12]

I spent a few days in the town shortly after ground had been broken on the new Islamic Center of Murfreesboro (ICM) and found all the classic elements that have allowed the Muslim Brotherhood's disciples to gain footholds in communities across the United States. For starters, Murfreesboro's tiny Muslim community consisted of no more than 250 families who had quietly worshipped at a much smaller facility for years. According to ICM's 2009 annual report, the mosque had only forty-five active members overall. So why the sudden need for a gargantuan 52,000-square-foot facility—built right next door to a Christian church, no less? And who exactly was paying for this very expensive structure serving a mostly working-class congregation of (presumably) modest means?

The mosque's imam, Ossama Bahloul (a graduate of Egypt's Al-Azhar University, an institution notorious for spewing anti-Semitic and anti-American bile) offered few answers to these questions but lots of reassuring smiles and pleas for tolerance and peaceful coexistence—even after an ICM board member was suspended for posting pro-jihad slogans and photos on MySpace. That same board member—whose MySpace page included a picture celebrating murderous Hamas founder Sheikh Ahmed Yassin—was quietly reinstated shortly thereafter.

There was also the not-so-small matter of the literature found at the ICM, which included pamphlets from Muslim Brotherhood–tied groups, and the mosque's official reading list, which contained a roll call of MB ideologues before curiously disappearing from the ICM website. Likewise, YouTube footage of a January 2009 anti-Israel rally sponsored by the ICM in downtown Murfreesboro and featuring shouts of "Allahu Akbar" was also scrubbed from the Web shortly after the ICM gained approval to build the new mega-mosque. This was no coincidence: local residents were in the process of filing a series of appeals against the mosque and the ICM's hierarchy was trying desperately to conceal all traces of its Ikhwan-inspired Islamism until the mammoth structure was safely built.

When my cameraman and I found Imam Bahloul in the parking lot of the original ICM, he declined to speak on the record. Asked about the ICM's Brotherhood-heavy reading list and allegations that the mosque was tied to the Ikhwan, he responded, with a straight face, "They're in this country? I didn't know that." Back in Sheepshead Bay, that's called *chutzpah*.

But Bahloul needn't have worried. The Rutherford County (TN) Commission, petrified of earning the dreaded "Islamophobe" label, green-lighted the mosque after only seventeen days and with no input from local residents—even though it often takes churches and other religious facilities in the area up to a year to gain such approval. When Murfreesboro residents (who, like the homeowners in Sheepshead Bay, only learned of the mosque plans after approval had already been granted) loudly protested, state and national media dutifully castigated them as anti-Muslim rednecks and zealots.

The Civil Rights Division of the Obama Justice Department essentially sealed the deal for the ICM's construction when it filed an amicus brief in October 2010 declaring DOJ's "vigorous" support for the new mega-mosque in the heart of American Christendom. This was followed by a DOJ lawsuit against Rutherford County demanding that the mosque be permitted to open.[13] The Obama administration ultimately got its way, and Assistant Attorney General Thomas Perez (who, at the time of this writing, was in line to be the next Secretary of Labor) spoke at the mosque's grand opening in November 2012 where he warned of—you guessed it—Islamophobia.[14]

Surprised that the federal government would get involved in a community quarrel? Don't be. The Obama Justice Department has shown a troubling and persistent habit of meddling in local mosque controversies like in Murfreesboro, repeatedly strong-arming townspeople and weighing in on the side of Islamists. The administration's efforts in this regard are led by the DOJ's Civil Rights Division, which, as of this writing, has opened investigations into a whopping twenty-eight cases nationwide involving local denials of mosque construction applications.[15] A few notable examples:

■ In December 2012, shortly after the Department of Justice opened an investigation, the zoning commission for the town of Norwalk, Connecticut (population: 86,000), dropped its previous opposition to the construction of a 27,000-square-foot mega-mosque. The commission had opposed the Al-Madany Islamic Center—which will reportedly feature a towering, eighty-foot minaret—over zoning and parking issues before caving to DOJ pressure.

The current Islamic center in Norwalk serves a hundred families. The new facility, which will cost an estimated $3.5 million, will have the capacity to hold a thousand worshippers.[16] Where are the funds coming from and why the need for Norwalk's small Muslim population to have such a large complex? Frankly, the Obama administration doesn't care, as long as more mosques are constructed and the traditional Judeo-Christian fabric of America is further eroded in the process.

■ In the small town of St. Anthony, Minnesota (population: just over 8,000), the Department of Justice opened a formal investigation in October 2012 after the local city council rejected a proposal to open a 13,000-square-foot Islamic center in a building located in an area dedicated to light industrial use only. A Christian group's proposal was rejected on the same grounds in 2011.[17] The DOJ was curiously absent in that case but not this time around.

The space for the proposed Abu Huraira Islamic Center was purchased for $1.9 million—again, a very tidy sum for a small congregation of only two hundred people.[18,19] DOJ reportedly got involved after the Minnesota chapter of the notorious Council on American-Islamic

Relations (CAIR) requested an investigation. The lesson: when a Hamas-linked group that was an unindicted co-conspirator in the largest terrorism financing trial in American history talks, the Obama administration listens—and acts.

■ In March 2010, in Lomita, California—a town of just over 20,000 people located in Los Angeles County—the city council unanimously rejected a proposed expansion of the Islamic Center of the South Bay into a much larger, two-story facility. The council cited neighbors' concerns and a likely increase in traffic as the main reasons behind its decision. Sounds reasonable enough—but not to the Obama administration.

In November 2011, the Department of Justice launched an investigation of Lomita city officials over alleged discrimination.[20] Once again, the local CAIR chapter led the charge. In the end, the DOJ found no evidence that the officials engaged in religious discrimination. But Lomita eventually came to a settlement with the Islamic center and the federal government that required the city to reconsider the mosque's redevelopment plans. That means the mosque expansion may yet happen.[21] "It surprises me that the federal government would spend so many resources second-guessing this pretty basic land-use decision," said Lomita City Attorney Christi Hogin.[22] In truth, she and the people of Lomita learned the hard way that when it comes to promoting Islamism at the expense of American interests, this particular federal government is full of surprises—of the worst kind.

■ Let's get ready for what's been dubbed the "Largest Islamic Project in America." It's a massive Islamic center planned, yet again, for a rural area—this time in Howard County, Maryland. The Dar us-Salaam mosque would reportedly hold up to five thousand people and cover some sixty-six acres of land. The price tag? An astronomical $8 million. As of this writing, the sale has not been completed; locals are up in arms about the plan and have vowed to fight.[23] Rest assured the Department of Justice is up for a battle as well—and not on the side of the locals.

The cases described above are far from isolated. According to a 2012 Pew Research Forum study, no less than fifty-three proposed Islamic centers and mosques have met community resistance in recent years from coast to coast.[24] Contrary to elite opinion, the American people are not stupid. When they see a multi-million-dollar mega-mosque proposed for a rural area with only a smattering of Muslims, they begin to ask serious questions. Years of watching Islamist fanatics burn American flags and kill U.S. soldiers and civilians will have that kind of effect on folks.

At the end of the day, however, the widespread resistance to creeping Islamization has had little noticeable effect. A 2011 study found that the number of mosques in America had nearly *doubled* over the span of a decade, from 1,209 in 2000 to 2,106 in 2011—or an increase of 74 percent in just eleven years.[25] That means that roughly four in ten mosques in the United States have opened since the year 2000. These are simply astounding numbers, made all the more jarring when one considers that the mosque-building craze has occurred mostly *after* 9/11. During that same span, the Muslim population in the United States has grown by 67 percent, more than doubling since 9/11 and making Islam the fastest growing religion in America.[26] The Muslim presence is growing in particular in the South and Midwest, areas where the traditional, Judeo-Christian, God-and-country ethos of the United States has always been strongest. Yes, folks, America is so viciously Islamophobic that Muslims are beating down the doors to settle here and build mosques in droves—and our government is rolling out the prayer mat.

In a sane society, an ongoing, existential struggle against Islamists—of both the violent and stealth variety—would mean fewer mosques, not more. But the West, including the United States, isn't too concerned with self or cultural preservation these days. Besides, the new iPhone is out and Honey Boo Boo is on the tube—so who has time to worry about depressing stuff like jihad and sharia? Better to bury our heads in the latest gadgets, watch the Kardashians, and have another brew. It'll all work out in the end: after all, in Barack we trust, and he shall protect and provide.

———

It's estimated that at least 10 percent (or roughly 157 million) of the world's Muslims subscribe to the al-Qaeda/MB model. The highly respected Middle East expert Daniel Pipes believes the number could be as high as 15 percent.[27] No matter how you slice it, that's a whole lot of violence-minded Islamic supremacists. And remember, most of these estimates came before the Islamist explosion (no pun intended) brought on by the so-called Arab Spring.

By the way, a good number of those terror-supporting, 10-to-15-percenters hail from countries like Egypt, Yemen, Somalia, and Pakistan—the same places that are providing a sizable chunk of the ever-increasing Muslim arrivals to America's shores, where a rapidly expanding mosque network awaits them with doors open and indoctrination program at the ready. A comprehensive 2011 study by the Washington-based Center for Security Policy found that 81 percent of U.S. mosques feature Islamic texts that promote violence.[28] According to the study's authors:

> Of the 100 mosques surveyed, 51% had texts on site rated as severely advocating violence; 30% had texts rated as moderately advocating violence; and 19% had no violent texts at all. Mosques that presented as Sharia adherent were more likely to feature violence-positive texts on site than were their non-Sharia-adherent counterparts. In 84.5% of the mosques, the imam recommended studying violence-positive texts. The leadership at Sharia-adherent mosques was more likely to recommend that a worshiper study violence-positive texts than leadership at non-Sharia-adherent mosques. Fifty-eight percent of the mosques invited guest imams known to

promote violent jihad. The leadership of mosques that featured violence-positive literature was more likely to invite guest imams who were known to promote violent jihad than was the leadership of mosques that did not feature violence-positive literature on mosque premises.[29]

The study found that one popular tract at U.S. mosques is none other than Muslim Brotherhood luminary Sayyid Qutb's *Milestones*, which has helped inspire the jihadist careers of al-Qaeda and many others. With incendiary literature like this so commonplace, is it any coincidence that several American mosques have been the scenes of terrorist plotting and fundraising over the past three decades?[30] Of course, the U.S. government's unspoken response to these frightening statistics is a collective shrug, followed by a phalanx of DOJ lawyers who'll ensure that still more mosques are built.

It's also no coincidence that pricey mega-mosques are popping up in areas with miniscule Muslim populations. Rest assured MAS officials knew full well the heavily Jewish demographics around Voorhies Avenue when they made the Sheepshead Bay purchase. It's also a certainty that the Islamists behind the sprawling Islamic Center of Murfreesboro were well aware of the reaction they would receive when they proposed building a mega-mosque in the devoutly Christian heart of the Bible Belt, right next to a Baptist church, no less. These moves are direct, calculated challenges by Islamists against Judeo-Christian civilization. As I wrote in *The Terrorist Next Door*:

> Throughout the West, mosques are often built right next door to, or directly across the street from, churches or synagogues. I've been to many mosques in the United States and Europe…and seen this phenomenon firsthand. Just for kicks, take a few minutes and check out the location of your local

mosques. I guarantee that many will either be in close proxim-
ity to Christian churches or synagogues, or will occupy buildings that are renovated churches. You'll also notice that
minarets at U.S. and European mosques will usually be built
higher than the steeples of neighboring churches. All this is no
accident. Again: domination is the name of the game, and
bigger is better.[31]

That helps explain why the Brotherhood-connected Muslim American
Society, around the same time it acquired the Sheepshead Bay property,
also attempted to purchase an empty Roman Catholic convent in nearby
Staten Island. That attempt failed, a rare victory for mosque opponents
in the Age of Obama. Not to worry, though: MAS simply opened a
mosque in another heavily Catholic neighborhood nearby—in a building
that formerly housed a Hindu temple.[32]

Yes, symbolism abounds with Islamists, as the proposed mega-
mosque at Ground Zero—sight of the most lethal jihadist attack in U.S.
history—clearly showed. It's no secret that historically, when Muslims
conquer an area, they build a large mosque to symbolize Islam's domination over the newly vanquished territory. It's the Islamic version of the
Roman victory arch. Some of the most notable examples are The Dome
of the Rock and the Al-Aqsa Mosque in Jerusalem—which are built atop
the remains of the ancient Jewish Temple—and the Ayasofya Mosque,
formerly known as the Hagia Sophia Church of Constantinople before
the Ottoman Turks conquered the city in 1453, mosque-ifying the church
and changing the city's name to Istanbul.

For the Muslim Brotherhood, building mosques in decidedly non-
Muslim areas is about much more than symbolism. According to the
Brotherhood's own documents, select "Islamic centers" are Ikhwan
beachheads and command centers. What follows is an eye-opening passage from the 1991 MB Explanatory Memorandum captured by FBI

agents (and detailed in Chapter Two) that reveals the integral role mosques play in the Brotherhood's strategic, long-range plan to conquer America. Yes, I said conquer:

Understanding the role and the nature of work of "The Islamic Center" in every city with what achieves the goal of the process of settlement:

The center we seek is the one which constitutes the "axis" of our Movement, the "perimeter" of the circle of our work, our "balance center", the "base" for our rise and our "Dar al-Arqam" to educate us, prepare us and supply our battalions in addition to being the "niche" of our prayers.

This is in order for the Islamic center to turn—in action not in words—into a seed "for a small Islamic society" which is a reflection and a mirror to our central organizations. The center ought to turn into a "beehive" which produces sweet honey. Thus, the Islamic center would turn into a place for study, family, battalion, course, seminar, visit, sport, school, social club, women gathering, kindergarten for male and female youngsters, the office of the domestic political resolution, and the center for distributing our newspapers, magazines, books and our audio and visual tapes.

In brief we say: we would like for the Islamic center to become "The House of Dawa" and "the general center" in deeds first before name. *As much as we own and direct these centers at the continent level, we can say we are marching successfully towards the settlement of Dawa' in [the United States].*

Meaning that the "center's" role should be the same as the "mosque's" role during the time of God's prophet, God's prayers and peace be upon him, when he marched to "settle" the Dawa' in its first generation in Madina. [F]rom the mosque, he drew the Islamic life and provided to the world the most magnificent and fabulous civilization humanity knew. *This mandates that, eventually, the region, the branch and the Usra turn into "operations rooms" for planning, direction, monitoring and leadership for the Islamic center in order to be a role model to be followed.*[33] [emphasis added]

Again, those are the words of a top Muslim Brotherhood strategist, lifted straight from an official Brotherhood document penned only two decades ago. Some conclusions here; first, judging by the massive spike in mosque building since the Explanatory Memorandum was written in 1991, the Ikhwan's strategy is working to perfection.

Second, we must assume that the countless Islamic centers nationwide that are currently run by MB-linked groups and individuals are indeed considered by the Brotherhood as "the axis" of its subversive movement, "the base for [the MB's] rise" in America and the "beehive[s]" from which jihadist "battalions" will be supplied in any future coordinated action by Islamists on U.S. soil. These mosques would also ostensibly serve as "operations rooms" in such a scenario. And in the Brothers' view, the more mosques they "own and direct," the closer they are to their goal of transforming America into an Islamic state governed by sharia—or, in the very least, into a weakened, divided state dotted with self-governing Islamic enclaves governed by sharia.

These are the only logical conclusions that can be reached after reading the passages I included above from the Brotherhood's own Explanatory Memorandum. In that document, the Ikhwan lay out their gradualist plan for Islamizing America. Just as I take the Iranian regime at face value when it vows to wipe Israel and the United States off the map, so, too, do I regard with utmost seriousness the Muslim Brotherhood's desire to conquer the United States from within, in part through rampant mosque building. The Muslim Brothers are ruthless, committed, and ideologically driven. They mean business.

Of course, to the complacent, ignorant, liberal mind, the Brotherhood's plans sound completely outlandish and improbable—just as Hitler's did in *Mein Kampf*. But in the Brothers' view, these plans are perfectly feasible—and even more important, they firmly *believe* that they can make them happen. With a combination of generous global financing, patience, discipline, and fanatical commitment, the Ikhwan fully expect to make their sharia dreams a reality one day in America—or across large swaths of it.

———

It was I, my cameraman, a mosque, and a snail. All we needed were a rabbi and a Catholic priest—but given the locale, their absence was understandable.

I had just recorded a few reporter standups in front of the Islamic Center of Munich when the little fellow with the big shell gamely inched his way across the street in front of the mosque.

I had expected the Muslim Brotherhood's first beachhead in the West to be located in a heavily Islamicized area of Germany's third-largest city. Instead, it was tucked away on a leafy side street in a quintessentially Bavarian neighborhood so quiet and nondescript that a snail's journey could capture your attention. If not for the minaret rising high above the skyline, you would never know the Islamic center was there.

But any notion that snails were the street's only occupants was quickly put to rest when a young, hijab-clad woman and a bearded Arab man emerged from the mosque and walked toward us.

"Can we help you?" the woman asked suspiciously. "I noticed that you were filming."

I'd been through this drill countless times in my years of investigating radical mosques throughout the United States and Europe. Usually, once someone inside the mosque notices that there is a TV crew filming out front, a few of the mosque's congregants will hop in a car and drive by slowly a few times, talking on cell phones as they survey the scene. They may stop and ask us some questions or they may call the police. At other times, the imam may emerge from the mosque after talking to the advance team and approach us with questions of his own.

At all times, the encounters are uncomfortable and it is made abundantly clear that your presence—and that of your TV camera—is not welcome. But it really doesn't matter. As long as you do not stand directly on the mosque's property, you are perfectly within your rights to film. When I relay that information to the mosque-eteers, I'm usually met with grim silence as they silently curse the infidels' laws. Why, if only sharia were in effect, I'd have my microphone cord wrapped around my throat in no time. The vibe in Munich was no different.

"We've gotten a lot of bad coverage over the past few years," the hijab-clad woman shared as her bearded companion looked on intently. "Someone wrote a book about the mosque that was filled with lies."

I politely explained that I had come to the Islamic Center of Munich to document its pivotal role in the rise of Islam—really, Islamism—in modern Europe. The conversation was brief and to the point, and my cameraman and I departed without incident, with instructions to call later when the mosque's imam would be around. In the end, I had no luck reaching him—the snail proved much more approachable.

The supposed "book of lies" the woman referred to is called *A Mosque in Munich*, written by Pulitzer Prize–winning journalist Ian Johnson. In reality, it is a meticulously researched and sourced work that chronicles how the Islamic Center of Munich—an unassuming building in a quiet residential neighborhood—served as the Muslim Brotherhood's main entry point to the West in the 1960s, '70s, and '80s.[34]

"It was a refuge for senior key Brotherhood people," Johnson told me when I interviewed him about the mosque in June 2012. "The board of directors was a who's who of radical Islam people from Pakistan, Egypt, Syria, North Africa, and of course, Europe…people who were key members of the mosque in Munich moved to the United States and helped set up and organize Islam there as well."

So we've noticed.

"It really had nothing to do with Munich," Johnson continued. "It wasn't a local mosque for local Muslims. It was a political entity that was trying to organize political Islam around the world."

It's no surprise, then, that the Brotherhood designated its senior operative in Europe, Said Ramadan—father of Tariq—as the point man for getting such an important project off the ground. Ramadan, who led the Brotherhood's operations against Israel during the Jewish State's 1948 war for independence, was well connected with the oil-rich Saudi Royal Family, and had close ties with Islamists around the world.

"Initially, the mosque was an idea of the West Germans, who wanted to harness Islam for their political purpose in the Cold War," Johnson told me. "But the project was taken over by young students, mostly members or sympathizers with the Muslim Brotherhood. They took over the project and brought in Said Ramadan."

From Munich, the Brotherhood's message spread throughout Europe and the United States via the construction of mosques and Islamic schools, or madrassahs, and the founding of numerous Islamic organizations and bodies, all frequently backed by generous Saudi funding. In short, the Saudis (and increasingly today, other oil-rich Gulf states like Qatar) provide the money and the Brotherhood and its sympathizers supply the imams, ideology, and literature in Islamic centers across the West. I've seen it myself firsthand in frequent visits to Western mosques, in the form of Korans printed in Saudi Arabia, libraries filled with the works of Brotherhood ideologues like Qutb and al-Banna, and pamphlets by

Brotherhood-linked groups like CAIR, the Islamic Society of North America, and the Muslim American Society.

The Saudi/MB nexus dates back to Egyptian president Gamal Abdel Nasser's brutal crackdown on the Brotherhood, which prompted many top Ikhwan leaders to flee Egypt for Saudi Arabia. According to French terrorism expert Gilles Kepel, a sometimes uneasy but mutually beneficial relationship soon developed between the two Salafi heavyweights:

> After being driven out of Egypt in the 1950s and '60s, many Brothers found shelter in Saudi Arabia. The Saud family establishment was extremely hesitant and cautious vis-à-vis the Brotherhood, and they were never permitted access to the core of Saudi society, and to deal openly with religious issues. This was seen as the exclusive domain of the Wahhabis, who had formed an alliance with the ruling family.
>
> But the Saudi elites nonetheless saw the Brothers as useful because—to put it bluntly—they could read and write. While the Wahhabi ulama were ill at ease in dealing with the modern world, the Brothers were well traveled and relatively sophisticated. They knew foreign languages and, unlike the Wahhabi ulama, were aware that the earth was not flat. The Brothers had been in jail, had political experience, and were skilled in modern polemics that resonated widely with ordinary people. Most of all, they had stood courageously against Saudi Arabia's archenemies, the communists and secularists, and were eager to continue the fight.... More broadly speaking, a cross-fertilization of ideas took place between the exiled Brotherhood and the austere teachings of what might be described as the Wahhabi rank and file.[35]

Interestingly enough, as the Brotherhood's power and influence has grown over the years, the Saudi government has developed second thoughts about getting so cozy with a revolutionary movement specializing in regime change. As far back as 2002, Saudi Prince Nayef bin Abdul Aziz, the Royal Kingdom's Interior Minister until his death ten years later, reportedly lamented:

> The Brotherhood has done great damage to Saudi Arabia.... All our problems come from the Muslim Brotherhood. We have given too much support to this group.... The Muslim Brotherhood has destroyed the Arab world.... Whenever they got into difficulty or found their freedom restricted in their own countries, Brotherhood activists found refuge in the Kingdom which protected their lives.... But they later turned against the Kingdom....[36]

The Saudis realize, particularly now, in the wake of the so-called Arab Spring, that the Brotherhood has the Land of the Two Holy Mosques firmly in its crosshairs. That's one reason why in 2011, as revolution was beginning to sweep across the Middle East and North Africa, the Saudi Ministry of Education reportedly banned the works of Brotherhood leading lights Hassan al-Banna and Sayyid Qutb from Saudi libraries and schools and began investigating how the MB was using Saudi cash to spread its influence throughout the Islamic world.[37]

The Saudis may be too late. The Saudi Royals, certainly no strangers to fomenting jihadist incitement and chaos worldwide themselves, could be on the verge of being outmaneuvered by the Ikhwan in a strange case of jihadi comeuppance. But even if the relationship between the Brotherhood and the Saudi Royals unravels completely, the mosqueing of the West promises to continue. Indeed, Qatar and other Gulf States—

awash in oil money, sympathetic to the Brotherhood's ideology, and eager to stay on the right side of what they see as a rising Islamist wave—are ready and willing to open their considerable coffers.

Another player to watch in the mosque-building game is the Brotherhood-allied regime in Turkey. In 1998, while serving as mayor of Istanbul, Turkey's current prime minister, Recep Tayyip Erdogan, was imprisoned for four months after reciting a poem that included the lines, "the mosques are our barracks, the domes our helmets, the minarets our bayonets, and the faithful our soldiers."[38] Bear in mind that his conviction for inciting religious hatred occurred during a period when Turkey was still a secular nation. Since 2002, when it came under the stewardship of Erdogan and his Justice and Development Party (known as AKP), Turkey has drifted gradually but unmistakably toward becoming an Islamist state that is hostile to Israel and the West and embraces Islamic terror groups like Hamas.

Erdogan's AKP has used stealthy, Brotherhood-like tactics not only to consolidate power at home but also to project influence abroad—particularly in Germany and Austria. It's estimated that some 3.5 million Turks now live in Germany, while Austria boasts a 225,000-strong Turkish Muslim population. In both countries, multi-million-dollar megamosques financed by the Islamist-led Turkish government are sprouting up at an alarming rate.

I paid a visit to one of them, the newly built Cologne Central Mosque, in June 2012. With its massive domed structure, the mosque complex—which cost $40 million to build and takes up an entire city block—resembles a nuclear reactor (as some locals unhappily observed to me). Those features, combined with two 100-foot-plus-high minarets that are visible from blocks away, have made the Cologne Central Mosque one of the largest mosques in all of Europe. So large, in fact, that on several occasions during my visit, I witnessed passersby stop in their tracks and crane their necks skyward to take pictures of the imposing structure.[39]

Could the Turkish government's selection of Cologne for this mega, mega-mosque have anything to do with the nearby presence of Cologne's famed High Cathedral of St. Peter? The cathedral is a world-renowned historic landmark and symbol of German Catholicism—it's also the largest Christian building north of the Alps. Sounds like a symbolic challenge by the Turks to me. So does the growth of Turkish-run mosques in small German towns that I visited around Cologne, like Herten and Reckling-hausen. In Herten, for instance—where the population is now 10 percent Turkish Muslim and the Muslim population rapidly growing—I spent time at a large structure that locals call the "Blue Mosque," where the parking lot was filled with cars decorated with Turkish flags. Can you say, "unassimilated?"

I found the same problem across the border in the traditional Austrian town of Bad Voslau (population: 11,000), just outside Vienna. Ottoman Turkish armies reached the gates of Vienna twice—in 1529 and 1683—before being turned back by Western forces. Today, the Turks are waltzing into and around Vienna with little resistance. In 2010, a mosque official gave me a tour of the new Islamic Cultural Center of Bad Voslau, an elaborate complex that stirred, you guessed it, heated opposition from non-Muslim locals when it was first proposed. As you also probably guessed, approval for the $1 million-plus mosque was rammed through anyway by cowering city officials. According to locals I interviewed, the new mosque had not improved relations between local Turks and non-Muslims, as officials had promised. In fact, Bad Voslau's Turkish community—which is based mainly in an enclave around the mosque—had reportedly become even more insular and disconnected from mainstream German society.[40] Such news must positively warm the hearts of non-Muslim residents of Lanham, Maryland, outside Washington, D.C., where the Turkish government announced in May 2013 that it would be financing a fif-teen-acre, $100 million mega-mosque.[41]

What's happening in Lanham, Herten, Bad Voslau, and cities and towns across the West where Muslim populations are growing and mega-mosques are popping up is a phenomenon I call the "enclave effect." A Muslim Brotherhood–linked Islamic center opens—the beachhead is established. And rest assured, if you build it, they will come. The crowds get bigger and bigger each Friday for prayers, as worshippers travel from miles away to attend the spanking new mosque—which was supposedly built to serve the needs of the *local* Muslim population. Women in hijabs and men in Islamic garb become common sights around the neighborhood and shops pop up everywhere with signs written in Arabic. Soon, local non-Muslims who've lived in the neighborhood for years begin to move out and Muslims move in. Before long, an enclave is established: self-segregated and centered around a large Islamic center, or "beehive," as the Brotherhood calls it.

In Europe, many of these areas become no-go zones for non-Muslims where sharia law is enforced and even police are hesitant to enter. The Tower Hamlets section of East London, in the shadow of London's financial district, is well on its way to no-go status. I've walked the streets of this area on numerous occasions, spent time in its outdoor bazaars, and observed the massive flow of South Asian immigrants in and out of Friday prayers at the vast East London Mosque—which serves as the de facto British base for Jamaat-e-Islami, considered the South Asian branch of the Muslim Brotherhood. It's a stunning experience to see thousands of predominantly Pakistani and Bangladeshi Muslims dressed in Islamic garb spill out of the mosque and swarm the streets of East London, giving the area a distinctly non-Western, Islamicized feel.

In the summer of 2011, Islamists (reportedly in league with our old friend Anjem Choudary), put up posters around Tower Hamlets proclaiming it a "Sharia Controlled Zone" where "Islamic rules are enforced."[42] They wasted no time in getting busy "enforcing." Harassment of non-Muslims—particularly homosexuals, women, and alcohol consumers—at the hands of self-proclaimed "Muslim London Patrols" has become a regular occurrence in East London.[43] Britain's *Daily Mail* newspaper described the Tower Hamlets borough's descent into Islamist oblivion in stark detail:

> This vocal minority, who are causing increasing concern in the area, have lent this corner of the capital a new nickname—the Islamic republic of Tower Hamlets.... Residents have grown used to the fact that the council-run libraries are stocked with books and DVDs containing the extremist rantings of banned Islamist preachers. There is a Muslim faith school where girls as young as 11 have to wear face-covering veils. There are plans to spend hundreds of thousands of pounds of municipal money to build a set of Islamic arches—the so-called "hijab gates," which would look like a veil—at either end of Brick Lane, which is packed with Indian restaurants and clothes shops.... Bangladeshi-born Lutfur Rahman became the first directly elected mayor of Tower Hamlets. He originally stood as the Labour candidate but was deselected by the party amid allegations about his links with an organisation known as the Islamic Forum of Europe (IFE). The fundamentalist group believes in jihad and Islamic sharia law, and wants to turn Britain and other European countries into Islamic republics.... Leaders of the group want to impose hardline views on local communities. With bitter irony, it is said to have pocketed £10 million from the taxpayer by attracting state grants designed to "prevent violent extremism." ... "You basically have a large umbrella Islamist group that appears to have almost a stranglehold over a major council in the East End of London," said one local resident.[44]

All of this is happening against the will of native-born British citizens. According to a 2013 report by a London think tank, British Future, one out of three Brits sees the culture clash between immigrants and indigenous Brits as the primary cause of the country's problems. Seventy-five percent would like to see a reduction in immigration, with 51 percent desiring a large reduction.[45] Granted, Britain gets immigrants from around the world, but it seems likely that Catholic Poles, French job seekers, or other Europeans are less difficult to assimilate than sharia-governed Muslims. Between 2001 and 2011, the Muslim population of the UK doubled—from 1.5 million to 2.7 million (and those numbers don't include the country's many undocumented Muslim immigrants). In only ten years, Muslims grew from 3 percent to nearly 5 percent of the British population.[46] And there are no signs that British politicians have the will or desire to turn off the spigot.

No less an authority than the Brotherhood's global spiritual leader, Sheikh Yusuf al-Qaradawi—a leading proponent of the enclave effect—has said "We will conquer *Europe*, we will conquer America, not through the sword but through *dawah [proselytizing]*."[47] Remember: mosques, enclaves, victory. Spend time in passport control at London's Heathrow Airport, where it is common to see long lines of Muslim women in niqabs and bearded men in Salafi garb entering the country, and you'll get a glimpse of Britain's future.

––––––

Whether the issue is socialism, spiraling debt, or cultural disintegration, it's useful to look to Europe today for signs of what is coming to the United States tomorrow. The culture clash with Islam is clearly much more advanced on the Old Continent, but the Muslim Brotherhood and its American acolytes are working diligently to change that—and with the active assistance of the Obama administration.

Essam El Erian, a top Brotherhood official from Egypt who is also vice chairman of the country's ruling Freedom and Justice Party, was able to see the fruits of his organization's labor up close in late 2012, when he paid a visit to Brooklyn's MB-linked Al-Noor Islamic School. As Erian was speaking before a standing-room-only crowd, he was interrupted by anti-Brotherhood protestors, who were swiftly ushered out of the building by the NYPD.[48]

A few miles away from that event, in Sheepshead Bay, residents of Voorhies Avenue can relate to the protestors' plight.

"Everybody in America needs to stand together in our small communities such as Sheepshead Bay," one of the Bay People told me as we stood in front of the soon-to-be-opened Muslim American Society mosque. "As Sheepshead Bay goes, so goes America. It's coming to you. I kid you not, it's going to be in your neighborhood."

CHAPTER NINE

OCCUPY SHARIA: WHY THE LEFT HELPS THE BROTHERHOOD

"I'm particularly enthralled by the Occupy movement."

While it was common to hear liberal Democrats make such statements throughout the fall of 2011 during Occupy Wall Street's anarchic heyday, Anas Al-Tikriti—the man behind this particular statement—is no garden variety American leftist. For starters, his father is the leader of Iraq's Muslim Brotherhood. And much like Tariq Ramadan, son of another Brotherhood icon, the younger Al-Tikriti is also well-connected in the global Ikhwan universe yet, of course, denies membership in the organization.

Interestingly enough, when I met with Al-Tikriti in June 2012, he had just returned from a tour of the Middle East and North Africa where he met with MB officials in various countries. But as we sat in his spacious West London office overlooking Wembley Stadium, our conversation about the so-called Arab Spring quickly turned from Tahrir Square to Zuccotti Park.

"We saw youngsters emerge on the streets of New York, and Philadelphia, and Washington, raising banners saying your dictator and your tyrant was Hosni Mubarak, our tyrant was Goldman Sachs," Al-Tikriti told me. "It's a different challenge, but it's sort of a same approach to how we can create a different reality."

Al-Tikriti was clearly drawing a parallel between the Arab Spring uprisings and the Occupy Wall Street protests that broke out in major American cities shortly thereafter. Occupy was undoubtedly influenced by the tumult that swept throughout the Muslim world—the OWS website goes so far as to declare that the movement uses "the revolutionary Arab Spring tactic,"[1] and leaders from the demonstrations in Tahrir Square even traveled to New York City to conduct a tactical "teach-in" for Occupiers.[2] But there are glaring differences. While both sides do indeed want "a different reality," as Al-Tikriti suggested, the Islamists who won out in countries like Egypt and Tunisia desired Islamic states ruled by sharia law. The Occupiers, on the other hand, are a chaotic collection of anarchists, communists, and hardcore leftists who seem to have no coherent message other than "Capitalism, America, Jews: bad." Several commentators noted the overt anti-Semitism of much of the Occupy crowd.[3,4,5] God and religion are otherwise nowhere in the equation, although anti-Americanism has certainly become a pseudo-religion for many on the hard Left—a demographic that is, in most cases, militantly atheistic.

So how could Anas Al-Tikriti—an Islamist whose organization, the London-based Cordoba Foundation, was described in 2008 by future British Prime Minister David Cameron (then a member of parliament) as a "front for the Muslim Brotherhood"[6]—be so enthusiastic about the godless Occupy movement? And how could he have spent the better part of a decade working closely with leftist factions in Great Britain to oppose, among other things, the Iraq War and Israel's supposed "occupa-tion" of Palestinian land? As we'll see in this chapter, the budding Islamo/ leftist alliance exists because the two factions share common enemies— America, Israel, capitalism, and Judeo-Christian, Western civilization— and not because Islamists are eager to ditch the Koran in favor of Marx and Engels. Nevertheless, judging by Al-Tikriti's ready response, it seemed he had been asked the question before.

"How could you bring a Muslim or a Jew or a Buddhist or a seeker or a Christian together—I mean, how on earth could you do that?" Al-Tikriti mused in a flawless English accent befitting a man who's lived in the UK for most of his life. "You do that by saying, 'Okay, fine what would you want for your children?' You'd find invariably, they all want the same thing.… And once you do that you sort of transcend beyond the ideol-ogy. You transcend to another level whereby you could get people to talk about the mechanics of how they want to achieve their dreams. Once that happens, there's a level of appreciation and understanding that would blow your mind away. But you have to do it in a safe structure and in a safe area, in a way that isn't threatening, isn't condescending, isn't under-mining and with absolute respect and equality."

Which means that sharia, with its inherent *disrespect* for opposing views, would presumably have to be checked at the door. Or not. During the run-up to the second Iraq War, left-wing activists from the Stop the War Coalition (STWC) reportedly acquiesced to the demands of the Muslim Association of Britain—a Brotherhood-linked organization Al-Tikriti would later lead—to have halal food and segregation by sex dur-ing joint meetings and demonstrations.[7] I'm sure the radical feminist element of the STWC was just thrilled with those ground rules. Align yourself with sharia-driven Islamic supremacists and prepare for some serious compromises—on your end, not theirs.

After hearing Al-Tikriti's flowery explanation of his partnership with the Left, with all the talk of transcendence and common dreams, it becomes clear why he's been dubbed "one of the shrewdest UK-based Brotherhood activists."[8] Al-Tikriti is nothing like Anjem Choudary, the notoriously in-your-face British Salafi firebrand. In fact, Al-Tikriti even took some swipes at Choudary's "extremism" during our interview. Rather, Al-Tikriti—again, much like Tariq Ramadan—has spent considerable time and effort painting himself to gullible Western elites as a sort of anti-Choudary, while at the same time selling the Brotherhood as the "moderate" Islamist elixir to the global al-Qaeda virus.

And it works. The local council for Tower Hamlets borough in East London awarded Al-Tikriti's Cordoba Foundation £34,000 (the equivalent of more than $50,000) in taxpayer money over the course of 2007 and 2008 as part of the British government's Preventing Violent Extremism program. Ironically enough, Al-Tikriti's organization promptly used some of the funding to organize a panel featuring a known supporter of said violent extremism named Dr. Abdul Wahid. The not-so-good doctor is a leader of the UK branch of Hizb ut-Tahrir, a charming Islamist outfit that former British Prime Minister Tony Blair once promised to ban (but never did) due to its very public support for suicide bombings, wiping Israel off the map, and reestablishing the global caliphate. In the wake of the Hizb ut-Tahrir travesty, the Cordoba Foundation was forced to give some of the grant money back, and Tower Hamlets council later reportedly terminated its agreement with Al-Tikriti and company altogether.[9]

The Cordob-ites, seemingly unfazed, went on to co-sponsor an August 2009 London event where American-born al-Qaeda cleric Anwar al-Awlaki was scheduled to deliver a live video address. Al-Awlaki was the chief English-language propagandist for al-Qaeda's Yemen branch and later had a hand in several terrorist plots against the United States, including the Fort Hood massacre and the failed Underwear Bomber plot on Christmas Day 2009, which helped earn al-Awlaki a spot on the U.S. "kill list" of global terrorists. Al-Awlaki's appearance was ultimately forbidden by the local council, and the Cordoba Foundation tried to distance itself from him and the event.[10] But Al-Tikriti's ties to al-Awlaki—who was killed by a U.S. drone strike in Yemen in 2011—were longstanding, including a 2003 lecture tour of the UK, sponsored by the Muslim Association of Britain, of which Al-Tikriti was already a prominent member if not leader.[11]

Yet Al-Tikriti continues to have access to power brokers in the international media and world governments. He writes frequently for Britain's leading leftist newspaper, *The Guardian*, and advises various European leaders on Islamic issues, invariably lobbying them to embrace the Muslim Brotherhood.

During our wide-ranging discussion, Al-Tikriti decried the fact that most Western governments refuse to talk (at least publicly) with the Brotherhood's Palestinian branch, the terror group Hamas, saying:

> The more you isolate [Hamas], the more they'll be isolated, and the more they'll think in an isolated fashion. It's in our favor to actually communicate with these people. In terms of violence, let me tell you this: we had a similar situation in Iraq. We had, still have, a very similar situation in Afghanistan. You occupy any people, it doesn't matter whether they're Arabs or non-Arabs, it doesn't matter whether they're Muslims or non-Muslims, they will rise against their occupiers. They will resist occupation. The use of violence is just one way of resisting. People are resisting in an array of ways … this is what I tell the American State Department when I meet with them and when I meet with the Foreign Office here in London and when I speak to Catherine Ashton [the European Union's top foreign policy representative] in Europe. What do you expect when … you clasp someone's neck and strangle? They will kick out … and they'll try to gouge your eyes, try to scratch your neck … and if they had something in their

hands, they would hit you with it. That's the nature of human beings. I condemn the shedding of blood from anyone, anywhere, on any side of the fence. But when we talk about violence being used by someone who's being cornered, humiliated, rid of every single shred of life, it would be totally bemusing not to understand why that person...is responding in the way that they are.

Al-Tikriti's comments here are useful for a few reasons. 1) He paints a picture of Hamas—and, by extension, jihadists in Iraq and Afghanistan who are "resisting" occupying U.S. forces—not as bloodthirsty fanatics and killers but as oppressed, desperate victims. Those Hamas suicide bombers blowing up Israeli women and children—what choice do they have? They were pushed to violence as a very last resort in their struggle to survive under a brutal occupation by foreign invaders! This is the standard Ikhwan "defensive jihad" talking point when it comes to their Hamas brothers, and Al-Tikriti has mastered it. As we'll see, so has a good chunk of the radical Left. 2) Al-Tikriti delivers his remarks in an impassioned, eloquent style that sounds perfectly legitimate and convincing to the uninformed listener, which, unfortunately, describes most of today's Western journalists, academics, and lawmakers.

It's not difficult to see why Al-Tikriti has made such inroads among Western elites. Young (in his mid-forties), energetic, witty, and surrounded by a polite, well-groomed staff at his Cordoba Foundation offices, he is quite likable and outgoing. During our time together, it became clear that he was a seasoned speaker, disciplined with his messaging, and comfortable in front of a camera. He has spent most of his life living in Britain and is intimately acquainted with the local culture and customs (he spoke fondly of the country's weather and football teams as we chatted off camera). Because of all this, Al-Tikriti is walking catnip for agenda-driven, mainstream media types eager to portray Islam in the most positive light possible, or for Western government officials desperate to find devout Muslims who "understand the Islamic street" yet are non-threatening—at least on the surface.

Al-Tikriti also proved irresistible to radical leftists who were seeking a Muslim partner to help front massive anti-Iraq war demonstrations in Britain in 2002 and 2003. When the Stop the War Coalition (STWC) wanted to add a Muslim presence to its lily-white, socialist- and communist-dominated ranks for the sake of "diversity," it was impressed by Al-Tikriti and the Muslim Association of Britain organizing a large anti-Israel protest in London that attracted thousands of demonstrators (some of whom were waving the flags of Hamas and Hezbollah). Acceding to some sharia rules in order to form a partnership with the MAB seemed a small price to pay for adding Muslim allies to the coalition.

The seemingly unlikely pairing went on to lead several large demonstrations in London, with the MAB pushing the Palestinian issue alongside opposition to "Bush's war." According to the 2009 book, *The New Muslim Brotherhood in the West*, written by Italian terrorism expert Lorenzo Vidino: "MAB leaders, who have often openly expressed support for Hamas, imposed as a slogan for the movement the dual statement, 'No war in Iraq, justice for Palestine.'"[12] They received no argument from the STWC, which heartily agreed with the MAB's anti-Israel sentiments.

The STWC/MAB partnership—which drew hundreds of thousands of protestors to its events[13]—was a seminal one for the budding Islamo-leftist axis in the West. The two sides capitalized on their momentum and deepened their relationship further by forming a new political party in Great Britain called RESPECT/The Unity Coalition that participated in national and European elections in 2005. The party ran on a platform of socialism, pro-Palestinian activism, and opposition to the Iraq War. Its candidates, which included Al-Tikriti, fared poorly overall, with only George Galloway—a Marxist who has traveled to Gaza to publicly embrace Hamas leaders—winning a seat in parliament.

While RESPECT has mostly fizzled, its formation and continued existence show that committed Islamists and radical leftists are ready and willing to put aside sharp differences—at least temporarily—to further their shared hostility to Western capitalism, Western power, and, at bottom, Judeo-Christian, Western civilization.

Of his efforts to sell Western governments on engaging the Muslim Brotherhood, Al-Tikriti told me, "I think it's a very, very valid strategy. I think it will work, and I think it will be in [the West's] best interest." But it's hard to believe that Al-Tikriti or the radical Left have the West's best interests at heart.

═══

Anas Al-Tikriti is far from alone among prominent Islamists in his vocal support for Occupy Wall Street. Admiration for the OWS movement has been widespread among Islamic terror groups and non-violent Islamist organizations alike and cuts across Sunni/Shia sectarian lines.

IRAN

During an October 2011 address broadcast on Iranian state television, Supreme Leader Ali Khamenei donned the turban of Occupy Ayatollah, calling the protests that had started in New York City and spread to other American cities a harbinger of the West's demise. "They may crack down on this movement but cannot uproot it," Khamenei promised. "Ultimately, it will grow so that it will bring down the capitalist system and the West."

Not to worry, Mr. Ayatollah: our leaders are accomplishing that feat without Occupy's help.

Khamenei also railed against "the prevalence of top-level corruption, poverty and social inequality in America" and the supposed "heavy-handed treatment of [Occupy] demonstrators by U.S. officials."[14] Because as we all know, Iran treats its demonstrators with kid gloves.

Khamenei's statements were echoed by groups of Iranian university students who held pro-Occupy protests in front of the Swiss Embassy in Tehran (which hosts Iran's U.S. Interests Section). The students—who were undoubtedly directed by the Iranian regime—shouted anti-capitalist slogans, waved placards declaring themselves part of the "99 percent" (the OWS rallying cry) and burned American and Israeli flags.[15] Tehran University later hosted a contingent of U.S. college professors—including one Heather Gautney, a self-described "Occupy Wall Street activist" who teaches sociology at Fordham University—at a two-day conference supporting OWS. "I got the sense that they were trying to confirm impressions that they had, confirm things that they had read in the press," Gautney said of her hosts.[16]

Or more likely, they were helping promote the Iranian regime's propaganda, as when General Masoud Jazayeri, a top commander in Iran's Revolutionary Guard Corps, told an Iranian state-run news agency: "The failure of the U.S. president to resolve the Wall Street crisis will turn this economic movement into a political and social movement protesting the very structure of the U.S. government. A revolution and a comprehensive movement against corruption in the U.S. is in the making. The last phase will be the collapse of the Western capitalist system." Jazayeri called OWS an "American Spring," comparing it to the uprisings surging across the Middle East and North Africa.[17]

Wishful thinking on Jazayeri's part, as OWS eventually torpedoed itself amid spasms of rampant violence and debauchery by its adherents toward the end of 2011 and into 2012. If nothing else, though, his comments reflect how pleased the Iranians were to see the Great Satan and its infidel capitalist system under assault from within. In essence, the Occupiers were doing the Iranian regime's dirty work for it. It's no wonder Iranian president Mahmoud Ahmadinejad reportedly sought a meeting with Occupy leaders in New York during his 2012 trip to the UN General Assembly[18] and gave a shout-out to "the 99 percent" during his speech at Turtle Bay.[19]

HEZBOLLAH

Given that the paramilitary terror organization Hezbollah was created by Iran and serves as the mullahs' chief striking arm around the world, it comes as no surprise that the so-called "Party of God" was also on board with the Occupy movement. The Hezbollah website almoqawama.org ran glowing articles about OWS during the fall of 2011.[20] Occupy DC reportedly returned the favor, flying Hezbollah flags (and those of al-Qaeda and Hamas) at one of its rat-infested encampments in the nation's capital.[21]

That the Occupiers stood in solidarity with murderous terrorist groups should come as no surprise: one of the hallmarks of Occupy "zones" nationwide was their rampant violence. From Portland, Oregon, to Oakland, California, from Denver to Baltimore to New York City, OWSers clashed violently with police (and in some cases, each other) and had to be forcibly evicted from the tent cities they had set up. The situation in Oakland turned into near anarchy at times, as Occupiers ransacked the city's downtown area, stormed City Hall, attacked police, and shut down a local port in a series of uprisings over a period of months.[22] There were also several reports of women being sexually assaulted at OWS sites around the country.[23] By the time the OWS protests had died down in early 2012, thousands of Occupiers nationwide had been arrested for various forms of criminal activity. Bet you didn't hear about that on CNN, MSNBC, CBS, or other mainstream media news outlets that were busy lionizing the noble Occupiers while demonizing the Tea Party as dangerous, racist kooks.

Speaking of Occupy and terrorism, an organizer from Occupy Cleveland was arrested in May 2012 along with four cohorts (all of whom were also linked to the OWS movement) for plotting to blow up a bridge outside Cleveland as a supposed statement against the U.S. government. Columnist Rich Lowry correctly branded the Cleveland Five, "the left's homegrown terrorists...the pathetic sons of Occupy—rootless, underemployed, drunk on a sophomoric radicalism, alienated from the American system to the point of lawlessness.... If the Cleveland Five had been right-wing haters of the government, everyone in America would know their names by now. Instead, they're a neglected sign of what nastiness lurks in Occupy's fetid ideological stew."[24]

Make no mistake: the so-called Cleveland Five are the type of dark, disturbed souls at the very forefront of the Occupy movement. Yet President Obama readily embraced OWS in the fall of 2011 when it was at its anarchic height. "We are on their side," he told ABC News.[25] Ever the class warrior, he also opined approvingly that Occupy "protesters [we]re giving voice to a more broad-based frustration about how [America's] financial system works."[26] Officials in the Obama White House even adopted Occupy's "99 percent vs. the wealthy 1 percent" rhetoric.[27]

Just as violent Salafists are the Muslim Brotherhood's foot soldiers in Egypt and elsewhere, ready and willing to crack heads to enforce the sharia agenda (and giving the Brothers plausible deniability in the process), the Occupiers played a similar "dirty work" role for the Obama administration. Along with labor unions and radicals like the New Black Panther Party, the Occupiers used violence and intimidation in an effort to push the administration's class warfare agenda and divide Americans along class (and in the case of the Panthers, racial) lines in the run up to the 2012 election. If things got too hairy, "mainstream" Democrat politicians could always distance themselves from Occupy and rely on their media allies to not make a peep. The strategy clearly worked. From his perch in the Oval Office, Mr. Divide-and-Conquer himself looked on and smiled.

HAMAS

In September 2012, Ismail Haniyeh, Hamas's top political leader, drafted a statement of Hamas support for OWS. It was supposed to be read by Haniyeh's friend, the radical lawyer Stanley L. Cohen, at an Occupy protest coinciding with the start of the Democratic National Convention in Charlotte. According to the leftist, pro-Palestinian website Mondoweiss, Cohen ultimately did not end up reading the letter due to "extenuating circumstances." The text of Haniyeh's anti-American screed, however, was posted online and lined up perfectly with the unholy spirit of Occupy Wall Street:

> I send the heartfelt greetings of the Palestinian people, as we salute you in your fight against the American military machine, against its secrets and lies, and against its vision of an American world order maintained through coercion and control. You bring your protest straight to the heart of the political system, there in Charlotte, and we are there with you in spirit, we Occupy Charlotte with you!
>
> Gaza and the West Bank stand in solidarity with you, as we have stood against US military might for decades—we have been on the ugly receiving end of American policy for so long, fighting for our own freedom against Israeli and US control, that to know of your efforts gladdens our hearts....
>
> Like you, we want a stop to the endless wars promoted or fought by the United States; no more attacks on the Muslim world by American troops! We Palestinians want people to know the truth about US power, and its dirty deeds exposed

to the sunlight. Palestinians hail all those courageous truth-tellers and activists everywhere who have shattered the veil of secrecy, for making information public at terrible risk to themselves and their families, so that those who struggle for independence can know the truth.

Our struggle against Israel and its massive, high-tech military bought and paid for by US taxpayers will not be defeated.... Palestine will have justice, and it will need people of good conscience in America to stand up for us, and for the truth. Your presence and your voices there in Charlotte give American voters an alternative to the corrupt narrative of US power—you say, there is another way, there is another story, and you challenge the official secrets and lies of this government.

The American political process is now a global process—and we watch it from our corner of the world, waiting for some sign of change at the top. But meanwhile, it is the growing force from below that gives us hope. This movement is a global movement—our numbers are vast, we are legion, and we do not forget.[28]

Haniyeh's letter sounds like it could have been written by Michael Moore. In short, America is a militaristic bully, and its capitalist-imperialist system must be abolished. This is the kind of rhetoric that makes Occupiers swoon, especially when delivered by a non-white, "oppressed" Third Worlder like Haniyeh. And Haniyeh knows his audience: he intentionally avoids any mention of Islam lest he turn off Occupy's decidedly irreligious rabble. In addition, the way he melds America and Israel as joint capitalist-imperialist oppressors of the Palestinian "struggle" (just as Anas al-Tikriti and his ilk have done in Britain) is seamless. And with his closing statement that conjures images of a unified global resistance—

a revolutionary movement that transcends race or religion—he appeals directly to the "fight the power" ethos that is the very essence of the Left's destructive, utopian fantasies.

In short, Haniyeh's letter is pretty darn brilliant strategically, given its purpose: to rally American leftists who share Hamas's disdain for America, Israel, and capitalism, making them useful idiots in the Islamist cause. What else would you expect from the leader of the Muslim Brotherhood's Palestinian branch?

Haniyeh wasn't the first Islamic terrorist to use rhetoric designed to appeal to the American hard Left. While al-Qaeda was strangely silent on Occupy Wall Street, its leaders have weighed in on other pet leftist causes. In recent years, both current al-Qaeda leader Ayman al-Zawahiri and former AQ kingpin Osama bin Laden gave addresses blaming the United States for global warming, and Zawahiri not only railed against former President George W. Bush, the Iraq War, and the treatment of terrorists at Guantanamo Bay, he's also slammed the United States as a hopelessly racist society and referred to Colin Powell and Condoleezza Rice as "house slaves" working in the Bush administration.[29]

AMERICAN ISLAMISTS

On November 18, 2011, the New York branch of the Council on American-Islamic Relations (CAIR), helped organize a Friday prayer rally and march in lower Manhattan to protest police surveillance of Muslims. Some five hundred Muslims gathered in Foley Square and were later joined by at least fifty members of Occupy Wall Street in marching on police headquarters and chanting for NYPD Commissioner Ray Kelly's firing. Protestors waved signs that read, "NYPD Watches Us. Who Watches NYPD?"[30]

CAIR, though it poses as a mainstream, moderate Islamic organization, is, as we've seen, a Hamas-linked group that was named as an unindicted co-conspirator in the largest terrorism financing trial in

American history. CAIR doesn't like the United States in its current form. Ultimately, it would like the United States to be governed by sharia. So naturally, it gravitates to others who feel the same way—not about sharia, but about turning the existing order in America on its head. Hence, CAIR's relationship with Occupy Wall Street.

A few weeks before the anti-NYPD rally, CAIR-NY helped lead a Muslim prayer service in Manhattan's Zuccotti Park—the epicenter of Occupy Wall Street—complete with dozens of men in Muslim garb and women in hijabs chanting "We are the 99 percent." According to the Investigative Project on Terrorism, the Muslim demonstrators also chanted, "American Muslims have to stand with Occupy Wall Street," and portrayed themselves as victims of American racism and "Islamo-phobia."[31] It's the kind of language the Left laps up—and Islamists know it. So it should have come as no surprise when a Muslim lawyer who'd worked on cases with CAIR turned up as a leader of Occupy Orlando.[32] Occupy had been occupied.

CAIR was joined in its support for OWS by other well-known American Brotherhood front groups. The youth branch of the Muslim American Society (MAS)—an organization created by MB members—held an event in Zuccotti Park to stand in solidarity with "the protestors of Occupy Wall Street." The MAS flyer for the event declared the group "members of the 99 percent" and claimed it was Muslims' duty to "stand up against social and economic injustice."[33]

Likewise, the Islamic Circle of North America—another radical Brotherhood front closely linked to MAS—released a November 2011 press release in support of Occupy Wall Street that invoked classic leftist class warfare rhetoric:

> Real progress and development of a country depends on prosperity of society as a whole, not just that of a selected portion of society. Yet the income gap between the rich and the poor

continues to grow, and uneconomic recovery across the country has been uneven and unstable at best. Corporations are ruthlessly cutting jobs, leaving 10% of the entire population unemployed while Wall Street enjoys huge bonuses.

A report...by the Congressional Budget Office found that the average after-tax income for the top 1 percent of U.S. households had increased by 275 percent over the past three decades. Middle-income households saw just a 40 percent rise. For those at the bottom of the economic scale, the jump was 18 percent.

Despite government aid during the credit crisis, banks have been indifferent to the suffering of distressed homeowners and have made it extremely difficult to refinance homes. They have also restricted credit to small and mid-size businesses, essentially forcing them to close. Any attempt to improve the situation has been shot down by the Wall Street sponsored lobby.

ICNA sympathizes with the message of Occupy Wall Street protesters and supports their cause. These protesters are raising legitimate concerns regarding income disparity, unemployment and the state of our economy that cannot be ignored. As American Muslims we stand in solidarity with them across the country.[34]

Sounds a lot like the campaign ads run by the Obama administration during the 2012 election. Yet it was written by an Islamist organization that considers the Left as a bunch of godless infidels and libertines. Go figure.

———

Islamists weren't alone in pledging their full-throated support for Occupy Wall Street. A comprehensive list of Occupy boosters compiled by the conservative website Pajamas Media revealed that virtually every nefarious anti-American, anti-freedom dictatorship or movement you can think of lined up behind OWS. The list includes the North Korean regime, the Chinese Communist Party, the late Venezuelan tyrant Hugo Chavez, Nation of Islam leader Louis Farrakhan, the Communist Party USA, the American Nazi Party, and ex-Klansman David Duke, among others.[35]

From black separatists to white separatists, from Reds to brownshirts, from Marxists to Muslim extremists, all can agree on one thing: they *are* the 99 percent; they eagerly joined President Obama, Nancy Pelosi, and Joe Biden as supporters of the Occupy movement.

Interestingly, they offered no such support for the Tea Party movement. CAIR Executive Director Nihad Awad, for example, said in 2010 that, "the Tea Party and the Republican Party have given the green light for...people to defame and stereotype Muslims, and...these have led to violence against Muslims."[36] If you haven't heard of Tea Party violence against Muslims, that's because there wasn't any. But the reason why Islamists can come together with Occupiers and not Tea Party folks is because the Tea Partiers love America, venerate the Constitution and free markets, and want to make America stronger and more prosperous; the Occupiers hate America, loathe the free market, want to weaken the United States, overthrow capitalism, and divide the spoils among themselves. Islamists hate capitalism as much as any socialist Occupier does, because they seek to install a global Islamic financial system based on sharia precepts. Additionally, the Islamists and the radical Left both regard the United States—the standard bearer and chief protector of Judeo-Christian Western Civilization—as the Great Satan that must be destroyed.

So the next time you're tempted to scratch your head when you see Islamic totalitarian Mahmoud Ahmadinejad linking arms with secular Latin American Marxists, just remember: the enemy of my enemy is my friend. This phrase has never been more fitting than in the case of the alliance between hardcore Islamists and the hardcore Left. These two disparate, destructive factions certainly don't agree on everything, but they certainly do agree that the United States, its military, its Constitution, its capitalist economic system, its ally Israel, and its observant Jews and Christians are enemies to be destroyed.

I've seen this combined leftist-Islamist hatred of America and Israel, Christians and Jews, up close on a few occasions, most memorably, in a speech I delivered at Portland State University in May 2012. The PSU chapter of Christians United for Israel (CUFI), which had invited me to speak, placed posters around campus to promote the event. The posters featured American and Israeli flags, plus my picture. A few days prior to the event, the posters were vandalized, with pro-Palestinian slogans and swastikas scrawled over the Star of David. Other flyers around campus were torn down.

That was just a foretaste of what I would experience at the event. As I prepared to speak, more than fifty demonstrators filed into the room with masking tape over their mouths as a "silent protest" against lil' ol' me. According to a mass email that was sent out by a pro-Palestinian student group on the night before my appearance, I was a "fundamentalist, right-wing pundit" whose "racism," "hatred," "Islamophobia," and "intolerance" were not welcome at Portland State University. But apparently, defacing the Star of David with swastikas is perfectly acceptable.

My direct and immediate challenge to the protestors to debate me on the facts went unheeded. Instead, they stood up in unison and filed out of the room about twenty-five minutes into my speech, with a few waving anti-Israel signs and shouting mindless slogans about Israeli "apartheid" as they left. So the protest itself was completely ineffectual. But the makeup of the protestors was revealing: hijab and skullcap-clad Muslims, obviously very serious about their Islam, flanked by aging, tie-dyed ex-hippies and smarmy young leftists who looked like refugees from the local Occupy camp. It was the worst of both worlds and a telling sign of where things are headed.

These two divergent groups had joined together at PSU not because of any genuine camaraderie but due solely to their shared hatred for America, Israel, observant Jews, and professing Christians. Their protest was peaceful this time, but another taste the Islamists and the radical Left share is the taste for violence. Not only did the radical Left give a pass to the communist regimes of the twentieth century that killed about 100 million people—because you can't make a progressive utopian omelet without breaking a few eggs—but leftist radicals take it for granted that their causes merit violence, almost as much as any Islamist does.

Here on American soil, we saw the Weather Underground movement murder civilians and carry out terrorist attacks against U.S. government targets during the 1960s, 1970s, and 1980s in the name of the same sort of revolutionary Marxism that the Occupiers espouse today. That's the same Weather Underground, incidentally, that boasted Bill Ayers and Bernardine Dohrn among its ranks. If those names don't ring a bell, they should. In 1995, the two former domestic terrorists—now comfortably ensconced as college professors and still unrepentant about their crimes— held a fundraiser for Barack Obama at their Chicago home that marked the beginning of his foray into politics.[37]

The radical Left has a weakness for certain sorts of murderers. When disgruntled former LAPD officer Christopher Dorner went on a killing spree in February 2013—murdering four people, including two police officers, before dying himself during a standoff with police—he was cheered by Occupy Los Angeles, which posted a photo of the cold-blooded murderer on its official website with the caption, "Rest in Power Chris Dorner: Assassinated by The Police for Trying To Expose LAPD Corruption."[38]

That the anarchic miscreants of Occupy LA would lionize a demonic killer like Dorner, who left behind a manifesto revealing his hard-left worldviews (funny, the mainstream media didn't have much to say about that), came as no surprise. The Left's fetishes for revolution and totalitarianism, however, do not only exist on its fringes. Take Marc Lamont Hill, for instance. An associate professor of English education at Columbia University and a regular guest on cable news programs, he went on CNN and portrayed Dorner's trail of dead bodies as "kind of exciting":

> This has been an important public conversation that we've had, about police brutality, about police corruption, about state violence. As far as Dorner himself goes, he's been like a real life superhero to many people. Now don't get me wrong, what he did is awful, killing innocent people is bad.... Many people aren't rooting for him to kill innocent people, they're rooting for somebody who was wronged to get a kind of revenge against the system. It's almost like watching *Django Unchained* in real life. It's kind of exciting.[39]

Hill apparently believes it's an absolute gas to see innocent people slaughtered by a psychotic killer. Salon.com and Alternet, two widely read online leftist publications that ran stories sympathetic to Dorner, seemed to agree with Hill's glowing assessment. Salon, for instance, ran a piece called "Were Dorner's Complaints Legitimate?" that essentially went on to answer in the affirmative.[40]

But nothing compared to the Left's angst when Venezuelan tyrant Hugo Chavez died of cancer in March 2013. Chavez, a close ally of Iran and Hezbollah and an avowed enemy of the United States, was mourned by the likes of the BBC, which announced his death in solemn tones,[41] and the widely read liberal Huffington Post website, which one writer dubbed a "Hugo Chavez Fanpage" for its fawning remembrances of

Chavez' supposed legacy. "Hugo Chavez was a man of many talents," read one top story at HuffPo. "He played ball, sang songs, pulled out pistols, and got down and groovy—and that is precisely how we'll remember the Venezuelan leader."[42] Personally, I'll remember Chavez as a crude Marxist thug who jailed political opponents, shut down opposition media, funded Colombian narco-terrorists, and openly rooted for the demise of the United States and Israel, while working closely with the Iranian regime to help make it happen. But to each his own, I guess.

Celebrity leftists like Sean Penn, Oliver Stone, Michael Moore, and former President Jimmy Carter also praised the late dictator,[43] and professional race-baiter Jesse Jackson Sr. led a delegation to Chavez' funeral in Caracas, saying he was "deeply saddened" by the tyrant's passing.[44] Another Democrat, New York Congressman Gregory Meeks, also attended the funeral, and his Democrat colleague, New York Congressman José Serrano, mourned Chavez from afar, tweeting, "Hugo Chavez was a leader that understood the needs of the poor. He was committed to empowering the powerless. R.I.P. Mr. President."[45]

Just as elements of the Left recast a brutal despot like Hugo Chavez as a devoted champion of workers and the poor, or a crazed murderer like Christopher Dorner as a sort of heroic whistleblower fighting a corrupt system, so, too, do they excuse Islamic suicide bombers as oppressed victims rising up against occupation and imperialism.

In his landmark 2004 book, *Unholy Alliance: Radical Islam and the American Left,* conservative commentator David Horowitz writes that the Islamo-leftist alliance, like the Hitler-Stalin pact of 1939 that brought together two divergent ideologies, seems incomprehensible on the surface. In the late 1930s, American leftists liked to call themselves "anti-fascists." Yet, they turned on a dime when Josef Stalin signed the non-aggression pact with Hitler's National Socialist regime. As Horowitz explains, "When it came to choosing between the interests of the Soviet state and their 'progressive agendas'—even their opposition to Fascism—American

Communists and their progressive allies did not hesitate to choose the former." This same impulse, Horowitz writes, animated leftist opposition to the war against the Taliban in Afghanistan in the wake of 9/11. By extension, it drives the broader leftist romance with Islamists today. "The readiness of a large segment of the Left to actively oppose America's war against the Taliban indicated that their opposition to America was greater than their support for 'progressive values,'" Horowitz notes. "In short, they had become 'frontier guards' for any opponent of American power."[46]

And what better way to confront American power than to demonize the U.S. military? On the very day U.S. forces invaded Iraq in 2003, a leftist (what else?) anthropology professor named Nicholas De Genova made abundantly clear which side he wanted to win, telling an audience of three thousand at Columbia University, "I personally would like to see a million Mogadishus." De Genova was referring to the slaughter of nineteen U.S. servicemen in Somalia during 1993's Black Hawk Down incident. He added:

> U.S. patriotism is inseparable from imperial warfare and white supremacy. U.S. flags are the emblem of the invading war machine in Iraq today. They are the emblem of the occupying power. The only true heroes are those who find ways that help defeat the U.S. military.[47]

"C'mon, Stakelbeck," you might be tempted to say. "This De Genova guy is just another wacked out, lefty college professor. He's in no way representative of the average liberal, who loves and supports the U.S. military." Oh, really? Have you tuned in to that bastion of mainstream liberal thought, MSNBC, lately? One week before Memorial Day 2012, MSNBC host Chris Hayes said he was "uncomfortable" calling fallen American military members, "heroes" because such a phrase, according to the painfully effete Hayes, would be "rhetorically proximate to justi-fications for more war." Whatever that means. Hayes later apologized for his comments after receiving a firestorm of criticism. But a few months later, his fellow leftist MSNBC colleague, Melissa Harris-Perry, doubled down, telling viewers of her weekend show—correctly—that the U.S. military is "despised as an engine of war by many progressives."[48] Funny, Islamists feel the same way. No wonder the two sides get along so well.

Virtually all of the above-named examples, whether they excused the murderous behavior of Christopher Dorner, exalted the tyranny of Hugo Chavez, or castigated the U.S. military, hail from mainstream institutions. Some work for major television networks, others for widely read publica-tions, and still others for prestigious Ivy League universities. Some have Oscar-winning Hollywood pedigrees and one was a former American president. This is extremely telling because it shows how the so-called fringe has become mainstream in the Democrat party—as President Obama and other leading Democrats' support for Occupy Wall Street showed.

Remember, these are the same Democrats who, at their national convention in 2012, booed lustily at the suggestion that God and an undivided Jerusalem should be included in their party's official platform. And the same Democrats who, from President Obama on down, have gone all in with the Muslim Brotherhood. Presidents Harry Truman and John F. Kennedy, while not perfect by any stretch of the imagination, would not recognize their party today. Both were military veterans, defenders of America's national interests, and staunch anti-communists. Henry "Scoop" Jackson, Daniel Moynihan, and other prominent, hawk-ish Democrats of previous eras would find that today the national secu-rity wing of the Democrat Party does not exist.

Instead, Democrats are falling over themselves to embrace and appease an Islamist enemy that seeks America's destruction. This disturb-ing reality was on full display in March 2011 when New York Congress-man Peter King had the temerity—ten years after 9/11 and a decade into a supposed war against Islamist extremism—to hold the first of what would be a series of hearings on Muslim radicalization in America. King, who was then chairman of the House Homeland Security Committee, was blasted, one after another, by his Democrat colleagues on the panel as a bigoted, Islamophobic McCarthyite for daring to suggest that the American Muslim community might have a terrorism problem (the arrests of dozens upon dozens of American Muslims on terror charges over the past few years clearly bears King's argument out).

I attended that first hearing and remember leaving it extremely discouraged. By the end of the proceedings, it was clear that an entire side of the political aisle had decided to not only take a pass on confronting the Islamist enemy, but to attack anyone who dared even broach the subject. Their targets included Dr. Zuhdi Jasser, a devout Muslim and true moderate who bravely testified about the danger of the Muslim Brotherhood in America only to be slammed by the Democrats on the panel as little more than a pawn of conservatives and Islam haters.

Essentially, the Democrats on the panel were willfully running interference for Islamists. To see it played out, live and in person, was a truly disturbing experience, given that the Islamists themselves see their conflict with America as an existential struggle. The spectacle was complete when one of the witnesses, Minnesota Congressman Keith Ellison, a not-so-moderate friend of Muslim Brotherhood–linked groups like CAIR, began weeping theatrically during his testimony as he recounted the story of a Muslim first responder in New York City who died on 9/11.

Ellison, the first Muslim congressman in American history, turned on the waterworks while trying to make a point that his co-religionists were being unfairly stigmatized as being hostile to America. Perhaps he should have a chat with his Democrat colleague in the House, Indiana Representative André Carson—who happens to be the nation's second elected Muslim congressman. During a 2012 speech given to the Brotherhood-tied

Islamic Circle of North America (ICNA), Carson didn't seem very fond of the United States in its current form. He openly fantasized about a female Muslim president "with a hijab on" in the Oval Office[49] and suggested that America's school system should be patterned after Islamic madrasas.[50] The people of Indiana's seventh district, who elected Carson to Congress, must be so proud.

Ellison and Carson, much like Anas Al-Tikriti and his brethren in Great Britain, manage to seamlessly blend their Islamism with hard-left policies. The reason it works, despite obvious contradictions, is simple: at the end of the day, both the Islamists and the Left seek to unravel the traditional fabric of the United States (and Great Britain); this is the ultimate culture war, and it is why Islamists have no trouble collaborating with leftists who celebrate social liberalism that the Islamists otherwise oppose. Islamists take advantage of the Left's moral relativism, its default approval for non-Western, non-Judeo-Christian forces, and its tendency to pathologize any opposition to its causes as bigotry and "phobia." For instance, Islamists and leftists alike applauded in August 2011 when the George Soros–funded Center for American Progress—which *Time* magazine once dubbed "Obama's Idea Factory in Washington"[51]—released a study called "Fear, Inc.: The Roots of the Islamophobia Network in America."

The 132-page hit job targeted a long list of terrorism and Islam experts, like Steven Emerson and Daniel Pipes, as well as conservative voices in the media and political realms, including Sean Hannity, Glenn Beck, Rush Limbaugh, Newt Gingrich, *National Review*, and myself, for supposedly stirring up anti-Muslim hatred.[52] Interestingly enough, those same claims were echoed one year later in a similar report by the Muslim Public Affairs Council (MPAC), yet another Brotherhood-influenced group that is a favorite of the Obama administration. MPAC's founder, Salam Al-Marayati, was even sent by the Obama State Department to represent the United States at a 2012 human rights conference in Warsaw, despite his past support of Hezbollah and his claim—later recanted—that Israel was behind the 9/11 attacks.[53]

The report by Al-Marayati's organization aimed to "expose" what it called the "Top 25 Pseudo-Experts on Islam." I was proud to once again make the list, along with courageous colleagues like Frank Gaffney, David Horowitz, Brigitte Gabriel, and others. MPAC's case against our expertise rested on the fact that most of us do not hold degrees in Islamic studies.[54] That is why, according to MPAC, retired General Jerry Boykin—a highly decorated, founding member of Delta Force who has stared down Islamic jihadists face to face in hotspots around the world—is not qualified to discuss the Islamist threat. Neither, apparently, is Dr. Zuhdi Jasser, a practicing Muslim and medical doctor also targeted in MPAC's diatribe. As for myself, I may not have learned about the finer points of Islam from a Marxist, anti-American college professor who applauds suicide bombers, but hey, I have interviewed and spent hours with current and former members of some of the world's most notorious Islamist groups, including al-Qaeda, Hamas, the Muslim Brotherhood, Hizb ut-Tahrir, the Libyan Islamic Fighting Group, and al-Muhajiroun. I've also spent time in mosques and Islamic enclaves throughout America and Europe, traveled in the Middle East, and interviewed top lawmakers and intelligence officials from the U.S., EU, and Israel about these issues. Oh, and I've conducted endless background research, going through stacks of books and articles, and hours of broadcast material on Islam, Islamism, terrorism, and related topics for twelve years; in fact, as part of my job, I do that nearly every day. But, sorry: not qualified.

Just a few weeks before MPAC's report was released, it held a teleconference with the Center for American Progress and another longtime liberal bastion, the Southern Poverty Law Center, to discuss "The Real World Impact of Hate Rhetoric in America."[55] Or, as I refer to it: "The

Dangerous Impact that Patriotic, Anti-Jihad Truth Tellers Are Having on Islamo-leftist Efforts to Fundamentally Transform America."

———

America talks about truth, justice, and the American way and most Americans think they are the nicest people and greatest nation in the history of the world yet your government and military have for more than 230 years been one of the world's foremost and most prolific liars as well as one of its most unjust regimes and one of the greatest violators of America's professed values.

Today, as well as yesterday, America's armed forces engage in mass casualty aerial bombing much of which is now fully automated as if you are dealing with money transfers and not matters of life and death. And much of which depends on so-called intelligence from satellites and spy planes which sorry to say don't distinguish between friend, foe, and innocent bystander, in the same way that white phosphorus and depleted uranium also pick their victims indiscriminately.

Today, as yesterday, America's homesick, half-mad soldiers rape, pillage, and murder then plant weapons and fabricate reports to cover up their evil deeds.

And today, more than ever before America's military and intelligence services are guilty of the most atrocious forms of torture and unlawful and arbitrary detention of innocents in Iraq, Afghanistan, Guantanamo, and elsewhere, including on American soil.[56]

Who said it? Was it Bill Ayers? Noam Chomsky? Sean Penn? A Castro brother? Perhaps an Occupy Wall Street leader in Zuccotti Park? Try

Adam Gadahn—also known as Azzam the American—al-Qaeda's chief English-language propagandist, making an obvious rhetorical appeal to America's leftists. Just as the Aytaollah Khomeini accepted communist and socialist support in the 1979 Iranian revolution against the Shah before turning on them with executions and mass arrests, so too do Islamists see western leftists as allies of convenience, useful idiots, to help take down America and the West.

The Left believes it can utilize the Islamists—yet another aggrieved minority—as foot soldiers to help hammer away at the hated Judeo-Christian, capitalist power structure, but really has very little idea who it is getting in bed with—not that it cares. The Left is now winning—decisively—in virtually all facets of American life, and their man is in the White House.

The Muslim Brotherhood and their ilk know that without their collaboration with the Left, and without the protection they receive from Democrats who treat them as just another minority interest group, they would be far less powerful. The Brothers also know that if they ultimately succeed and are in a position to impose sharia, the Left will dutifully fall in line.

A BROTHERHOOD WORLD

A merica is losing the great civilizational struggle of our time. As we've seen throughout this book, the Brotherhood's "Civilization Jihad" strategy is being used with increasing success in the United States—and with the full participation and support of the Obama administration and its leftist allies. And really, that gets to the heart of the matter. While both the Clinton and Bush administrations frequently embraced Brotherhood front groups, the Obama White House is empowering them to a degree that would have been unimaginable just a few years ago, even granting them a say in counterterrorism and Middle East policymaking.

The Obama administration has also thrown the gates wide open to unchecked Muslim immigration (not to mention Muslims on student visas) that is changing the face of even small towns in the American

271

heartland and the Bible Belt. At the same time, mosque-building continues at a breathtaking pace, with the full backing and protection of the Obama Department of Justice. In addition, while Islamic terror plots are hatched with alarming regularity by American citizens, the U.S. government doggedly refuses to even associate Islam with terrorism or utter the word "jihad," except to praise it as a form of New Age-y spiritual cleansing.

Witness President Obama's reaction to the April 2013 Boston bombings: initially, he neglected to call the bombing terrorism, and then he steadfastly avoided mentioning the Islamist motivations of the bombers.[1] Move along folks, nothing to see here: just two lone wolves, no larger jihadist threat. Obama's media minions, after openly hoping that the Boston bombers were American-born, white, right-wing, anti-government extremists, quickly fell into line with the administration's "See No Islam" narrative once the terrorists' obvious jihadist intentions emerged. The ever-shameless *New York Times* ran a piece twelve days after the attacks questioning whether Tamerlan Tsarnaev's failed boxing career was what led him on the path to Islamic jihad—anything but Islam itself.[2]

The Tsarnaev brothers' attendance at a Muslim Brotherhood–linked mosque brings up an interesting point. As we've seen throughout this book, perpetrators of Islamic terrorism—not only in the United States but around the world—are frequently inspired by the teachings of Muslim Brotherhood ideologues like Hassan al-Banna and Sayyid Qutb. The MB's totalitarian ideology and teachings on violent jihad have long served as the prime gateway for Islamists, whether they're of the stealth or violent variety.

Nowhere is that seen more clearly today than in the Middle East and North Africa, two regions where, if the Brotherhood itself doesn't get you (usually through the ballot box), al-Qaeda jihadists waving copies of Qutb's *Milestones* will. The dominoes are falling so fast in the Islamist direction throughout the Muslim world that some form of a renewed caliphate, or at least, some kind of regional emirate, feels inevitable.

From the Muslim Brotherhood to al-Qaeda to Turkey's Justice and Development Party to Iran's ayatollahs, there is certainly no shortage of influential actors pining to unite the Muslim ummah into one powerful entity with first, Israel, and then, the West, in its line of fire.

For example, Egypt and Iran, after decades of zero diplomatic relations, are now rapidly warming to each other in the post-Mubarak era. Serious theological and geopolitical differences obviously still exist between the two countries, but the immediate prospect of eliminating Israel, raising the price of world oil, and menacing the West should be enough to bridge the Sunni/Shia divide, at least for a short while.

What is definite is that war is coming to the Middle East and may already be at hand by the time you read this. The trigger will almost certainly be Iran, in some form or fashion—either through its nascent nuclear weapons program, its continued pursuit of state-supported terrorism, its possible activation of its proxies, Hezbollah and Hamas, against Israel, or its decision to escalate the civil war in Syria, where it is now largely directing the Assad forces. Whatever the cause, cataclysmic events will be unfolding in the Middle East—likely sooner rather than later—that will make you forget all about domestic political squabbles in the United States.

From its open support of the Muslim Brotherhood (both at home and abroad) and the so-called Arab Spring, to its refusal to acknowledge the Islamist enemy, to its appeasement of the Iranian regime, to its isolation of Israel, the Obama administration has been playing with fire for some time—and the United States is very close to being burnt in a serious way as a result. The Obama administration believes it can "flip" die-hard, revolutionary Islamists like Egypt's president, Mohammed Morsi, into American allies; it believes it can entrust Islamists like him to achieve peace in the Middle East; and it believes it can win the support of the Muslim Brotherhood to crack down on al-Qaeda. But the responsibility of governing will not moderate the committed ideologues of the Muslim

Brotherhood, just as it did not moderate the Taliban, Iran's mullahs, or the MB's Palestinian branch, Hamas.

Take a good look at Brussels and Londonistan—where, as I write this, Londoners are reeling after two Islamic jihadists shouting "Allahu Akbar" beheaded a British soldier in broad daylight. The stakes are that high and the hour is getting that late. Events are unfolding in the Middle East and in America's own backyard at a pace that is almost too rapid to follow. To turn the tide, America must, for starters:

- Ban all Muslim Brotherhood–related groups currently operating on U.S. soil. As we saw in the MB's Explanatory Memorandum, these organizations possess a clearly seditious agenda that is a threat to America's national security.
- Impose a moratorium on Muslim immigration and student visas for the foreseeable future.
- Closely scrutinize the funding sources and ideology of any proposed new mosque. This can be done at the local level, barring federal interference. Any trace of Islamist funding, anti-Semitic inclinations, or Brotherhood influence must be a deal-breaker.
- Withdraw financial support from Islamist regimes around the world, beginning with Egypt. The Muslim Brotherhood is an avowed enemy of the United States, and its ruling regimes, in Egypt and elsewhere, should not receive one American cent or U.S. military aid. Period.
- Hold the Islamist regime in Turkey accountable for its radical words and actions. Turkey, under Recep Tayyip Erdogan, has expansionist, sharia-fueled aims and fiercely anti-Israel leanings that will eventually bring it into conflict with U.S. interests. In some cases, it already has (as in the Erdogan government's refusal to allow U.S. troops to

operate out of Turkey—a fellow NATO country—in the run-up to the 2003 Iraq invasion).

- Ensure, by any means necessary, that Iran never develops a nuclear weapon.

- Work for regime change in Iran, which is the source of much of the world's Islamic terror. As we saw with the Reagan administration's support of pro-democracy forces in Poland during the 1980s, working for regime change does not have to include military action.

- Stand publicly, proudly, and forcefully with the Jewish State of Israel—the Middle East's only democracy—against the Islamists.

- Support genuine Muslim moderates—while recognizing their limitations and difficult position. Not every mosque is a terror hotbed nor, obviously, is every Muslim a terrorist. I've worked with courageous moderate Muslims who fervently oppose the Brotherhood's totalitarian Islamism. Many of them are "cultural Muslims" who were raised Muslim but are not very observant. They are allies because they want to remain sharia-free. Unfortunately, if the so-called Arab Spring has proven anything, it's that casual, cultural Muslims are on the run and Koran-waving, Islamic fundamentalists are on the rise. Many moderate Muslims are unwilling to go public (remember that big "Muslims against Terrorism" march on the Mall in Washington, D.C.? Me neither). And their post-modern, Islam-lite is a very tough sell in a large majority of American mosques where Muslim Brothers are the gatekeepers.

I realize the above policy prescriptions will send the Democrat Party, the mainstream media, Islamist pressure groups like CAIR, and the weak-kneed GOP establishment into an absolute tizzy. But let's face it: even without Dr. Stakelbeck's prescriptions, the mere existence of this book would have been enough to spark cries of "Islamophobe," "racist," "bigot," "alarmist," "Christianist," and "right-wing nut job" from the usual quarters until the end of my days. I knew that going in, and as you might have guessed after reading the first few chapters, I could not care less.

I'm just thirty-seven years old, yet the America I grew up in is fading away before my eyes. For the sake of the country and my children, I refuse to be silent. We are entering dangerous times, and I would rather tell the truth boldly, while I still have the platform, and leave all the consequences to God. I believe that the United States is the greatest nation in the history of the world, a gift from God above, and eminently worth fighting for. I also believe that there are millions more Americans who feel the same way as I do: watchmen and women on the wall who will proclaim the truth, without concerns over political correctness or hurt feelings, until their last breath. If the long battle against Islamism is to be won, it will be won by what we, as concerned American citizens, do. Our government and the mainstream media have checked out almost completely, and in many cases are running interference for the enemy. Needless to say, thank God for the internet and the rise of alternative media.

I am pessimistic about America's future and the unchecked rise of global Islamism. But I have an unbreakable faith in the God of Abraham, Isaac, and Jacob. It's what keeps me going. All is not lost. Yet.

On the other hand, I'm also a brutal realist. And the way things are lining up, it appears that, before spring and renewal, we may be destined to suffer through a long, harsh Islamist Winter. It's up to us.

ACKNOWLEDGMENTS

Much has happened in the two years since the release of my first book for Regnery, *The Terrorist Next Door*, and I have a lot of folks to thank: some are new and some are repeat offenders.

My lovely wife, Lori, has once again been a rock through this whole demanding process, full of love, support, understanding and above all, patience. Lor, your sacrifices and support are appreciated more than you know. I love you and thank God that he put us together.

My beautiful daughters, Juliana and Leah, bring such joy to my life and are my reason for being. Girls, one day you will understand why Daddy had to disappear once in awhile to "go get some writing done." You are and will always be my little angels from heaven. I love you both dearly.

To everyone at Regnery Publishing, especially Harry Crocker and Marji Ross: thank you from the bottom of my heart for the opportunity to write this book and sound the alarm. I couldn't be with a better team. You guys are the best in the business and I am grateful for your support. Harry also provided impeccable editing to the manuscript, and Maria Ruhl was a huge help in putting it all together down the stretch.

To my friend and colleague Patrick Poole, who graciously shared his vast knowledge about the Muslim Brotherhood throughout the writing of this book. Patrick's expert insights were invaluable, particularly in the writing of Chapter Seven. He is simply one of America's very finest investigative journalists and researchers and the Muslim Brotherhood's worst nightmare.

To my mom, Agnes, my brother, Fred, and my sister, Judy: thank you for a lifetime of love and support and for encouraging me throughout the writing of this book and in everything I do. God couldn't have chosen a better family for me, and I know Dad is smiling down on us from heaven.

To the entire CBN family, particularly Pat and Gordon Robertson and Michael Little: thank you for providing me the opportunity to fulfill the Lord's calling on my life. I am eternally grateful.

To the entire CBN News team for their overflowing friendship, camaraderie, prayers, and support. I've said it before and I'll say it again: I'll stack our team up against anyone's in the news biz.

I particularly want to thank CBN's News Director, Rob Allman, and Washington, D.C., Bureau Chief, Robin Mazyck, for their leadership, wisdom, and wise counsel throughout our time together and for allowing me the freedom to spread my wings in so many ways. You have been more than just bosses: you have been friends and always accessible. Thank you for your endless support and confidence.

To the entire CBN News Washington, D.C., Bureau: you guys are family and I still have a blast coming to work every day. To all the reporters, shooters, directors, and editors: thank you for your dedication, friendship, and for making me look good: not an easy task.

Special thanks go to my CBN D.C. colleagues Tracy Winborn, the executive producer of CBN's *Stakelbeck on Terror* show, and Matthew Keedy, the creative genius who makes the show look great week after week. Tracy is a prayer warrior and great friend, and has been a blessing for our newsroom. Matt has been my partner in crime since I started at CBN and I am blessed to work with such a talented, steady hand that makes it all so fun.

CBN Senior Political Correspondent David Brody has been a great friend, mentor, and kindred spirit since we met and I'm thankful for all the laughs and the legendary train rides home. Oy gevalt indeed.

Special thanks also go to videographer/editor extraordinaire Ian Rushing, who accompanied me on the overseas trips described in this book and never flinched, no matter how dicey the situation became. The sky is the limit for you, my friend.

To CBN's entire Jerusalem Bureau, especially my great friend Chris Mitchell: thank you for always being such gracious hosts and wonderful brothers and sisters in Christ whenever I am in the Land of Israel.

To the entire team and membership of Christians United for Israel (CUFI), especially Pastor John Hagee and his lovely wife, Diana Hagee, David Brog, Ari Morgenstern, Pastor Victor Styrsky, Pastor Jay Bailey, Pastor Scott and Cindy Thomas, Shari Dollinger, and Velvet Ridings. Thank you for your support, friendship, and for providing me with the opportunities to sound the alarm about the dire threats facing America and Israel.

A special shout-out goes to David Brog and "Off the Record" Ari Morgenstern, my unofficial advisors, good buddies, and fellow warriors for the cause. And also to Victor Styrsky and his beautiful wife, Marita: thank you for your prayers, encouragement, and wise counsel. You are a blessing to me.

To my friend Glenn Beck and the team at TheBlaze TV, especially Joel Cheatwood, Tiffany Siegel, Jenna Diaco, Virginia Grace, Raj Nair, Joe Weasel, and the entire Dallas crew: thanks for the opportunities and for being a beacon of truth.

Thanks to Fox News for giving me the opportunity to spread the word to a wide audience: special thanks go to Sean Hannity, Neil Cavuto, Judge Jeanine Pirro, and their incredible teams.

To my dear friends Edwin Black and Carol DiSalvo, thank you for all the meals, laughs, support, and advice. Looking forward to many more.

To my razor-sharp attorney, Alexis Soterakis of Coran Ober P.C.: thanks for your guidance, dedication, and for always being ready and willing whenever needed.

To my friends Bill Koenig and Bill Salus for their insights into the Middle East and what's coming.

To the Middle East Media Research Institute (MEMRI) the Investigative Project on Terrorism (IPT), and the *Global Muslim Brotherhood Daily Report*: three indispensable sources of information that I leaned on heavily throughout the writing of this book.

To all of the brave men and women I've worked with through the years that have sounded the alarm about the dangers of the Muslim Brotherhood: keep up the fight and never waver.

To all of my "fixers," and hosts around the world who helped make many of the stories described in this book possible. You know who you are. Thank you.

To all my dear friends from Fox Chase, Philadelphia: you are a source of endless inspiration, motivation, and fond memories. There will be a Rec in heaven where we will all have a good laugh together. Of that, I'm sure. There's no place I would have rather grown up. Thank you.

Writing a book is a massive, often trying undertaking—but greatly rewarding. The final three weeks of getting this book finished were particularly challenging for a few reasons. But somehow, I got through it, with Philippians 4:13 always in mind: "I can do all things through Christ who strengthens me."

Indeed, I could not have completed this book without the steady, comforting presence of the Lord Jesus Christ. Yeshua. Thank you, Lord, for coming into my life in a powerful, personal way, and making all things new.

> Trust in the Lord with all your heart
> And lean not on your own understanding;
> In all your ways acknowledge Him,
> And He will make your paths straight
> (Proverbs 3:5–6)

His love endures forever.

—Erick Stakelbeck
May 25, 2013
Washington, D.C.
Psalm 91
Isaiah 54

NOTES

PROLOGUE

1. Ian Johnson, *A Mosque in Munich: Nazis, the CIA, and the Rise of the Muslim Brotherhood in the West* (Boston, New York: Mariner Books, 2010), p. 230.
2. Lorenzo Vidino, *The New Muslim Brotherhood in the West* (New York: Columbia University Press, 2010), p. 152.
3. "EXCLUSIVE: European Muslim Brotherhood Youth Organization Announces Green Initiative; VP Of Group Is Daughter Of Rachid Ghannouchi," *Global Muslim Brotherhood Daily Report*, December 23, 2012, http://globalmbreport. org/?p=7751.
4. Vidino, *The New Muslim Brotherhood in the West*, p. 153.
5. Johnson, *A Mosque in Munich*, p. 229.
6. "Der Herr der Moscheen," *Kölner Stadt-Anzeiger*, December 19, 2007, http:// www.ksta.de/koeln-uebersicht/der-herr-der-moscheen,16341264,13295774. html.

7.   Mohamed Akram, "An Explanatory Memorandum on the General Strategic
     Goal for the Brotherhood in North America," Investigative Project on
     Terrorism, May 19, 1991, http://www.investigativeproject.org/document/id/20.
8.   Johnson, *A Mosque in Munich*, p. 231.
9.   Ibrahim Farouk El-Zayat, "Ibrahim El-Zayat: I am not a member of the MB,"
     Ikwhanweb, February 12, 2007, http://www.ikhwanonline.info/article.
     php?id=2409.
10. Johnson, *A Mosque in Munich*, p. 235.
11. Al-Masry Al-Youm, "Names released of Islamists pardoned by Morsy," *Egypt
     Independent*, July 31, 2012, http://www.egyptindependent.com/news/names-
     released-islamists-pardoned-morsy.
12. Vidino, *The New Muslim Brotherhood in the West*, p. 46.

CHAPTER ONE

1.   Fred Lucas, "Obama Has Touted Al Qaeda's Demise 32 Times since Benghazi
     Attack," CNSNews.com, November 1, 2012, http://cnsnews.com/news/article/
     obama-touts-al-qaeda-s-demise-32-times-benghazi-attack-0.
2.   "#3476 Mohamed Morsi during Elections Campaign: Jihad Is Our Path, Death
     for the Sake of Allah Is Our Most Lofty Aspiration, the Shari'a Is Our
     Constitution," Middle East Media Research Institute, May 13, 2012, http://
     www.memritv.org/clip/en/3476.htm.
3.   Ibid.
4.   "The Muslim Brotherhood," Investigative Project on Terrorism, http://www.
     investigativeproject.org/documents/misc/135.pdf.
5.   Youssef Nada with Douglas Thompson, *Inside the Muslim Brotherhood*
     (London: Metro Publishing, 2012), p. 29.
6.   Husain Haqqani, "The Politicization of American Islam," *Current Trends in
     Islamist Ideology* (Hudson Institute Center on Islam, Democracy and the
     Future of the Muslim World) 6 (March 2008), http://www.currenttrends.org/
     research/detail/the-politicization-of-american-islam.
7.   Tom Heneghan, "Many in Muslim world want sharia as law of land: survey,"
     Reuters, April 30, 2013, http://www.reuters.com/article/2013/04/30/us-islam-
     views-survey-idUSBRE93T0TK20130430.
8.   Andrew C. McCarthy, "Huge Flaw in Pew Survey on Muslim Views about
     Sharia," National Review Online, May 1, 2013, http://www.nationalreview.
     com/corner/347095/huge-flaw-pew-survey-muslim-views-about-sharia.

9. "Egyptian Cleric Safwat Higazi Launches MB Candidate Mohamed Morsi's Compaign: Morsi Will Restore the 'United States of the Arabs' with Jerusalem as Its Capital," Middle East Media Research Institute, May 1, 2012, http://www.memritv.org/clip_transcript/en/3431.htm.

10. "Egyptian Cleric Safwat Higazi: 'The Day Will Come When We Will Be the Masters of the World," Middle East Media Research Institute, August 14, 2012, http://www.memritv.org/clip_transcript/en/3543.htm.

11. "Egyptian Cleric Safwat Higazi Launches MB Candidate."

12. "Morsi in 2010: No to Negotiations with the Blood-Sucking, Warmongering 'Descendants of Apes and Pigs"; Calls to Boycott U.S. Products," Middle East Media Research Institute, September 23, 2010, http://www.memri.org/clip_transcript/en/3702.htm.

13. Robert Satloff and Eric Trager, "Getting Egypt's Morsi to give up his 9/11 'truther' talk," *Washington Post*, September 11, 2012, http://articles.washingtonpost.com/2012-09-11/opinions/35497583_1_morsi-qaeda-al-qaeda.

14. Aya Batrawy, "Egypt president's wife: Don't call me first lady," *Mercury News*, June 28, 2012, http://www.mercurynews.com/breaking-news/ci_20964211/egypt-presidents-wife-dont-call-me-first-lady.

15. Lawrence Wright, *The Looming Tower: Al-Qaeda and the Road to 9/11* (New York: Vintage Books, 2011), p. 26.

16. Clare Lopez, "Egypt Woos Hezbollah," The Clarion Project, December 30, 2012, http://www.clarionproject.org/analysis/egypt-pursues-hezbollah.

17. Sayyid Qutb, *Milestones* (Salimah-Kuwait: International Islamic Federation of Student Organizations, 1978), pp. 112–13.

18. Ibid.

19. Dina Samak, "Will El-Shater nomination split Egypt's Brotherhood?" ahramonline, April 4, 2012, http://english.ahram.org.eg/NewsContentPrint/1/0/38392/Egypt/0/Will-ElShater-nomination-split-Egypts-Brotherhood.aspx.

20. "Differing Views of Qaradawi's Tahrir Square Speech," Investigative Project on Terrorism, March 31, 2011, http://www.investigativeproject.org/2731/differing-views-of-qaradawi-tahrir-square-speech.

21. "Inevitable: Muslim Brotherhood at the White House this week for talks on Egypt; Updated: Salafist presidential candidate disqualified?" Hot Air, April 4, 2012, http://hotair.com/archives/2012/04/04/inevitable-muslim-brotherhood-at-the-white-house-this-week-for-talks-on-egypt/.

22. Kareem Fahim, "In Upheaval for Egypt, Morsi Forces Out Military Chiefs," *New York Times*, August 12, 2012, http://www.nytimes.com/2012/08/13/world/middleeast/egyptian-leader-ousts-military-chiefs.html?pagewanted=all&_r=0.

23. Andrew C. McCarthy, "Are We Really Back to Relying on the Egyptian Military to Save the Day?" National Review Online, January 30, 2013, http://www.nationalreview.com/corner/339254/are-we-really-back-relying-egyptian-military-save-day-andrew-c-mccarthy.

24. Bill Gertz, "Egypt's Muslim Brotherhood filling pro-Western military's ranks with Islamists," *Washington Times*, March 29, 2013, http://www.washingtontimes.com/news/2013/mar/29/egypts-muslim-brotherhood-filling-pro-western-mili/?page=all.

25. "Protestors attack U.S. diplomatic compounds in Egypt, Libya," CNN, September 12, 2012, http://edition.cnn.com/2012/09/11/world/meast/egpyt-us-embassy-protests.

26. David D. Kirkpatrick, Helene Cooper, and Mark Landler, "Egypt, Hearing From Obama, Moves to Heal Rift From Protests," *New York Times*, September 13, 2012, http://www.nytimes.com/2012/09/14/world/middleeast/egypt-hearing-from-obama-moves-to-heal-rift-from-protests.html?pagewanted=all.

27. Thomas Joscelyn, "Al Qaeda Responsible for 4 Attacks on U.S. Embassies in September," *Weekly Standard*, October 3, 2012, http://www.weeklystandard.com/blogs/al-qaeda-responsible-4-attacks-us-embassies-september_653460.html?page=1.

28. Ruth Whitehead, "Muslim Brotherhood 'paying gangs to go out and rape women and beat men protesting in Egypt' as thousands of demonstrators pour on to the streets," *Daily Mail*, December 1, 2012, http://www.dailymail.co.uk/news/article-2241374/Muslim-Brotherhood-paying-gangs-rape-women-beat-men-protesting-Egypt-thousands-demonstrators-pour-streets.html.

29. Gregg Re, "Egyptian journalist tours brutal Muslim Brotherhood torture facility," *Daily Caller*, December 9, 2012, http://dailycaller.com/2012/12/09/egyptian-journalist-tour-brutal-muslim-brotherhood-torture-facility/.

30. Peter Beaumont, "Mohamed Morsi signs Egypt's new constitution into law," *The Guardian*, December 26, 2012, http://www.guardian.co.uk/world/2012/dec/26/mohamed-morsi-egypt-constitution-law.

31. Peter Baker and David D. Kirkpatrick, "Egyptian President and Obama Forge Link in Gaza Deal," *New York Times*, November 21, 2012, http://www.

nytimes.com/2012/11/22/world/middleeast/egypt-leader-and-obama-forge-link-in-gaza-deal.html?pagewanted=all.

32. Robert Spencer, "Jimmy Carter All Over Again," *FrontPage Magazine*, February 7, 2012, http://frontpagemag.com/2012/robert-spencer/jimmy-carter-all-over-again/.

33. "Morsi mouths 'Amen' as Egyptian preacher urges 'Allah, destroy the Jews,'" The Times of Israel, October 21, 2012, http://www.timesofisrael.com/in-morsis-presence-egyptian-preacher-urges-allah-destroy-the-jews/.

34. Elhanan Miller, "'Holy Jihad is the only way to deal with Israel, says Egypt's Muslim Brotherhood chief," The Times of Israel, October 11, 2012, http://www.timesofisrael.com/holy-jihad-is-the-only-way-to-deal-with-israel-says-egypts-muslim-brotherhood-chief/.

35. "Sheik Yusuf al-Qaradawi: Theologian of Terror," Anti-Defamation League archive website, updated March 15, 2011, http://archive.adl.org/NR/exeres /788C5421-70E3-4E4D-BFF4-9BE14E4A2E58,DB7611A2-02CD-43AF-8147-649E26813571,frameless.htm.

36. "Sheik Yusuf al-Qaradawi: Theologian of Terror," Anti-Defamation League, May 3, 2013, http://www.adl.org/anti-semitism/muslim-arab-world/c/sheik-yusf-al-qaradawi.html.

37. Ibid.

38. Erick Stakelbeck, "Brotherhood's 'Lenin' Plotting Islamic Super-State," CBN News, January 12, 2012, http://www.cbn.com/cbnnews/world/2012/January/ Brotherhoods-Lenin-Plotting-Islamic-Super-State-/.

39. "Sheikh Yousuf Al-Qaradhawi: Allah Imposed Hitler On the Jews to Punish Them—'Allah Willing, the Next Time Will Be at the Hand of the Believers,'" Middle East Media Research Institute, February 3, 2009, http://www.memri. org/report/en/0/0/0/0/0/0/3062.htm.

40. Praveen Swami, "Mediator in Taliban-U.S. talks backed Kashmir jihad," *The Hindu*, December 29, 2011, http://www.thehindu.com/news/article2755817. ece.

41. Ibid.

42. Tzvi Ben Gedalyahu, "Egyptians: We Want Nuclear Bombs and to Break Treaty with Israel," Arutz Sheva, October 21, 2012, http://www.israelnationalnews. com/News/News.aspx/161145#.UX7R4YI3524.

43. Edmund Sanders, "Egypt decries Israeli attack that killed 3 of its soldiers," *Los Angeles Times*, August 20, 2011, http://articles.latimes.com/2011/aug/20/ world/la-fg-israel-egypt-tension-20110820.

44. Jack Khoury and Reuters, "Egypt's Muslim Brotherhood blames Sinai attack on Mossad," *Haaretz*, August 6, 2012, http://www.haaretz.com/news/diplomacy-defense/egypt-s-muslim-brotherhood-blames-sinai-attack-on-mossad-1.456403.

45. Erick Stakelbeck, "Global Jihad? Al Qaeda Expands to Africa, Beyond," CBN News, March 17, 2013, http://www.cbn.com/cbnnews/world/2013/March/Global-Jihad-Al-Qaeda-Expands-to-Africa-Beyond/.

46. Maxim Lott, "US gives 4 more F-16 fighter jets to Egyptian government despite outcry," Fox News, April 11, 2013, http://www.foxnews.com/politics/2013/04/11/us-gives-4-more-f-16-fighter-jets-to-egyptian-government/.

47. Ibid.

48. Al-Masry Al-Youm, "US teargas shipment arrives in Suez," *Egypt Independent*, April 8, 2013, http://www.egyptindependent.com/news/us-teargas-shipment-arrives-suez.

49. Julian Pecquet, "Congress blocked Kerry from offering more aid to Egypt," *The Hill*, March 9, 2013, http://thehill.com/blogs/global-affairs/middle-east-north-africa/287129-congress-blocked-kerry-from-offering-egypt-more-aid.

50. "Morsi in 2010: No to Negotiations with the Blood-Sucking, Warmongering 'Descendants of Apes and Pigs.'"

51. Jane Kinninmont, "Egypt and President Mohammed Morsi make a good impression on the West," *The Telegraph*, November 22, 2012, http://www.telegraph.co.uk/news/worldnews/middleeast/9696397/Egypt-and-President-Mohammed-Morsi-make-a-good-impression-on-the-West.html.

CHAPTER TWO

1. Steve Merley, "The Federation of Islamic Organizations in Europe," NEFA, October 1, 2008, available on Scribd, http://www.scribd.com/doc/27710280/The-Federation-of-Islamic-Organisations-in-Europe-NEFA-Foundation.

2. Ibid.

3. Ian Johnson, *A Mosque in Munich: Nazis, the CIA, and the Rise of the Muslim Brotherhood in the West* (Boston, New York: Mariner Books, 2010), p. 128.

4. Daniel Pipes, "Islamism's Unity," National Review Online, October 30, 2012, http://www.nationalreview.com/articles/331975/islamism-s-unity-daniel-pipes.

5. Jeffrey Goldberg, "The Modern King in the Arab Spring," *The Atlantic*, March 18, 2013, http://www.theatlantic.com/magazine/archive/2013/04/monarch-in-the-middle/309270/?single_page=true.

6. Deborah Amos and Nabih Bulos, "Sea of Syrian Refugees Threatens to Overload Jordan," NPR, May 2, 2013, http://www.npr.org/2013/05 /02/180595881/sea-of-syrian-refugees-threatens-to-overload-jordan.

7. Ben Hubbard, "Islamist Rebels Create Dilemma on Syria Policy," *New York Times*, April 27, 2013, http://www.nytimes.com/2013/04/28/world/middleeast/ islamist-rebels-gains-in-syria-create-dilemma-for-us.html?pagewanted=all.

8. "Saudi Prince Al-Waleed Bin Talal: The Arab Spring Is 'Arab Destruction,' No Regime Is Immune to It; MB Smell Spreads in Saudi Arabia; Iran Cannot Be Trusted," Middle East Media Res Research Institute, April 28, 2013, http:// www.memri.org/report/en/0/0/0/0/0/0/7150.htm.

9. "UAE charges 'plotters linked to Muslim Brotherhood,'" BBC, January 28, 2013, http://www.bbc.co.uk/news/world-middle-east-21226174.

10. "UAE appreciates Kuwait's cooperation in Muslim Brotherhood cell case," Gulf News, March 30, 2013, http://gulfnews.com/news/gulf/uae/government/ uae-appreciates-kuwait-s-cooperation-in-muslim-brotherhood-cell- case-1.1164740.

11. William Maclean, "Dubai police chief says Muslim Brotherhood sows subversion in the Gulf," Reuters, April 3, 2013, http://blogs.reuters.com/ faithworld/2013/04/03/dubai-police-chief-says-muslim-brotherhood- sows-subversion-in-the-gulf/.

12. Brief No. 07-4778 from the U.S. fourth circuit court of appeals case *United States of America v. Sbri Benkahla*, available on the Investigative Project on Terrorism website, http://www.investigativeproject.org/documents/case_ docs/542.pdf#page=58.

13. Oren Dorell, "Mosque that Boston suspects attended has radical ties," *USA Today*, April 25, 2013, http://www.usatoday.com/story/news/nation/2013/ 04/23/boston-mosque-radicals/2101411/.

14. Michelle Malkin, "What say you now, Grover Norquist?" MichelleMalkin. com, July 30, 2004, http://michellemalkin.com/2004/07/30/what-say-you-now- grover-norquist/.

15. "Alamoudi: 'You can be violent anywhere else..," Investigative Project on Terrorism, December 28, 1996, http://www.investigativeproject.org/261/ alamoudi-you-can-be-violent-anywhere-else.

16. Sylvain Besson, *La conquête de l'Occident: Le projet secret des Islamistes* (Paris: Le Seuil, 2005).

17. Youssef Nada with Douglas Thompson, *Inside the Muslim Brotherhood* (London: Metro Publishing, 2012), pp. 217–18.

18. Patrick Poole, "The Muslim Brotherhood 'Project,'" *FrontPage Magazine*, May 11, 2006, http://archive.frontpagemag.com/readarticle.aspx?artid=4476.
19. Olivier Guitta, "The Cartoon Jihad," *Weekly Standard*, February 20, 2006, http://www.weeklystandard.com/Content/Public/Articles/000/000/006/704xewyj.asp?page=2.
20. Besson, *La conquête de l'Occident*, p. 31.
21. Poole, "The Muslim Brotherhood 'Project.'"
22. Ibid.; the full English text of "The Project" was first published along with this analysis by *FrontPage Magazine*, Patrick Poole, "The Muslim Brotherhood 'Project' (Continued)," May 11, 2006, http://www.frontpagemag.com/readArticle.aspx?ARTID=4475.
23. *From Dawa to Jihad: The Various Threats from Radical Islam to the Democratic Legal Order* (Leidschendam: AIVD, 2004), p. 40, available on the Investigative Project on Terrorism website, http://www.investigativeproject.org/documents/testimony/49.pdf.
24. Poole, "The Muslim Brotherhood 'Project.'"
25. Documents # ISE-SW 1B41/0000855 through # ISE-SW 1B41/0000858 available on the United States District Court, Northern District of Texas, website, http://www.txnd.uscourts.gov/judges/hlf2/09-25-08/Elbarasse%20Search%204.pdf.
26. Mohammed Akram, "An Explanatory Memorandum On the General Strategic Goal for the Group In North America," May 22, 1991, Government Exhibit Elbarasse Search–3, 3:04-CR-240-G, US v. HLF, et al., http://www.txnd.uscourts.gov/judges/hlf2/09-25-08/Elbarasse%20Search%203.pdf.
27. Jason Trahan, "Muslim Brotherhood's papers detail plan to seize U.S.," *Dallas Morning News*, September 17, 2007, http://www.dallasnews.com/news/crime/headlines/20070917-muslim-brotherhood-s-papers-detail-plan-to-seize-u.s..ece.
28. Documents # ISE-SW 1B41/0000855 through # ISE-SW 1B41/0000858, p. 5.
29. Ibid., p. 7.
30. Ibid.
31. Ibid., see also Investigative Project on Terrorism, http://www.investigativeproject.org/documents/misc/20.pdf.
32. Eric Rich and Jerry Markon, "VA. Man Tied to Hamas Held as Witness," *Washington Post*, August 25, 2004, http://www.washingtonpost.com/wp-dyn/articles/A28476-2004Aug24_2.html.

33. "A man and 6 of the Brotherhood in the White House!" *Rose El-Youssef*, December 22, 2012, http://www.rosa-magazine.com/news/3444/%D8%B 1%D8%AC%D9%84%D9%886-%D8%A5%D8%AE%D9%88%D 8%A7%D9%86-%D9%81%D9%89%D8%A7%D9%84%D8 %A8%D9%8A%D8%AA-%D8%A7%D9%84%D8%A3%D8%A8%D9% 8A%D8%B6.

34. John Rossomando, "Egyptian Magazine: Muslim Brotherhood Infiltrates Obama Administration," Investigative Project on Terrorism, January 3, 2013, http://www.investigativeproject.org/3869/egyptian-magazine-muslim-brotherhood-infiltrates.

35. Steve Emerson and John Rossomando, "A Red Carpet for Radicals at the White House," Investigative Project on Terrorism, October 21, 2012, http://www.investigativeproject.org/3777/a-red-carpet-for-radicals-at-the-white-house.

36. Joseph Abrams, "FBI Cuts Ties With CAIR Following Terror Financing Trial," Fox News, January 30, 2009, http://www.foxnews.com/politics/2009/01/30/fbi-cuts-ties-cair-following-terror-financing-trial/.

37. Niraj Warikoo, "FBI ditches training materials criticized as anti-Muslim," *USA Today*, February 20, 2012, http://usatoday30.usatoday.com/news/nation/story/2012-02-20/fbi-anti-muslim-training/53168966/1.

38. Matt Williams, "FBI accused of 'dropping the ball' on prior questioning of Tamerlan Tsarnaev," *The Guardian*, April 21, 2013, http://www.guardian.co.uk/world/2013/apr/21/fbi-tamerlan-tsarnaev-questioning.

39. "Military Recruiting Center Shooting Suspect Under FBI Investigation," Fox News, June 2, 2009, http://www.foxnews.com/story/2009/06/02/military-recruiting-center-shooting-suspect-under-fbi-investigation/.

40. Associated Press, "Old friends recall Obama's college years," Politico, May 16, 2008, http://www.politico.com/news/stories/0508/10402.html.

41. "OBAMA FLASHBACK: THE DAY I'M INAUGURATED MUSLIM HOSTILITY WILL EASE," Breitbart.com, September 14, 2012, http://www.breitbart.com/Breitbart-TV/2012/09/14/FLASHBACK-Obama-The-Day-Im-Inaugurated-Muslim-Hostility-Will-Ease.

42. Nicholas D. Kristof, "Obama: Man of the World," *New York Times*, March 6, 2007, http://www.nytimes.com/2007/03/06/opinion/06kristof.html?_r=0.

43. Rossomando, "Egyptian Magazine: Muslim Brotherhood Infiltrates Obama Administration."

44. "President Obama Announces Special Envoy to the Organization of the Islamic Conference," WhiteHouse.gov, February 13, 2010, http://www.whitehouse.gov/the-press-office/president-obama-announces-special-envoy-organization-islamic-conference.

45. Ryan Mauro, "Rashad Hussain's Troubling Ties," *FrontPage Magazine*, February 18, 2010, http://frontpagemag.com/2010/ryan-mauro/rashad-hussains-troubling-ties/.

46. "OBAMA AL-ARABIYA INTERVIEW: FULL TEXT," *Huffington Post*, February 27, 2009, http://www.huffingtonpost.com/2009/01/26/obama-al-arabiya-intervie_n_161127.html.

47. Kevin Glass, "America's Reputation in the Muslim World Is Worse Than Ever," *TownHall*, September 13, 2012, http://townhall.com/tipsheet/kevinglass/2012/09/13/americas_reputation_in_the_muslim_world_is_worse_than_ever.

48. Erick Stakelbeck, *The Terrorist Next Door: How the Government Is Deceiving You about the Islamist Threat* (Washington, D.C.: Regnery Publishing, Inc., 2011), pp. 35, 36.

49. Marc Ambinder, "'Brotherhood' Invited To Obama Speech By U.S.," *The Atlantic*, June 3, 2009, http://www.theatlantic.com/politics/archive/2009/06/-brotherhood-invited-to-obama-speech-by-us/18693/.

50. "2009 TRANSCRIPT: President Obama Delivers Speech to Muslim World in Cairo, Egypt," Fox News, October 20, 2012, http://foxnewsinsider.com/2012/10/20/2009-transcript-president-obama-delivers-speech-to-muslim-world-in-cairo-egypt/.

51. "Obama: Muslims suffered most from extremism," *Washington Times*, September 25, 2012.

52. Tamim Elyan and Shaimaa Fayed, "Egypt Christians vent fury after clashes kill 25," Reuters, October 10, 2011, http://www.reuters.com/article/2011/10/10/us-egypt-copts-clashes-idUSTRE7981Q220111010.

53. Keith Koffler, "Obama Calls for Restraint by Egypt's Christians," White House Dossier, October 13, 2011, http://www.whitehousedossier.com/2011/10/13/obama-calls-for-restraint-egypts-christians/.

54. Sheryl Gay Stolberg, "Obama Pointedly Questioned by Students in India," *New York Times*, November 7, 2010, http://www.nytimes.com/2010/11/08/world/asia/08prexy.html?_r=0.

55. Stakelbeck, *The Terrorist Next Door*, pp. 193–95.

56. Katrina Trinko, "Obama: 'The Future Must Not Belong To Those Who Slander the Prophet of Islam,'" National Review Online, September 25, 2012, http://www.nationalreview.com/corner/328483/obama-future-must-not-belong-those-who-slander-prophet-islam-katrina-trinko.

57. Jason Howerton, "JOE BIDEN TO FATHER OF FORMER NAVY SEAL KILLED IN BENGHAZI: 'DID YOUR SON ALWAYS HAVE BALLS THE SIZE OF CUE BALLS?'" The Blaze, October 25, 2012, http://www.theblaze.com/stories/2012/10/25/joe-biden-to-father-of-former-navy-seal-killed-in-benghazi-did-your-son-always-have-balls-the-size-of-cue-balls/.

58. Greg Risling and Linda Deutsch, "Mark Basseley Youssef, 'Innocence Of Muslims' Producer, Sentenced To Year in Prison," *Huffington Post*, November 7, 2012, http://www.huffingtonpost.com/2012/11/07/mark-basseley-youssef-prison-sentence_n_2090279.html.

59. Tiffany Gabbay, "FREE SPEECH THAT MOCKS ISLAM IS NATIONAL SECURITY THREAT FOR U.S., PROMINENT NJ IMAM TELLS THEBLAZE," The Blaze, September 20, 2012, http://www.theblaze.com/stories/2012/09/20/free-speech-that-mocks-islam-is-national-security-threat-for-u-s-prominent-nj-imam-tells-theblaze/.

60. Andrew C. McCarthy, *Spring Fever: The Illusion of Islamic Democracy* (New York, NY: Encounter Digital, 2013), pp. 123–24.

61. Nina Shea, "A perverse 'Process': Hillary's free-speech follies," *New York Post*, updated December 17, 2011, http://www.nypost.com/p/news/opinion/opedcolumnists/perverse_process_orKksIN05i0UKsRMCs6r0J.

CHAPTER THREE

1. Caroline Fourest, *Brother Tariq: The Doublespeak of Tariq Ramadan.* (Encounter Books, 2008), p. 28.

2. Olivier Guitta, "The State Dept. Was Right: To deny Tariq Ramadan a visa," *Weekly Standard*, October 16, 2006, http://www.weeklystandard.com/Content/Public/Articles/000/000/012/800naxnt.asp?page=1

3. Paul Berman, "Who's Afraid of Tariq Ramadan," *The New Republic*, June 4, 2007.

4. "Apologists or Extremists: Tariq Ramadan," Investigative Project on Terrorism, updated March 8, 2010, http://www.investigativeproject.org/profile/111#_ftn9.

5. Julia Preston, "Suit Backing Muslim Scholar Challenges Part of Patriot Act," *New York Times*, January 25, 2006, http://www.nytimes.com/2006/01/25/politics/25cnd-muslim.html.
6. Fourest, *Brother Tariq: The Doublespeak of Tariq Ramadan*, p. 231.
7. Daniel Pipes, Why Revoke Tariq Ramadan's U.S. Visa?" *New York Sun*, August 27, 2004, available on DanielPipes.org, http://www.danielpipes.org/2043/why-revoke-tariq-ramadans-us-visa.
8. Fourest, *Brother Tariq: The Doublespeak of Tariq Ramadan*, p. 96.
9. Ibid.
10. Allan Nadler, "Tariq Ramadan Gets a Hero's Welcome, and Cold Shoulders, at Religion Scholars Confab," *Forward*, November 11, 2009, http://forward.com/articles/118781/tariq-ramadan-gets-a-hero-s-welcome-and-cold-sho/.
11. "McCain Calls for More Military Support to Anti-Qaddafi Forces During Libya Visit," Fox News, April 22, 2011, http://www.foxnews.com/politics/2011/04/22/mccain-travels-libya-meet-rebel-forces/.
12. Matthias Küntzel, *Jihad and Jew-Hatred: Islamism, Nazism and the Roots of 9/11* (Telos Press Publishing, 2009), pp. 14–15.
13. David Blair, "'The Americans love Pepsi Cola, but we love death,'" *The Telegraph*, September 24, 2001, http://www.telegraph.co.uk/news/worldnews/asia/afghanistan/1341470/The-Americans-love-Pepsi-Cola-but-we-love-death.html.
14. Itamar Marcus and Nan Jacques Zilberdik, "Hamas: Martyrdom death for Allah is ideal 'We love death more than you love life' 'You [Israel] scare us with what we love,'" Palestinian Media Watch, December 9, 2012, http://palwatch.org/main.aspx?fi=157&doc_id=8094.
15. Küntzel, *Jihad and Jew-Hatred*, p. 15.
16. "The Way of Jihad: Complete Text by Hassan Al Banna founder of the Muslim Brotherhood," Militant Islam Monitor, January 16, 2005, http://www.militantislammonitor.org/article/id/379.
17. Ibid.
18. Küntzel, *Jihad and Jew-Hatred*, pp. 16–18.
19. Ian Johnson, *A Mosque in Munich: Nazis, the CIA, and the Rise of the Muslim Brotherhood in the West* (Boston, New York: Mariner Books, 2010), p. 111.
20. Ibid.
21. Ibid.
22. Fourest, *Brother Tariq: The Doublespeak of Tariq Ramadan*, p. 29.
23. Küntzel, *Jihad and Jew-Hatred*, p. 9.

24. Edwin Black, *The Farhud: Roots of the Arab-Nazi Alliance in the Holocaust* (Washington, D.C.: Dialog Press, 2010), p. 332–33.

25. Matthias Kuntzel, "Islamic Antisemitism and Its Nazi Roots," Matthias Kuntzel's website, April 2003, http://www.matthiaskuentzel.de/contents/islamic-antisemitism-and-its-nazi-roots.

26. Fourest, *Brother Tariq: The Doublespeak of Tariq Ramadan*, p. 45.

27. P. Bogdanor, "Understanding the Arab-Israeli Conflict," *New York Times*, August 2, 1948.

28. Fereydoun Hoveyda, *The Broken Crescent: The "Threat" of Militant Islamic Fundamentalism* (Praeger Publishers, 2002).

29. Ibid.

30. "NEW YORK TIMES 1948–1949 Muslim Brotherhood's Terrorist Activities Made the Headlines," *Point de Bascule*, June 10, 2011, http://pointdebasculecanada.ca/index.php?option=com_content&view=article&id=1364-new-york-times-1948-1949-muslim-brotherhoods-terrorist-activities-made-the&catid=9&Itemid=103.

31. Jamie Weinstein, "New York Times Cairo bureau chief: Muslim Brotherhood is 'moderate, regular old political force,'" *Daily Caller*, December 7, 2012, http://dailycaller.com/2012/12/07/new-york-times-cairo-bureau-chief-muslim-brotherhood-is-moderate-regular-old-political-force/#ixzz2FLXhieEb.

32. Fourest, *Brother Tariq: The Doublespeak of Tariq Ramadan.*, pp. 33–34.

33. Richard P. Mitchell, *The Society of the Muslim Brothers* (Oxford University Press, 1993), p. 151.

34. Hassan Mneimneh, "The Islamization of Arab Culture," *Current Trends in Islamist Ideology* (Hudson Institute Center on Islam, Democracy and the Future of the Modern World) 6 (March 2008).

CHAPTER FOUR

1. "About Us" section, Ikhwanonline.net, 2003, http://web.archive.org/web/20080708095806/http://ikhwanonline.net/Article.asp?ArtID=120&SecID=0.

2. Melissa Eddy and Nicholas Kulish, "Koran Giveaway in Germany Has Some Officials Worried," *New York Times*, April 16, 2012, http://www.nytimes.com/2012/04/17/world/europe/germany-koran-giveaway-worries-officials.html?_r=0.

3. Yassin Musharbash, "The Third Generation: German Jihad Colonies Sprout Up in Waziristan," *Der Spiegel*, April 5, 2010, http://www.spiegel.de/

international/germany/the-third-generation-german-jihad-colonies-sprout-up-in-waziristan-a-687306.html.

4. Erick Stakelbeck, "Nazism to 'Salafism': Islamists Threaten Germany," CBN News, September 2, 2012, http://www.cbn.com/cbnnews/world/2012/August/Nazism-to-Salafism-Islamists-Threaten-Germany/.

5. "German intelligence chief warns of Islamist attacks following clashes with Salafis," Al Arabiya News, May 22, 2012, http://english.alarabiya.net/articles/2012/05/22/215765.html.

6. "Suspicious Luggage: Police Arrest Suspects in Bonn Bomb Case," *Der Spiegel*, December 11, 2012, http://www.spiegel.de/international/germany/bag-containing-explosive-material-shuts-down-bonn-train-station-a-872176.html.

7. "Kosovan Albanian admits killing two US airmen in Frankfurt terror attack," *The Guardian*, August 31, 2011, http://www.guardian.co.uk/world/2011/aug/31/kosovan-albanian-admits-killing-airmen.

8. Michael Stürzenberger, "Sharia Court in the Heart of Munich," Politically Incorrect, December 2, 2011, http://www.pi-news.org/2011/12/sharia-court-in-the-heart-of-munich/.

9. Maximilian Popp, "Parallel Justice: Islamic 'Arbitrators' Shadow German Law," *Der Spiegel*, September 1, 2011, http://www.spiegel.de/international/germany/parallel-justice-islamic-arbitrators-shadow-german-law-a-783361.html.

10. Souad Mekhennet, "Munich Imam Tries to Dull Lure of Radical Islam," *New York Times*, May 15, 2010, http://www.nytimes.com/2010/05/16/world/europe/16imam.html?pagewanted=all&_r=.

11. Allan Hall, "Muslim imam who lectures on non-violence in Germany is arrested for beating up his wife," *Daily Mail*, December 2, 2010, http://www.dailymail.co.uk/news/article-1335024/Muslim-imam-Sheikh-Adam-lectures-non-violence-arrested-wife-beating.html.

12. Irene Kleber, "Imam Abu Adam: 'Jetzt muss die Wunde heilen,'" *Abendzeitung*, February 14, 2011, http://www.abendzeitung-muenchen.de/inhalt.imam-abu-adam-jetzt-muss-die-wunde-heilen.487d28d2-f03f-4f19-b6e4-500cece25ed1.html.

13. Gilles Kepel, "The Brotherhood in the Salafist Universe," *Current Trends in Islamist Ideology* (Hudson Institute Center on Islam, Democracy and the Future of the Modern World) 6 (February 2008), http://www.currenttrends.org/research/detail/the-brotherhood-in-the-salafist-universe.

14. Lorenzo Vidino, *The New Muslim Brotherhood in the West* (New York: Columbia University Press, 2009), pp. 91–92.

15. Harold Rhode, "Can Muslims Reopen the Gates of *Ijtihad?*" Gatestone Institute, June 15, 2012, http://www.gatestoneinstitute.org/3114/muslims-ijtihad.

16. Eli Lake, "Member of Egyptian Terror Group Goes to Washington," *Daily Beast*, June 21, 2012, http://www.thedailybeast.com/articles/2012/06/21/member-of-egyptian-terror-group-goes-to-washington.html.

17. Jordy Yager, "Napolitano: Egyptian lawmaker from terrorist group was thoroughly 'vetted,'" *The Hill*, July 25, 2012, http://thehill.com/homenews/news/240041-napolitano-egyptian-terrorist-lawmaker-thoroughly-vetted#ixzz2HMLINdrd.

18. "Remarks by the President at Iftar Dinner," WhiteHouse.gov, August 10, 2012, http://www.whitehouse.gov/the-press-office/2012/08/10/remarks-president-iftar-dinner.

19. Gerard W. Gawalt, "America and the Barbary Pirates: An International Battle Against an Unconventional Foe," Library of Congress, http://memory.loc.gov/ammem/collections/jefferson_papers/mtjprece.html.

20. Erick Stakelbeck, "Stakelbeck on Terror Show: One-one-One with UK Islamist Anjem Coudary," CBN News, August 8, 2012, http://blogs.cbn.com/stakelbeckonterror/archive/2012/08/08/stakelbeck-on-terror-one-on-one-with-uk-islamist-anjem-choudary.aspx.

21. Andrew G. Bostom, "'Islamophobia' is a Sacralized Islamic Objective," American Thinker, October 3, 2012, http://www.americanthinker.com/blog/2012/10/islamophobia_is_a_sacralized_islamic_objective.html#ixzz2AYs436A1.

22. "Obama Adminstration Corrects Clapper's Claim That Muslim Brotherhood Is 'Secular,'" Fox News, February 10, 2011, http://www.foxnews.com/politics/2011/02/10/administration-corrects-dni-clapper-claim-muslim-brotherhood-secular/.

23. "The Muslim Brotherhood Movement in Support of Fighting American Forces in Iraq," Middle East Media Research Center, September 3, 2004, http://www.memri.org/report/en/print1209.htm.

24. "Muslim Brotherhood General Guide Muhammad Mahdi 'Akef's Weekly Sermon Calls for Attacks in Palestine, Iraq, and Afghanistan: Direct Energy Of Resistance At Real Enemy 'Concealed In Jerusalem,'" Middle East Media

Research Institute, April 20, 2007, http://www.thememriblog.org/blog_personal/en/1303.htm.

25. "Sheikh Yousuf Al-Qaradhawi: Resistance in Iraq is a Duty of Every Muslim," Middle East Media Research Institute, December 14, 2004, http://www.memri.org/report/en/0/0/0/0/0/0/1275.htm.

26. Houda Trabelsi, "Leaked Ghannouchi tape raises salafism concerns," Magharebia, October 15, 2012, http://www.magharebia.com/cocoon/awi/xhtml1/en_GB/features/awi/features/2012/10/15/feature-01.

27. Daniel Pipes, "Islamism's Unity," National Review Online, October 30, 2012, http://www.nationalreview.com/articles/331975/islamism-s-unity-daniel-pipes.

28. Eric Trager, "Egypt's Muslim Brotherhood Sticks With Bin Laden," *The Atlantic*, May 3, 2011, http://www.theatlantic.com/international/archive/2011/05/egypts-muslim-brotherhood-sticks-with-bin-laden/238218/.

29. "Egyptian Brotherhood Supreme Guide Considers Bin Laden A 'Mujahadeed," *Global Muslim Brotherhood Daily Report*, May 26, 2008, http://globalmbreport.org/?p=885.

30. Caroline Fourest, *Brother Tariq: The Doublespeak of Tariq Ramadan* (Encounter Books, 2008), p. 103.

31. "The Muslim Brotherhood: Understanding its Roots and Impact," Foundation for Defense of Democracies, http://www.defenddemocracy.org/the-muslim-brotherhood-understanding-its-roots-and-impact/.

32. "Muslim Students Association (MSA)," Investigative Project on Terrorism, updated July 9, 2008, http://www.investigativeproject.org/profile/166.

33. Erick Stakelbeck, "Muslim Student Group a Gateway to Jihad?" CBN News, August 29, 2011, http://www.cbn.com/cbnnews/us/2011/march/muslim-student-group-a-gateway-to-jihad/.

34. Ibid.

35. Chris Hawley, "New York Police Department monitored Muslim students all over the Northeast," Christian Science Monitor, February 20, 2012, http://www.csmonitor.com/USA/Latest-News-Wires/2012/0220/New-York-Police-Department-monitored-Muslim-students-all-over-the-Northeast.

36. "Egypt leader Mohammed Morsi vows to free Omar Abdel-Rahman, infamous blind sheik jailed in U.S.," CBS News, June 29, 2012, http://www.cbsnews.com/8301-202_162-57463933/egypt-leader-mohammed-morsi-vows-to-free-omar-abdel-rahman-infamous-blind-sheik-jailed-in-u-s-/.

37. Jason Howerton, "EGYPT'S PRESIDENT MORSI: 'I WILL DO EVERYTHING IN MY POWER TO SECURE FREEDOM' FOR THE BLIND

SHEIKH," The Blaze, September 28, 2012, http://www.theblaze.com/stories/egypts-morsi-i-will-do-everything-in-my-power-to-secure-freedom-for-the-blind-sheikh/.

38. "Exclusive: Wolf Blitzer interviews Egyptian President Morsy," CNN, January 7, 2013, http://situationroom.blogs.cnn.com/2013/01/07/exclusive-wolf-blitzer-interviews-egyptian-president-morsy/.

39. Erica Ritz, "SOURCE: STATE DEPARTMENT CONSIDERING TALKS TO TRANSFER 'BLIND SHEIKH' TO EGYPT," The Blaze, September 17, 2012, http://www.theblaze.com/stories/source-obama-administration-in-talks-to-transfer-blind-sheikh-to-egypt/.

40. "Egypt's President Mursi pardons 'revolutionaries,'" BBC, October 9, 2012, http://www.bbc.co.uk/news/world-middle-east-19877428.

41. Thomas Joscelyn, "Osama bin Laden on the Muslim Brotherhood," Threat Matrix, May 10, 2012, http://www.longwarjournal.org/threat-matrix/archives/2012/05/osama_bin_laden_on_the_muslim.php.

CHAPTER FIVE

1. Giulio Meotti, "Op-Ed: The Red Cross' War Against the Jews," Arutz Sheva, December 10, 2011, http://www.israelnationalnews.com/Articles/Article.aspx/10969.

2. Reuters, "Hamas rejects Red Cross demand to prove Shalit is alive," Haaretz, June 23, 2011, http://www.haaretz.com/news/diplomacy-defense/hamas-rejects-red-cross-demand-to-prove-shalit-is-alive-1.369250.

3. "The Covenant of the Islamic Resistance Movement—Hamas: From the MEMRI Archives," Middle East Media Research Institute, May 26, 2011, http://www.memri.org/report/en/0/0/0/0/0/0/5319.htm.

4. Ibid.

5. Ibid.

6. Ibid.

7. Jonathan Masters, "Hamas," Council on Foreign Relations, updated November 27, 2012, http://www.cfr.org/israel/hamas/p8968#p9.

8. Erick Stakelbeck, "American Victims of Palestinian Terror Seek Justice," CBN News, February 2, 2012, http://www.cbn.com/cbnnews/us/2012/February/American-Victims-of-Palestinian-Terror-Seek-Justice/.

9. Matthew Levitt, Hamas: Politics, Charity and Terrorism in the Service of Jihad (Yale University Press, 2006), p. 12.

10. Katie Cella, "Hamas runs summer camps for kids in Gaza," *Foreign Policy*, July 18, 2012, http://blog.foreignpolicy.com/posts/2012/07/18/hamas_summer_camps_for_kids_in_gaza.

11. "Q&A: Gaza conflict," BBC, January 18, 2009, http://news.bbc.co.uk/2/hi/middle_east/7818022.stm.

12. Shmulik Hadad, "Sderot: Those who can afford it have already left," Ynetnews, March 19, 2008, http://www.ynetnews.com/articles/0,7340, L-3520956,00.html.

13. Meital Yasur-Beit Or, "Study: Half of Sderot's toddlers suffering from PTSD," Ynetnews, June 30, 2009, http://www.ynetnews.com/articles/0,7340, L-3739071,00.html.

14. "The Truth Behind Hamas' Funding," Israel Defense Forces, January 21, 2012, http://www.idfblog.com/hamas/2012/01/21/the-truth-behind-hamas-funding/.

15. Levitt, *Hamas: Politics, Charity and Terrorism*, p. 206.

16. "The Covenant of the Islamic Resistance Movement," Middle East Media Research Institute.

17. Author interview with Azzam al-Tamimi, conducted via email on August 13, 2012.

18. Assam Tamimi, *Hamas: A History From Within* (Olive Branch Press, 2011), p. 46.

19. Ibid., p. 50.

20. Author interview with Azzam al-Tamimi, conducted via email on August 13, 2012.

21. Ibid.

22. Ibid.

23. "Sheik Yousuf Al-Qaradhawi Incites against Jews, Arab Regimes, and the U.S., and Calls on Muslims to Boycott Starbucks, Marks and Spencer," Middle East Media Research Institute, January 9, 2009, http://www.memritv.org/clip_transcript/en/1979.htm.

24. "Leading Sunni Scholar Sheik Yousuf Al-Qaradhawi Supports Suicide Bombings in Palestine and Declares: 'I Am Against the Peace Process,'" Middle East Media Research Center, December 17, 2010, http://www.memritv.org/clip_transcript/en/2731.htm.

25. Erick Stakelbeck, "Hamas in America," *The Sun*, September 24, 2004, http://www.nysun.com/opinion/hamas-in-america/2222/.

26. Reuters, "Mashal seeks pact to defeat Israel, U.S.," *Haaretz*, April 20, 2004, http://www.haaretz.com/print-edition/news/mashal-seeks-pact-to-defeat-israel-u-s-1.120141.

27. Arnon Regular, "Palestinians rally to show their support for Iraqi uprising," *Haaretz*, April 11, 2004, http://www.haaretz.com/print-edition/news/palestinians-rally-to-show-their-support-for-iraqi-uprising-1.119287.

28. Levitt, *Hamas: Politics, Charity and Terrorism*, p. 12.

29. Tim McGirk, "New Calls by Hamas Militants to Target the U.S.," *Time*, October 13, 2006, http://www.time.com/time/world/article/0,8599,1546101,00.html.

30. "Deputy Speaker of Hamas Parliament Calls on Muslims to Annihilate Jews and Americans," Israel Defense Forces, August 22, 2012, http://www.idfblog.com/hamas/2012/08/22/deputy-speaker-of-hamas-parliament-calls-on-muslims-to-annihilate-jews-and-americans/.

31. Richard Spencer, "Osama bin Laden dead: Hamas condemns killing of bin Laden," *The Telegraph*, May 2, 2011, http://www.telegraph.co.uk/news/worldnews/asia/pakistan/8488479/Osama-bin-Laden-dead-Hamas-condemns-killing-of-bin-Laden.html.

32. Tamimi, *Hamas: A History From Within*, p. 271.

33. Levitt, *Hamas: Politics, Charity and Terrorism*, p. 206.

34. Kouichi Shirayanagi, "Tunisian Jewish Community Horrified, Demanding Quick Government Response in Aftermath of Haniyeh Visit," Tunisia Live, January 11, 2012, http://www.tunisia-live.net/2012/01/11/tunisian-jewish-community-horrified-demanding-quick-government-response-in-aftermath-of-haniyeh-visit/.

35. Robert Zaretsky, "Out of Tune," *Tablet*, January 17, 2012, http://www.tabletmag.com/jewish-news-and-politics/88249/out-of-tune-3.

36. "Gaza leader promises 'difficult days' for Israel," AFP, January 8, 2012, www.google.com/hostednews/afp/article/ALeqM5hCH-8LI0oT-qtJws7Z-ICzRrM3ZQ?docId=CNG.befd8261ddab57b82fa93d007250aad6.581.

CHAPTER SIX

1. Michael Rubin, "Turkey's Turning Point," National Review Online, April 14, 2008, http://www.nationalreview.com/content/turkeys-turning-point.

2. "Frank Gaffney on Gulen schools," YouTube, February 23, 2011, http://www.youtube.com/watch?feature=player_embedded&v=W_UbiI9cFnI.

3.　Joe Lauria, "Reclusive Turkish Imam Criticizes Gaza Flotilla," *Wall Street Journal*, June 4, 2010, http://online.wsj.com/article/SB10001424052748704 025304575284721280274694.html.

4.　Maximilian Popp, "Der Spiegel: The Shadowy World of the Islamic Gülen Movement," *Der Spiegel*, August 8, 2012, http://turkishpoliticsupdates. wordpress.com/2012/08/08/der-spiegel-the-shadowy-world-of-the-islamic-gulen-movement/.

5.　Claire Berlinski, "Who Is Fethullah Gülen?" *City Journal* 22, no. 4 (Autumn 2012), http://www.city-journal.org/2012/22_4_fethullah-gulen.html.

6.　"GULEN & AKP & ERDOGAN: Anatomy Of A Power Struggle," Turkish Forum, February 5, 2013, http://www.turkishnews.com/en/content/2013/02/05/ gulen-akp-erdogan-anatomy-of-a-power-struggle/.

7.　Lauria, "Reclusive Turkish Imam Criticizes Gaza Flotilla."

8.　Fuad Aliyev, "The Gulen Movement in Azerbaijan," Hudson Institute, December 27, 2012, http://www.currenttrends.org/research/detail/the-gulen-movement-in-azerbaijan.

9.　Lauria, "Reclusive Turkish Imam Criticizes Gaza Flotilla."

10.　James C. Harrington, "Fethullah Gülen's legal cases in Turkey and U.S. immigration case," Fethullah Gülen official website, updated January 25, 2012, http://en.fgulen.com/about-fethullah-gulen/life/3835-fethullah-gulens-legal-cases-in-turkey-and-us-immigration-case.

11.　Rubin, "Turkey's Turning Point."

12.　Berlinski, "Who Is Fethullah Gülen?"

13.　"Two Important Points in Gülen-Pope Meeting," Fethullah Gülen official website, February 11, 1998, http://www.fethullahgulen.org/fethullah-gulens-life/dialogue-activities/meeting-with-the-pope-john-paul-ii/25151-two-important-points-in-gulen-pope-meeting.

14.　Erick Stakelbeck, "The Gülen Movement: A New Islamic World Order?" CBN News, June 4, 2011, http://www.cbn.com/cbnnews/world/2011/May/The-Gulen-Movement-The-New-Islamic-World-Order/.

15.　Berlinski, "Who Is Fethullah Gülen?"

16.　Popp, "Der Spiegel: The Shadowy World of the Islamic Gülen movement."

17.　Berlinski, "Who Is Fethullah Gülen?"

18.　Ibid.

19.　Popp, "Der Spiegel: The Shadowy World of the Islamic Gülen movement."

20.　Berlinski, "Who Is Fethullah Gülen?"

21. Martha Woodall and Claudio Gatti, "WikiLeaks files detail U.S. unease over Turks and charter schools," *The Inquirer*, April 4, 2011, http://articles.philly.com/2011-04-04/news/29380536_1_charter-schools-fethullah-gulen-truebright-science-academy.

22. Ibid.

23. Dan Bilefsky and Sebnem Arsu, "Turkey Feels Sway of Reclusive Cleric in the U.S.," *New York Times*, April 24, 2012, http://www.nytimes.com/2012/04/25/world/middleeast/turkey-feels-sway-of-fethullah-gulen-a-reclusive-cleric.html?pagewanted=all&_r=0.

24. Popp, "Der Spiegel: The Shadowy World of the Islamic Gülen movement."

25. Ibid.

26. "An interview with Fethullah Gülen for the Muslim World Journal," *The Muslim World Journal* 95, no. 3 (July 2005), pp. 456–57, available online "RE-ESTABLISHING CALIPHATE," Gulen Movement, March 10, 2012, http://www.gulenmovement.us/fethullah-gulen-caliphate.html.

27. "Erdoğan hopes Islamic scholar Gülen returns to Turkey soon," *Today's Zaman*, June 15, 2012, http://www.todayszaman.com/news-283601-.html.

28. "Gülen says prefers staying longer in US to avoid 'harming positive things,'" *Today's Zaman*, June 17, 2012, http://www.todayszaman.com/news-283711-gulen-says-prefers-staying-longer-in-us-to-avoid-harming-positive-things.html.

29. Andrew C. McCarthy, *Spring Fever: The Illusion of Islamic Democracy* (New York, NY: Encounter Digital, 2013), p. 59.

30. Ibid.

31. "Turkey's charismatic pro-Islamic leader," BBC, November 4, 2002, http://news.bbc.co.uk/2/hi/europe/2270642.stm.

32. Daniel Pipes, "Erdogan dreams of full sharia law in Turkey," The Australian, January 1, 2013, http://www.theaustralian.com.au/national-affairs/opinion/erdogan-dreams-of-full-sharia-law-in-turkey/story-e6frgd0x-1226545827254.

33. "Erdogan meets Hezbollah delegation," NOW news, November 26, 2010, https://now.mmedia.me/lb/en/nownews/erdogan_meets_hezbollah_delegation.

34. "Erdogan: Hezbollah not linked to Hariri assassination," Ynetnews, November 29, 2010, http://www.ynetnews.com/articles/0,7340,L-3991289,00.html.

35. Caroline Glick, "The Meaning and Consequences of Israel's Apology to Turkey," *FrontPage Magazine*, March 25, 2013, http://frontpagemag.com/2013/caroline-glick/the-meaning-and-consequences-of-israels-apology-to-turkey/.

36. McCarthy, *Spring Fever: The Illusion of Islamic Democracy*, p. 97.

37. Ibid., p. 101.

38. Yaakov Katz, "'Erdogan and Turkish government supported IHH,'" *Jerusalem Post*, January 24, 2011, http://www.jpost.com/Middle-East/Erdogan-and-Turkish-government-supported-IHH.

39. Tzvi Ben Gedalyahu, "Turkey Punishes Israel, Blocks It from NATO Summit," Arutz Sheva, April 23, 2012, http://www.israelnationalnews.com/News/News.aspx/155031#.UVC_Lhk3524.

40. Herb Keinon, "White House slams Erdogan's Zionism remark," *Jerusalem Post*, March 3, 2013, http://www.jpost.com/Diplomacy-and-Politics/White-House-slams-Erdogans-Zionism-remark.

41. Sam Ser, "Erdogan's planned Gaza visit concerns US," The Times of Israel, March 28, 2013, http://www.timesofisrael.com/erdogans-planned-gaza-visit-concerns-state-dept/.

42. Ibid.

43. Paul Richter, "Turkish Prime Minister Erdogan poses challenge for Obama," *Los Angeles Times*, October 10, 2011, http://articles.latimes.com/2011/oct/10/world/la-fg-us-turkey-20111011.

44. Daniel Halper, "Obama Gives Erdogan the 'Hug Treatment,'" *Weekly Standard*, November 3, 2011, http://www.weeklystandard.com/blogs/obama-hugs-erdogan_607704.html.

45. "Remarks by President Obama and Prime Minister Erdogan of Turkey after Bilateral Meeting," WhiteHouse.gov, March 25, 2012, http://www.whitehouse.gov/the-press-office/2012/03/25/remarks-president-obama-and-prime-minister-erdogan-turkey-after-bilatera.

46. Neil Munro, "Obama, Turkey's Islamist prime minister discuss nukes, teenagers," *Daily Caller*, March 26, 2012, http://dailycaller.com/2012/03/26/obama-turkeys-islamist-prime-minister-discuss-nukes-teenagers/.

47. Benjamin Harvey, Gregory Viscusi, and Massoud A. Derhally, "Arabs Battling Regimes See Erdogan's Muslim Democracy as Model," Bloomberg, February 4, 2011, http://www.bloomberg.com/news/2011-02-04/arabs-battling-regimes-see-erdogan-s-muslim-democracy-in-turkey-as-model.html.

48. "Erdogan says favors Bashir over Netanyahu," Ynetnews, November 8, 2009, http://www.ynetnews.com/articles/0,7340,L-3802150,00.html.

49. "Turkish Prime Minister says 'assimilation is a crime against humanity,'" The Local, February 11, 2008, http://www.thelocal.de/politics/20080211-10293.html#.UVM7aRk3524.

50. Marc J. Fink, "Stunner: Turkey Infiltrating Native American Tribes—and May Get Congressional Help," Islamist Watch, October 5, 2012, http://www.islamist-watch.org/11261/stunner-turkey-infiltrating-native-american.

51. "Erdogan Gets Warm Welcome in Cairo," *Wall Street Journal*, September 13, 2011, http://online.wsj.com/article/SB1000142405311190353280457656723246207798.html.

52. "Egypt's Islamists warn Erdogan: Don't seek Middle East domination," *Haaretz*, September 14, 2011, http://www.haaretz.com/news/diplomacy-defense/egypt-s-islamists-warn-erdogan-don-t-seek-middle-east-domination-1.384446.

53. "Assad: Erdogan thinks he's Caliph, new sultan of the Ottoman (EXCLUSIVE)," RT, November 9, 2012, http://rt.com/news/assad-interview-exclusive-syria-265/.

54. Jeffrey Goldberg, "The Modern King in the Arab Spring," *The Atlantic*, March 18, 2013, http://www.theatlantic.com/magazine/archive/2013/04/monarch-in-the-middle/309270/?single_page=true.

55. "Turkey: 17,000 new mosques built under Erdogan," ANSAmed, February 19, 2013, http://www.ansamed.info/ansamed/en/news/sections/generalnews/2013/02/19/Turkey-17-000-new-mosques-built-Erdogan_8274135.html.

56. Laurent Leylekian, "Armenia, Israel and Wild Turkey," *Asbarez*, October 18, 2011, http://asbarez.com/98735/armenia-israel-and-wild-turkey/.

57. "Judge to al Qaeda, Iran, Taliban: Pay $6B for 9/11," CBS News, September 11, 2012, http://www.cbsnews.com/8301-201_162-57483418/judge-to-al-qaeda-iran-taliban-pay-6b-for-9-11/.

58. Peter Bergen, "Strange bedfellows—Iran and al Qaeda," CNN, March 10, 2013, http://www.cnn.com/2013/03/10/opinion/bergen-iran-al-qaeda.

59. Eben Kaplan, "The Al-Qaeda-Hezbollah Relationship," Council on Foreign Relations, August 14, 2006, http://www.cfr.org/terrorist-organizations/al-qaeda-hezbollah-relationship/p11275.

60. Erick Stakelbeck, "Iranian Video Says Mahdi is 'Near,'" CBN News, April 3, 2011, http://www.cbn.com/cbnnews/world/2011/march/iranian-regime-video-says-mahdi-is-near-/.

61. Erick Stakelbeck, "'Mahdi Video' Exposure Rattles Iranian Regime," CBN News, April 20, 2011, http://www.cbn.com/cbnnews/world/2011/april/mahdi-video-exposure-rattles-iranian-regime/.

62. Reza Kahlili, "IRAN LEADER: WE MUST PREP FOR 'END OF TIMES,'"
     WND, July 8, 2012, http://www.wnd.com/2012/07/iran-leader-we-must-prep-
     for-end-of-times/.

63. Erick Stakelbeck, "Iranian Regime Continues Push to Unite Muslim World
     Against Israel and the West," CBN News, September 20, 2011, http://blogs.
     cbn.com/stakelbeckonterror/archive/2011/09/20/iranian-regime-continues-
     push-to-unite-muslim-world-against-israel.aspx.

64. Erick Stakelbeck, "Iran's Ayatollah Khamenei Calls for 'Islamic Power bloc,'"
     CBN News, November 9, 2011, http://blogs.cbn.com/stakelbeckonterror/
     archive/2011/11/09/irans-ayatollah-khameini-calls-for-islamic-power-bloc.
     aspx.

65. "FM DAVUTOĞLU: WHY ARE WE REFERRED TO AS NEO-
     OTTOMANS?" Sabah, March 4, 2013, http://english.sabah.com.tr/
     national/2013/03/04/fm-davutoglu-why-are-we-referred-to-as-neoottomans.

66. "DAVUTOĞLU MEETS WITH THE 'LAST OTTOMANS,'" Sabah, March
     9, 2013, http://english.sabah.com.tr/national/2013/03/09/davutoglu-meets-
     with-the-last-ottomans.

CHAPTER SEVEN

1. Patrick Poole, "My Neighbor, the Hamas Leader," PJ Media, August 3, 2012,
    http://pjmedia.com/blog/my-neighbor-the-hamas-leader/?singlepage=true.

2. Patrick Poole, "Hometown Jihad: Blowback," *FrontPage Magazine*, May 24,
    2006, http://archive.frontpagemag.com/readArticle.aspx?ARTID=4319.

3. "Columbus, Ohio Muslim Leader Says 9/11 Planned by Americans, Praises
    the Wanted Al-Qaeda-Linked Yemenite Sheikh Al-Zindani," Middle East
    Media Research Institute, May 19, 2006, http://www.memri.org/report/
    en/0/0/0/0/0/0/1695.htm#_edn15.

4. Borzou Daragahi, "Rift over Shiites is seen in Bahrain's royal court," *Los
    Angeles Times*, July 7, 2007, http://articles.latimes.com/2007/jul/07/world/
    fg-bahrain7.

5. "Ohio terror sheikh, Fiqh Council of North America member Salah Sultan:
    Jews killed President Kennedy, advocates Islamic theocracy in US elections,"
    Central Ohioans Against Terrorism, September 17, 2008, http://
    ohioagainstterror.blogspot.com/2008/09/ohio-terror-sheikh-noor-center-
    resident.html.

6. "As Gaza Fighting Continues, Egyptian Clerics Intensify Antisemitic
    Statements; Columbus, Ohio Muslim Scholar/Leader Dr. Salah Sultan:

Muhammad Said That Judgment Day Will Not Come Until Muslims Fight the Jews and Kill Them; America Will Suffer Destruction," Middle East Media Research Institute, December 30, 2008, http://www.memri.org/report/en/0/0/0/0/0/0/3021.htm.

7. "#2443—Blood Libel on Hamas TV—President of the American Center for Islamic Research Dr. Sallah Sultan: Jews Murder Non-Jews and Use Their Blood to Knead Passover Matzos," Al-Aqsa TV (Hamas/Gaza), March 31, 2010, video clip available on the Middle East Media Research Center TV Monitor Project, http://www.memritv.org/clip/en/2443.htm.

8. "#2726—Pro-Hamas Islamic Scholars Abd Al-Jabbar Sa'id and Sallah Sultan Rejoice over Israeli Casualties in Mount Carmel Fire," Al-Aqsa TV (Hamas/Gaza), December 9, 2010, video clip available on the Middle East Media Research Center website, http://www.memritv.org/clip/en/0/0/0/0/0/0/2726.htm.

9. "Article on Muslim Brotherhood Website: U.S. Terrorism Worse than Bin Laden's," Middle East Media Research Center, May 9, 2011, http://www.memri.org/report/en/0/0/0/0/0/0/5269.htm.

10. "Muslim Brotherhood Leader: 'Every Israeli who enters Egypt—tourist or not—should be killed,'" Translating Jihad, September 26, 2011, http://www.translatingjihad.com/2011/09/muslim-brotherhood-leader-every-israeli.html.

11. Patrick Poole, "My Neighbor, the Hamas Leader."

12. Kerry Picket, "PICKET: (VIDEO) Romney takes sharp turn from Obama policy and names 'radical Islamic terrorism' as a threat," *Washington Times*, July 25, 2012, http://www.washingtontimes.com/blog/watercooler/2012/jul/25/picket-video-romney-takes-sharp-turn-current-obama/.

13. Lorenzo Vidino, *The New Muslim Brotherhood in the West* (New York: Columbia University Press, 2010), pp. 43–52.

14. Major Thomas Dailey, Kansas City Police Dept.–Counterterrorism Division, "The Role of Local Law Enforcement in Countering Violent Extremism," Testimony before the U.S. Senate Committee on Homeland Security and Governmental Affairs, Oct. 30, 2007, pp. 1–2, to access, click the following url and click "Download Testimony" under Major Thomas Dailey, http://www.hsgac.senate.gov/hearings/the-role-of-local-law-enforcement-in-countering-violent-islamist-extremism.

15. Rick Montgomery, "Calls for 'oceans of blood' came during Kansas Muslim convention," *Knight Rider*, February 3, 2002.

16. Government document available on the Investigative Project on Terrorism website, http://www.investigativeproject.org/redirect/Ikhwan_in_American-Zeid_Al-Nomann.

17. Ibid.

18. Ibid.

19. Ibid.

20. Steven Merley, "The Muslim Brotherhood in the United States," *Research Monographs on the Muslim World* (Hudson Institute Center on Islam, Democracy and the Future of the Muslim World), Series 2, no. 3 (April 2009), http://www.currenttrends.org/doclib/20090411_merley.usbrotherhood.pdf.

21. Ian Johnson, *A Mosque in Munich: Nazis, the CIA, and the Rise of the Muslim Brotherhood* (Mariner Books, 2011), p. 195.

22. Mary Jacoby, "Terror raid warrant names Al-Arian," *St. Petersburg Times*, March 21, 2002.

23. Mary Beth Sheridan, "Man suspected of Bin Laden link accused of fraud," *Washington Post*, August 9, 2005, http://www.washingtonpost.com/wp-dyn/content/article/2005/08/08/AR2005080801492.html.

24. "Mousa Abu Marzook," Research Center, Investigative Project on Terrorism, http://www.investigativeproject.org/case/532.

25. FBIS-NES, October 8, 1992.

26. Yehudit Barsky, "Focus on Hamas: Terror by Remote Control," *Middle East Quarterly*, June 1996, http://www.meforum.org/300/focus-on-hamas-terror-by-remote-control.

27. Daniel Greenfield, "How the World Saved Hamas 20 Years Ago," *FrontPage Magazine*, November 26, 2012, http://frontpagemag.com/2012/dgreenfield/how-the-world-saved-hamas-20-years-ago/.

28. Ibid.

29. Larry Cohler-Esses, "Hamas Wouldn't Honor a Treaty, Top Leader Says," *Forward*, April 19, 2012, http://forward.com/articles/155054/hamas-wouldn-t-honor-a-treaty-top-leader-says/?p=2.

30. Neil MacFarquhar, "Terror suspect freed by U.S.; Flies to Jordan," *New York Times*, May 6, 1997, http://www.nytimes.com/1997/05/06/world/terror-suspect-freed-by-us-flies-to-jordan.html.

31. Cohler-Esses, "Hamas Wouldn't Honor a Treaty."

32. "Bylaws of the Palestine Committee of the Muslim Brotherhood," Investigative Project on Terrorism, http://www.investigativeproject.org/document/id/24.

33. Government Exhibit Philly Meeting – 5, p. 14, http://www.txnd.uscourts.gov/judges/hlf2/09-29-08/Philly%20Meeting%205.pdf.

34. "DOJ: CAIR's Unindicted Co-Conspirator Status Legit," Investigative Project on Terrorism, March 12, 2010, http://www.investigativeproject.org/1854/doj-cairs-unindicted-co-conspirator-status-legit.

35. Action Memorandum from Dale L. Watson, Assistant Director, Counterterrorism Division, Federal Bureau of Investigation, to R. Richard Newcomb, Director, Office of Foreign Asset Control, Department of the Treasury, November 5, 2001, p. 9, http://www.investigativeproject.org/documents/case_docs/466.pdf.

36. Ibid., p. 12.

37. Government Exhibit Philly Meeting 3E, 3:04-CR-240-G, US v. HLF, et al., p. 3, http://www.txnd.uscourts.gov/judges/hlf2/09-29-08/Philly%20Meeting%203E.pdf.

38. Government Exhibit Philly Meeting 4, 3:04-CR-240-G, US v. HLF, et al., p. 10, http://www.txnd.uscourts.gov/judges/hlf2/09-29-08/Philly%20Meeting%204.pdf.

39. Government Exhibit Philly Meeting – 11E, 3:04-CR-240-G, US v. HLF, et al., p. 2, http://www.txnd.uscourts.gov/judges/hlf2/09-29-08/Philly%20Meeting%2011E.pdf.

40. Government Exhibit Philly Meeting – 8, 3:04-CR-240-G, US v. HLF, et al., p. 4, 11, http://www.txnd.uscourts.gov/judges/hlf2/09-29-08/Philly%20Meeting%208.pdf.

41. Government Exhibit Philly Meeting – 7E, 3:04-CR-240-G, US v. HLF, et al., p. 5, http://www.txnd.uscourts.gov/judges/hlf2/09-29-08/Philly%20Meeting%207E.pdf.

42. Philly Meeting – 4, pp. 12–13.

43. Philly Meeting – 4E, p. 3, http://www.txnd.uscourts.gov/judges/hlf2/09-29-08/Philly%20Meeting%204E.pdf.

44. Matthew Levitt, *Hamas: Politics, Charity and Terrorism in the Service of Jihad* (Yale University Press, 2006), p. 147.

45. InvestigativeProject, "Esam Omeish in front of the Israeli Embassy," YouTube, September 27, 2007, http://www.youtube.com/watch?v=sb8jKzrvT6I.

46. InvestigativeProject, "Esam Omeish at Jerusalem Day Rally," YouTube, September 27, 2007, http://www.youtube.com/watch?v=Lajn3zOoWt4.

47. Amy Gardner and Anita Kumar, "Va. Muslim Activist Denies Urging Violence," *Washington Post*, September 29, 2007, http://www.washingtonpost.com/wp-dyn/content/article/2007/09/28/AR2007092800789.html.

48. "Virginia Governor Tim Kaine Accepts Resignation of Controversial Appointee," Fox News, September 27, 2007, http://www.foxnews.com/story/0,2933,298278,00.html.

49. Noreen S. Ahmed-Ullah, Sam Roe, and Laurie Cohen, "A rare look at secretive Brotherhood in America," *Chicago Tribune*, September 19, 2004.

50. Phone Directory, Exhibit 003-0079, 3:04-CR-240-G, US v. HLF, et al., p. 2, http://counterterrorismblog.org/site-resources/images/1992_Phone_Directory.pdf.

51. Department of Justice, "Brief for the United States," Fourth Circuit Court of Appeals, *U.S. v. Sabri Benkahla* 07-4778 (VA ED), p. 58.

52. Esam Omeish, "MAS President Letter to the Washington Post," Muslim American Society, September 16, 2004, http://www.unitedstatesaction.com/documents/omeish/www-masnet-org_pressroom_release-asp_nycmexs4.pdf.

53. "Esam S Omeish," Elections, Virginia Public Access Project, http://www.vpap.org/candidates/profile/elections/109248.

54. "Esam S Omeish," Money In, List Donors, Virginia Public Access Project, http://www.vpap.org/candidates/profile/money_in_donors/109248?end_year=2009&start_year=2009.

55. "Esam Omeish," Investigative Project on Terrorism, http://www.investigativeproject.org/documents/misc/711.pdf.

CHAPTER EIGHT

1. Noreen S. Ahmed-Ullah, Sam Roe, and Laurie Cohen, "A rare look at secretive Brotherhood in America," *Chicago Tribune*, September 19, 2004, http://www.chicagotribune.com/news/watchdog/chi-0409190261sep19,0,3008717.story.

2. "Overwhelming majority oppose mosque near Ground Zero," CNN, August 11, 2010, http://politicalticker.blogs.cnn.com/2010/08/11/overwhelming-majority-oppose-mosque-near-ground-zero/.

3. Isabel Vincent and Melissa Klein, "No community programs at 'Ground Zero' mosque a year after the controversy," *New York Post*, December 9, 2012, http://www.nypost.com/p/news/local/manhattan/it_mosque_rade_E4bLtxvo3yIwrCnYm1fRLP.

4. Ahmed-Ullah, Roe, and Cohen, "A rare look at secretive Brotherhood."

5.   "Introducing the Muslim American Society," Investigative Project on Terrorism, September 18, 2007, http://www.investigativeproject.org/472/introducing-the-muslim-american-society.

6.   Sharon Otterman, "A Planned Mosque Inches Along, but Critics Remain," *New York Times*, September 7, 2012, http://www.nytimes.com/2012/09/08/nyregion/mosque-being-built-in-brooklyn-continues-to-face-opposition.html?pagewanted=all&_r=0.

7.   Michael Paulson, "Making Peace, and prayers: Mosque opens its doors as controversy fades," *Boston Globe*, September 15, 2008, available on the Muslim American Society website, http://www.masboston.org/content.php?action=view&id=113&module=newsmodule.

8.   Jeff Jacoby, "The Boston mosque's Saudi connection," *Boston Globe*, January 10, 2007, http://www.boston.com/news/globe/editorial_opinion/oped/articles/2007/01/10/the_boston_mosques_saudi_connection/?page=full.

9.   Stephen Schwartz on Islam and Wahhabism in a Q & A by Kathryn Jean Lopez, "The Good & the Bad," National Review Online, November 18, 2002, http://old.nationalreview.com/interrogatory/interrogatory111802.asp.

10.   Haviv Rettig, "Expert: Saudis have radicalized 80% of US mosques," *Jerusalem Post*, December 5, 2005, http://www.jpost.com/International/Article.aspx?id=6635.

11.   Rebecca Hamilton, "After 9/11, An East Village Mosque Reaches Out to Its Neighbors," The Local East Village, September 9, 2011, http://eastvillage.thelocal.nytimes.com/2011/09/09/after-911-an-east-village-mosque-reaches-out-to-its-neighbors/.

12.   Erick Stakelbeck, *The Terrorist Next Door: How the Government Is Deceiving You About the Islamist Threat* (Washington, D.C.: Regnery Publishing, Inc., 2011), pp. 17–21.

13.   "Justice Department Files Lawsuit Requiring Rutherford County, Tenn., to Allow Mosque to Open in City of Murfreesboro," Department of Justice website, July 18, 2012, http://www.justice.gov/opa/pr/2012/July/12-crt-883.html.

14.   "Assistant Attorney General Perez Speaks at the Grand Opening of the Islamic Center of Murfreesboro," Department of Justice website, http://www.justice.gov/crt/opa/pr/speeches/2012/crt-speech-1211181.html.

15.   Ottermn, "A Planned Mosque Inches Along."

16.   Ryan Mauro, "DOJ Forces Mega-Mosque on Norwalk, CT Community," The Clarion Project, December 23, 2012, http://www.clarionproject.org/analysis/cry-islamophobia-and-win.

17.   Aaron Rupar, "St. Anthony council rejects Islamic center; 'Islam is evil,' says one opponent," City Pages, June 13, 2012, http://blogs.citypages.com/blotter/2012/06/st_anthony_council_rejects_islamic_center_islam_is_evil_says_one_opponent.php.

18.   Rose French, "Feds launch formal investigation into St. Anthony mosque rejection," StarTribune, October 29, 2012, http://www.startribune.com/local/blogs/176309071.html.

19.   Rose French, "St. Anthony City Council rejects Islamic center plan," StarTribune, June 13, 2012, http://www.startribune.com/local/158785005.html?refer=y.

20.   "Lomita under investigation over rejection of Islamic Center expansion," Los Angeles Times, November 18, 2011, http://latimesblogs.latimes.com/lanow/2011/11/federal-authorities-investigating-lomita-after-its-rejection-of-islamic-center-expansion.html.

21.   Nick Green, "Lomita to reconsider mosque's plans under terms of lawsuit settlement," Mercury News, January 16, 2013, http://www.mercurynews.com/california/ci_22389961/lomita-reconsider-mosques-plans-under-terms-lawsuit-settlement.

22.   "Lomita under investigation over rejection of Islamic Center expansion."

23.   Arthur Hirsch, "Mosque plan called too large for rural Howard County," Baltimore Sun, November 8, 2012, http://www.baltimoresun.com/news/maryland/howard/bs-md-ho-sunday-mosque-20121108,0,7633340.story.

24.   "Controversies Over Mosques and Islamic Centers Across the U.S.," Pew Research Center's Forum on Religion & Public Life, September 27, 2012, http://www.google.com/url?sa=t&rct=j&q=&esrc=s&source=web&cd=7&ved=0CFEQFjAG&url=http%3A%2F%2Ffeatures.pewforum.org%2Fmuslim%2F2012Mosque-Map.pdf&ei=h1z4UOznD-bX0QGKu4F4&usg=AFQjCNGYDpYgbzWBOKgWp_MUDyPBjcu1BQ.

25.   Ihsan Bagby, "The American Mosque 2011," US Mosque Study 2011, Report Number 1, January 2012, www.faithcommunitiestoday.org/sites/faithcommunitiestoday.org/files/The%20American%20Mosque%202011%20web.pdf.

26.   Meghan Neal, "Number of Muslims in the U.S. doubles since 9/11," New York Daily News, May 3, 2012, http://www.nydailynews.com/news/national/number-muslims-u-s-doubles-9-11-article-1.1071895.

27.   Daniel Pipes, "How Many Islamists?" Daniel Pipes.org, May 17, 2005 (updated January 26, 2013), http://www.danielpipes.org/blog/2005/05/how-many-islamists.

28. Mordechai Kedar and David Yerushalmi, "Shari'a and Violence in American Mosques," *Middle East Quarterly* (Middle East Forum)18 (Summer 2011), http://www.meforum.org/2931/american-mosques.

29. Mordechai Kedar and David Yerushalmi, "Correlations between *Sharia* Adherence and Violent Dogma in U.S. Mosques," Mapping *Shari'a*, http://mappingsharia.com/

30. Stakelbeck, *The Terrorist Next Door*, 29–34.

31. Ibid., p. 28.

32. Joseph Berger, "Protests of a Plan for a Mosque? That Was Last Year," *New York Times*, August 18, 2011, http://www.nytimes.com/2011/08/19/nyregion/mosque-opens-quietly-on-staten-island.html.

33. Mohamed Akram, "An Explanatory Memorandum on the General Strategic Goal for the Brotherhood in North America," Investigative Project on Terrorism, May 19, 1991, http://www.investigativeproject.org/document/id/20.

34. Ian Johnson, *A Mosque in Munich: Nazis, The CIA, and the Rise of the Muslim Brotherhood in the West* (Mariner Books, 2010).

35. Gilles Kepel, "The Brotherhood in the Salafist Universe," *Current Trends in Islamist Ideology* (Hudson Institute Center on Islam, Democracy and the Future of the Modern World) 6 (February 2008), http://www.currenttrends.org/research/detail/the-brotherhood-in-the-salafist-universe.

36. "Saudi Minister of Interior, Prince Nayef Ibn Abd-Al-Aziz: 'Who Committed the Events of September 11 ... I think They [the Zionists] are Behind these Events ... [Arab] Mass Media Should Condemn Terrorism, Warn Arab Nationals of it, and Let Our Voice be Heard by the World," Middle East Media Research Institute, December 3, 2002, http://www.memri.org/report/en/0/0/0/0/0/0/772.htm#_edn1.

37. Dore Gold, "Wary of the Muslim Brotherhood," *Israel Hayom*, December 2, 2011, http://www.israelhayom.com/site/newsletter_opinion.php?id=940.

38. "Turkey's charismatic pro-Islamic leader," BBC, November 4, 2002, http://news.bbc.co.uk/2/hi/europe/2270642.stm.

39. Erick Stakelbeck, "Turkish Mega Mosque in Germany Sparks Controversy," CBN News, October 14, 2012, http://www.cbn.com/cbnnews/world/2012/October/Turkish-Mega-Mosque-in-Germany-Sparks-Controversy/.

40. Erick Stakelbeck, "New Mosque Rattles Small Austrian Town," CBN News, March 27, 2010, http://www.cbn.com/cbnnews/world/2010/March/Small-Town-Austrian-Mosque-Brings-Big-Opposition/.

41. Ryan Mauro, "Turkey Stakes Claim in America With $100 Million Mega-Mosque," The Clarion Project, May 21, 2013, http://www.clarionproject.org/analysis/turkey-stakes-claim-america-100-million-mega-mosque.

42. Rebecca Camber, "'No porn or prostitution': Islamic extremists set up Sharia law controlled zones in British cities," Daily Mail, July 28, 2011, http://www.dailymail.co.uk/news/article-2019547/Anjem-Choudary-Islamic-extremists-set-Sharia-law-zones-UK-cities.html.

43. Soeren Kern, "Muslim Gangs Enforce Sharia Law in London," Gatestone Institute, January 25, 2013, http://www.gatestoneinstitute.org/3555/sharia-law-london.

44. Tom Rawstorne, "Tower Hamlets Taliban: Death threats to women who don't wear veils. Gays attacked in the streets. And all in a borough at the heart of Britain's capital…" Daily Mail, May 13, 2011, http://www.dailymail.co.uk/news/article-1386558/Tower-Hamlets-Taliban-Death-threats-women-gays-attacked-streets.html#ixzz2Jf05uKns.

45. "State of the nation: Where is bittersweet Britain heading?" British Future, January 14, 2013, http://www.britishfuture.org/publication/state-of-the-nation-2013/.

46. Douglas Murray, "It's Official: Muslim Population of Britain Doubles," Gatestone Institute, December 21, 2012, http://www.gatestoneinstitute.org/3511/britain-muslim-population-doubles.

47. John Mintz and Douglas Farah, "In Search Of Friends Among The Foes," Washington Post, September 11, 2004, http://www.washingtonpost.com/wp-dyn/articles/A12823-2004Sep10_3.html.

48. Liam Stack, "Anger and an Arrest as a Leader of Egypt's Muslim Brotherhood Visits Brooklyn," New York Times, December 10, 2012, http://thelede.blogs.nytimes.com/2012/12/10/anger-and-an-arrest-as-a-leader-of-egypts-muslim-brotherhood-visits-brooklyn/.

CHAPTER NINE

1. Home page, Occupy Wall Street website, http://occupywallst.org/.

2. Amy Goodman, "From Tahrir Square to Occupy Wall Street," The Guardian, October 26, 2011, http://www.guardian.co.uk/commentisfree/cifamerica/2011/oct/26/tahrir-square-occupy-wall-street.

3. Jennifer Rubin, "Occupy Wall Street: Does anyone care about the anti-Semitism?" Washington Post, October 17, 2011, http://www.washingtonpost.com/blogs/right-turn/post/occupy-wall-street-does-anyone-care-about-the-anti-semitism/2011/03/29/gIQA43p8rL_blog.html.

4. Caroline May, "Anti-Semitism at 'Occupy Wall Street'?" *Daily Caller*, October 7, 2011, http://dailycaller.com/2011/10/07/anti-semitism-at-occupy-wall-street/.

5. Tiffany Gabbay, "MORE ANTI-SEMITISM AT OCCUPY WALL ST.: PROTESTER CALLS JEWISH MAN 'DUMB MOTHERFU**ER,'" The Blaze, November 9, 2011, http://www.theblaze.com/stories/2011/11/09/more-anti-semitism-at-occupy-wall-st-protester-calls-jewish-man-dumb-motherfuer/.

6. David Cameron, "David Cameron: Speech to the Community Security Trust," Conservatives.com, March 4, 2008, http://www.conservatives.com/News/Speeches/2008/03/David_Cameron_Speech_to_the_Community_Security_Trust.aspx.

7. Lorenzo Vidino, *The New Muslim Brotherhood in the West* (New York: Columbia University Press, 2009), pp. 141–42.

8. James Brandon and Raffaello Pantucci, "UK Islamists and the Arab Uprisings," Hudson Institute, June 22, 2012, http://www.currenttrends.org/research/detail/uk-islamists-and-the-arab-uprisings.

9. Tom Whitehead, "Concerns over anti-extremism funding," *The Telegraph*, September 8, 2009, http://www.telegraph.co.uk/news/uknews/law-and-order/6151098/Concerns-over-anti-extremism-funding.html.

10. "Press Release—Response to accusations in the Centre for Social Cohesion Document," The Cordoba Foundation, November 11, 2009, http://www.thecordobafoundation.com/news.php?id=1&art=34.

11. "18-31.06.03: MAB 'To Be A Muslim. Think Globally, Act Locally' Campaign," Muslim Association of Britain, http://web.archive.org/web/20030601075509/http:/www.mabonline.net/branches/events/2bamuslim2003conf/2bamuslim2003conf.htm.

12. Vidino, *The New Muslim Brotherhood in the West*, p. 142.

13. Ibid.

14. J. David Goodman and Rick Gladstone, "Iran Sees Terror Plot Accusation as Diversion From Wall Street Protests," *New York Times*, October 13, 2011, http://www.nytimes.com/2011/10/13/world/middleeast/iran-sees-terror-plot-accusation-as-diversion-from-wall-street-protests.html?pagewanted=all&_r=0.

15. "Students Hold Demo in Sympathy with Wall Street Protests," *Tehran Times*, October 22, 2011, http://tehrantimes.com/index.php/politics/3816-students-hold-demo-in-sympathy-with-wall-st-protests-.

16. Mike Levine, "US professors travel to Iran to discuss Occupy Wall Street movement," Fox News, March 1, 2012, http://www.foxnews.com/

world/2012/03/01/us-professors-travel-to-iran-to-discuss-occupy-wall-street-movement/#ixzz2LCW1YPvs.

17. "Iran calls Wall Street protests 'American Spring,'" *USA Today*, October 9, 2011, http://usatoday30.usatoday.com/news/world/story/2011-10-09/iran-wall-street-protest/50713380/1.

18. Joe Coscarelli, "Occupy Wall Street Not Meeting With Ahmadinejad," *New York*, September 24, 2012, http://nymag.com/daily/intelligencer/2012/09/occupy-wall-street-not-meeting-with-ahmadinejad.html.

19. Neil MacFarquhar, "At U.N., Egypt and Yemen Urge Curbs on Free Speech," *New York Times*, September 26, 2012, http://www.nytimes.com/2012/09/27/world/united-nations-general-assembly.html?_r=0.

20. "The 99%: Official list of Occupy Wall Street's supporters, sponsors and sympathizers," PJ Media, October 31, 2011, http://pjmedia.com/zombie/2011/10/31/the-99-official-list-of-ows/.

21. Bill Gertz, "NUKE SCIENTIST EXCHANGE PLANNED," *Washington Times*, December 21, 2011, http://www.washingtontimes.com/news/2011/dec/21/inside-the-ring-105581724/?page=all#pagebreak.

22. Sarah Maslin Nir and Matt Flegenheimer, "Hundreds Held in Oakland Occupy Protest," *New York Times*, January 29, 2012, http://www.nytimes.com/2012/01/30/us/occupy-oakland-protest-leads-to-hundreds-of-arrests.html.

23. Kevin Fasick and Candice M. Giove, "Fiend attacks 'Occupy' protester in her tent," *New York Post*, October 30, 2011, http://www.nypost.com/p/news/local/manhattan/zuccotti_perv_Qd8v3hCAnspzJ7VGC9nJZP.

24. Rich Lowry, "Occupy's dark heart," *New York Post*, updated May 9, 2012, http://www.nypost.com/p/news/opinion/opedcolumnists/occupy_dark_heart_1AHsq1ZSEQOisADMXlek4L.

25. Daniel Halper, "Obama on Occupy Wall Street: 'We Are on Their Side,'" *Weekly Standard*, October 18, 2011, http://www.weeklystandard.com/blogs/obama-occupy-wall-street-we-are-their-side_598251.html.

26. Chris Isidore, "Obama, Cantor spar over Occupy Wall Street," CNN, October 7, 2011, http://money.cnn.com/2011/10/07/news/economy/occupy_wall_street/index.htm.

27. Glenn Thrush, "Obama Preoccupied? W.W. with the '99 percent'-ers," Politico, October 16, 2011, http://www.politico.com/politico44/perm/1011/obama_preoccupied_2e1e701c-9e52-4e29-a7a3-1d074659996b.html.

28. Allison Deger, "Open letter from Ismail Hanneya to Occupy Charlotte protesting the DNC: 'We salute you,'" Mondoweiss, September 6, 2012, http://

mondoweiss.net/2012/09/open-letter-from-ismail-hanneya-to-occupy-charlotte-protesting-the-dnc-we-salute-you.html.

29. "Zawahiri calls Colin Powell and Condi Rice 'house slaves,'" Hot Air, May 9, 2007, http://hotair.com/archives/2007/05/09/zawahiri-calls-colin-powell-and-condi-rice-house-slaves/.

30. "Muslims to NYPD: 'Respect us, we will respect you,'" Wall Street Journal, November 18, 2011, http://online.wsj.com/article/APf11f442532684f3696ff927109bf4a71.html.

31. "Is the Occupy Wall Street Movement Occupied?" Investigative Project on Terrorism, November 29, 2011, http://www.investigativeproject.org/3312/is-the-occupy-wall-street-movement-occupied.

32. "JIHAD ALERT—Is the Muslim Brotherhood directing Occupy Orlando?" The United West, October 17, 2011, http://theunitedwest.org/jihad-alert-is-the-muslim-brotherhood-directing-occupy-orlando/.

33. Ibid.

34. "ICNA's Stance on the Occupy Wall Street Protests," Islamic Circle of North America, November 2, 2011, http://www.icna.org/icnas-stance-on-the-occupy-wall-street-protests/.

35. "The 99%: Official list of Occupy Wall Street's supporters, sponsors and sympathizers," PJ Media, October 31, 2011, http://pjmedia.com/zombie/2011/10/31/the-99-official-list-of-ows/ .

36. Matt Cover, "CAIR Suggests Tea Party, GOP Are Behind Nationwide Anti-Muslim Campaign," News Busters, September 2, 2010, http://newsbusters.org/blogs/matt-cover/2010/09/02/cair-suggests-tea-party-gop-are-behind-nationwide-anti-muslim-campaign#ixzz2M4GeXAfZ.

37. Ben Smith, "Obama once visited '60s radicals," Politico, February 22, 2008, http://www.politico.com/news/stories/0208/8630.html.

38. Brandon Darby, "OCCUPY LA TO CHRISTOPHER DORNER: 'REST IN POWER,'" Breitbart.com, February 14, 2013, http://www.breitbart.com/Big-Government/2013/02/13/Occupy-LA-To-Cop-Killer-Rest-in-Power-For-Efforts-to-Expose-Corruption.

39. Rosie Gray, "The Christopher Dorner Fan Club Is More Mainstream Than You'd Think," BuzzFeed, February 13, 2013, http://www.buzzfeed.com/rosiegray/the-christopher-dorner-fan-club-is-more-mainstream-than-youd.

40. Natasha Lennard, "Were Dorner's complaints legitimate?" Salon.com, February 12, 2013, http://www.salon.com/2013/02/12/were_dorners_complaints_legitimate/.

41.   Michael Burleigh, "How typical of the Left to idolize a despot who gloried in attacking America and Britain," *Daily Mail*, updated March 7, 2013, http://www.dailymail.co.uk/news/article-2289326/How-typical-Left-idolise-despot-gloried-attacking-America-Britain.html.

42.   Joel B. Pollak, "HUFFINGTON POST IS JUST A HUGO CHÁVEZ FANPAGE NOW," Breitbart.com, March 6, 2013, http://www.breitbart.com/Big-Journalism/2013/03/06/Huffington-Post-Just-Hugo-Chavez-Fanpage-Now.

43.   Rich Lowry, "Hugo Chávez's Cheering Section," National Review Online, March 8, 2013, http://www.nationalreview.com/articles/342470/hugo-ch-vez-s-cheering-section-rich-lowry.

44.   Lisa Balde, "Rev. Jesse Jackson Attends Hugo Chavez Funeral," NBC Chicago, March 8, 2013, http://www.nbcchicago.com/blogs/ward-room/Rev-Jesse-Jackson-Attends-Hugo-Chavez-Funeral-196309381.html.

45.   Catalina Camia, "N.Y. Dem slammed for praising Hugo Chavez," *USA Today*, March 6, 2013, http://www.usatoday.com/story/onpolitics/2013/03/06/hugo-chavez-death-jose-serrano-congress/1966641/.

46.   David Horowitz, *Unholy Alliance: Radical Islam and the American Left* (Washington, D.C.: Regnery Publishing, Inc., 2004), pp. 20–21.

47.   Ibid., pp. 34–35.

48.   Melissa Harris Perry, "MSNBC's Melissa Harris-Perry: Progressives despise military as 'engine of war,'" Examiner.com, January 27, 2013, http://www.examiner.com/article/msnbc-s-melissa-harris-perry-progressives-despise-military-as-engine-of-war.

49.   Benny Johnson, "MUSLIM CONGRESSMAN: 'IMAGINE' THE FIRST FEMALE MUSLIM PRESIDENT WEARING 'A HIJAB' IN THE WHITE HOUSE," The Blaze, July 6, 2012, http://www.theblaze.com/stories/2012/07/06/muslim-congressman-imagine-the-first-female-muslim-president-wearing-a-hijab-in-the-white-house/.

50.   Mytheos Holt, "MUSLIM CONGRESSMAN: MODEL AMERICA'S SCHOOLS AFTER 'MADRASAS,'" The Blaze, July 5, 2012, http://www.theblaze.com/stories/2012/07/05/muslim-congressman-model-americas-schools-after-madrasas/.

51.   Michael Scherer, "Inside Obama's Idea Factory in Washington," *Time*, November 21, 2008, http://www.time.com/time/politics/article/0,8599,1861305,00.html.

52. Wajahat Ali et al., "Fear, Inc.: The Roots of the Islamophobia Network in America," Center for American Progress, August 26, 2011, http://www.americanprogress.org/issues/religion/report/2011/08/26/10165/fear-inc/.

53. Joseph Weber, "Selection of Israel critic for US delegation to human rights forum raises concern," Fox News, October 17, 2012, http://www.foxnews.com/politics/2012/10/17/watchdogs-oppose-appointment-israel-critic-al-marayati-to-us-delegation/.

54. "MPAC Releases 'Not Qualified: Exposing America's Top 25 Pseudo-Experts on Islam,'" Muslim Public Affairs Council, September 11, 2012, http://www.mpac.org/publications/mpac-releases-not-qualified-exposing-americas-top-25-pseudo-experts-on-islam.php#.UT_6A-g3524.

55. "You're Invited: National Community Calls on 'Real Impact of Hate in America' with Hate Experts," Muslim Public Affairs Council, August 15, 2012, http://www.mpac.org/events/youre-invited-natl-community-call-on-real-impact-of-hate-in-america-w-hate-experts.php#.UUCE4ug3524.

56. Jeffrey Imm, "Al-Qaeda's Gadahn—Transcript of January 6 Message," Counterterrorism Blog, January 6, 2008, http://counterterrorismblog.org/2008/01/gadahn_010608_transcript.php.

CONCLUSION

1. Josh Feldman, "O'Reilly And Krauthammer Blast Obama For Not Denouncing Radical Islam In Wake Of Boston Bombings," Mediaite, April 23, 2013, http://www.mediaite.com/tv/oreilly-and-krauthammer-blast-obama-for-not-denouncing-radical-islam-in-wake-of-boston-bombings/.

2. Deborah Sontag, David M. Herszenhorn, and Serge F. Kovaleski, "A Battered Dream, Then a Violent Path," *New York Times*, April 27, 2013, http://www.nytimes.com/2013/04/28/us/shot-at-boxing-title-denied-tamerlan-tsarnaev-reeled.html?pagewanted=all.

INDEX